D1004558

MARKET WIZARDS

Interviews with Top Traders

Jack D. Schwager

PERENNIAL LIBRARY

HARPER & ROW, PUBLISHERS, New York
Grand Rapids, Philadelphia, St. Louis, San Francisco
London, Singapore, Sydney, Tokyo, Toronto

This publication is designed to provide accurate and authoritative information in regard to the subject matter covered. It is sold with the understanding that the publisher is not engaged in rendering legal, accounting, or other professional service. If legal advice or other expert assistance is required, the services of a competent professional person should be sought.

*From a Declaration of Principles Jointly Adopted by
a Committee of the American Bar Association and a
Committee of Publishers and Associations*

A hardcover edition of this book was published in 1989 by the New York Institute of Finance. It is here reprinted by arrangement with the New York Institute of Finance, a division of Simon & Schuster, Inc.

MARKET WIZARDS: INTERVIEWS WITH TOP TRADERS. Copyright © 1989 by NYIF Corp. All rights reserved. Printed in the United States of America. No part of this book may be used or reproduced in any manner whatsoever without written permission except in the case of brief quotations embodied in critical articles and reviews. For information address Harper & Row, Publishers, Inc., 10 East 53rd Street, New York, NY 10022.

First PERENNIAL LIBRARY edition published 1990.

Library of Congress Cataloging-in-Publication Data

Market wizards : interviews with top traders / Jack D. Schwager.
    p. cm.
  "A Hardcover edition of this book is published by New York Institute of Finance" — T.p. verso.
  ISBN 0-06-097329-3
  1. Floor traders (Finance) — United States — Interviews. 2. Futures market — United States. 3. Financial futures — United States.
I. Schwager, Jack D., 1948–
HG4928.5.M37   1990
332.64′0973 — dc20   89-46228

      92 93 94 MPC 10 9 8 7 6 5 4 3

*To my wife Jo Ann
and my children
Daniel, Zachary, and Samantha
for the love they give
and, more important,
the love they receive.*

You've got to learn how to fall, before you learn to fly.

—Paul Simon

One man's ceiling is another man's floor.

—Paul Simon

If I wanted to become a tramp, I would seek information and advice from the most successful tramp I could find. If I wanted to become a failure, I would seek advice from men who had never succeeded. If I wanted to succeed in all things, I would look around me for those who are succeeding and do as they have done.

—Joseph Marshall Wade
(as quoted in a *Treasury of Wall Street Wisdom*
edited by Harry D. Schultz and Samson Coslow)

Contents

PART III   A LITTLE BIT OF EVERYTHING

PART IV   THE VIEW FROM THE FLOOR

PART V   THE PSYCHOLOGY OF TRADING

Preface

There are some amazing stories here:

- A trader who, after wiping out several times early in his career, turned a $30,000 account into $80 million
- A fund manager who achieved what many thought impossible—five consecutive years of triple-digit percentage returns
- A trader from small-town America who started out on a shoestring and has become one of the world's largest bond traders
- A former securities analyst who, during the past seven years, has realized an average *monthly* return of 25 percent (over 1,400 percent annualized), primarily trading stock index futures
- An electrical engineering graduate from MIT whose largely computerized approach to trading has earned his accounts an astounding 250,000 percent return over a sixteen-year period

These are but a sampling of the interviews contained in this book. In his own way, each of the traders interviewed has achieved incredible success.

What sets these traders apart? Most people think that winning in the markets has something to do with finding the secret formula. The truth is that any common denominator among the traders I interviewed had more to do with attitude than approach. Some of the traders use fundamental analysis exclusively, others employ only technical analysis, and still others combine the two. Some traders operate on a time horizon measured in hours or even minutes, while others typically implement positions that they intend to hold for months or even years. Although the trading methodologies varied widely, the forthcoming interviews reveal certain important commonalities in trading attitudes and principles.

Trading provides one of the last great frontiers of opportunity in our economy. It is one of the very few ways in which an individual can start with a relatively small bankroll and actually become a multimillionaire. Of course, only a handful of individuals (such as those interviewed here) succeed in turning this feat, but at least the opportunity exists.

While I hardly expect all readers of this book to transform themselves into super-traders—the world just doesn't work that way—I believe that these thought-provoking interviews will help most serious and open-minded readers improve their personal trading performance. It may even help a select few become super-traders.

Jack D. Schwager
Goldens Bridge, NY
May 1989

Acknowledgments

First and foremost, I would like to thank Stephen Chronowitz, who pored over every chapter in this book and provided a multitude of helpful suggestions and editing changes. I am indebted to Steve for both the quantity (hours) and quality of his input. I truly believe that whatever the merits of this work, it has benefited significantly from his contributions.

I am grateful to my wife, Jo Ann, not only for enduring nine months as a "book widow," but also for being a valuable sounding board—a role she performed with brutal honesty. Sample: "This is the worst thing you ever wrote!" (Needless to say, that item was excised from the book.) Jo Ann possesses common sense in abundance, and I usually followed her advice unquestioningly.

Of course, I would like to express my thanks to all the traders who agreed to be interviewed, without whom there would be no book. By and large, these traders neither need nor seek publicity, as they trade only for their own accounts or are already managing all the money they wish to. In many cases, their motives for participating were altruistic. For example, as one trader expressed it, "When I was starting out, I found biographies and interviews of successful traders particularly helpful, and I would like to play a similar role in helping new traders."

I wish to express my sincere appreciation to Elaine Crocker for her friendly persuasion, which made some of the chapters in this book possible. For advice, leads, and other assorted favors, I would like to thank Courtney Smith, Norm Zadeh, Susan Abbott, Bruce Babcock, Martin Presler, Chuck Carlson, Leigh Stevens, Brian Gelber, Michael Marcus, and William Rafter. Finally, I would like to thank three traders who were gracious enough to grant me lengthy interviews, which were not incorporated into this book: Irv Kessler, Doug Redmond, and Martin Presler (the former two because, in retrospect, I considered my line of question-

ing too esoteric and technical; the latter because publication deadlines
did not permit time for needed follow-up interviews and editing).

Prologue

The name of the book was *The Big Board* . . . . It was about an Earthling man and woman who were kidnapped by extraterrestrials. They were put on display in a zoo on a planet called Zircon-212.

These fictitious people in the zoo had a big board supposedly showing stock market quotations and commodity prices along one wall of their habitat, and a news ticker, and a telephone that was supposedly connected to a brokerage on Earth. The creatures on Zircon-212 told their captives that they had invested a million dollars for them back on Earth, and that it was up to the captives to manage it so that they would be fabulously wealthy when they were returned to Earth.

The telephone and the big board and the ticker were all fakes, of course. They were simply stimulants to make the Earthlings perform vividly for the crowds at the zoo—to make them jump up and down and cheer, or gloat, or sulk, or tear their hair, to be scared shitless or to feel as contented as babies in their mothers' arms.

The Earthlings did very well on paper. That was part of the rigging, of course. And religion got mixed up in it, too. The news ticker reminded them that the President of the United States had declared National Prayer Week, and that everybody should pray. The Earthlings had had a bad week on the market before that. They had lost a small fortune in olive oil futures. So they gave praying a whirl. It worked. Olive oil went up.

—Kurt Vonnegut Jr.
Slaughterhouse Five

If the random walk theorists are correct, then Earthbound traders are suffering from the same delusions as the zoo inhabitants of Kilgore Trout's novel. (Kilgore Trout is the ubiquitous science fiction writer in Kurt Vonnegut's novels.) Whereas the prisoners on Zircon-212 thought their decisions were being based on actual price quotes—they were not—real-life traders believe they can beat the market by their acumen or skill. If markets are truly efficient and random in every time span, then these traders are attributing their success or failure to their own skills or shortcomings, when in reality it is all a matter of luck.

After interviewing the traders for this book, it is hard to believe this view of the world. One comes away with a strong belief that it is highly unlikely that some traders can win with such consistency over vast numbers of trades and many years. Of course, given enough traders, some will come out ahead even after a long period of time, simply as a consequence of the laws of probability. I leave it for the mathematicians to determine the odds of traders winning by the magnitude and duration that those interviewed here have. Incidentally, the traders themselves have not a glimmer of doubt that, over the long run, the question of who wins and who loses is determined by skill, not luck. I, too, share this conviction.

My Own Story

Right out of graduate school, I landed a job as a commodity research analyst. I was pleasantly surprised to find that my economic and statistical analysis correctly predicted a number of major commodity price moves. It was not long thereafter that the thought of trading came to mind. The only problem was that my department generally did not permit analysts to trade. I discussed my frustration over this situation with Michael Marcus (first interview), with whom I became friends while interviewing for the research position he was vacating. Michael said, "You know, I had the same problem when I worked there. You should do what I did—open an account at another firm." He introduced me to a broker at his new firm, who was willing to open the account.

At the time, I was earning less than the department secretary, so I didn't exactly have much risk capital. I had my brother open a $2,000 account for which I acted as an advisor. Since the account had to be kept secret, I could not call in any orders from my desk. Every time I wanted to initiate or liquidate a position, I had to take the elevator to the building's basement to use the public phone. (Marcus' solution to the same problem is discussed in his interview.) The worst part of the situation was not merely the delays in order entry, which were often nerve-wracking, but the fact that I had to be very circumspect about the number of times I left my desk. Sometimes, I would decide to delay an order until the following morning in order to avoid creating any suspicion.

I don't remember any specifics about my first few trades. All I recall is that, on balance, I did only a little better than break even after paying commissions. Then came the first trade that made a lasting impression. I had done a very detailed analysis of the cotton market throughout the entire post–World War II period. I discovered that because of a variety of government support programs, only two seasons since 1953 could truly be termed *free markets* [markets in which prices were determined by supply and demand rather than the prevailing government program]. I correctly concluded that only these two seasons could be used in forecasting prices. Unfortunately, I failed to reach the more significant conclusion that existing data were insufficient to permit a meaningful market analysis. Based on a comparison with these two seasons, I inferred that cotton prices, which were then trading at 25 cents per pound, would move higher, but peak around 32–33 cents.

The initial part of the forecast proved correct as cotton prices edged higher over a period of months. Then the advance accelerated and cotton jumped from 28 to 31 cents in a single week. This latest rally was attributed to some news I considered rather unimportant. "Close enough to my projected top," I thought, and I decided to go short. Thereafter, the market moved slightly higher and then quickly broke back to the 29-cent level. This seemed perfectly natural to me, as I expected markets to conform to my analysis. My profits and elation were short-lived, however, as cotton prices soon rebounded to new highs and then moved unrelentingly higher: 32 cents, 33 cents, 34 cents, 35 cents. Finally, with my account equity wiped out, I was forced to liquidate the position. Not having much money in those days may have been one of my luckiest breaks, since cotton eventually soared to an incredible level of 99 cents—more than double the century's previous high price!

That trade knocked me out of the box for a while. Over the next few years, I again tried my hand at trading a couple of times. In each instance, I started with not much more than $2,000 and eventually wiped out because of a single large loss. My only consolation was that the amounts I lost were relatively small.

Two things finally broke this pattern of failure. First, I met Steve Chronowitz. At the time, I was the commodity research director at Hornblower & Weeks, and I hired Steve to fill a slot as the department's precious metals analyst. Steve and I shared the same office, and we quickly became good friends. In contrast to myself, a pure fundamental analyst, Steve's approach to the markets was strictly technical. (The fundamental analyst uses economic data to forecast prices, while the technical analyst employs internal market data—such as price, volume, and sentiment—to project prices.)

Until that time, I had viewed technical analysis with great skepticism. I tended to doubt that anything as simple as chart reading could be of any value. Working closely with Steve, however, I began to notice that his market calls were often right. Eventually, I became convinced that my initial assessment of technical analysis was wrong. I realized that, at least for myself, fundamental analysis alone was insufficient for successful trading; I also needed to incorporate technical analysis for the timing of trades.

The second key element that finally put me into the winner's column was the realization that risk control was absolutely essential to successful trading. I decided that I would never again allow myself to lose everything on a single trade—no matter how convinced I was of my market view.

Ironically, the trade that I consider my turning point and one of my best trades ever was actually a loss. At the time, the Deutsche mark had carved out a lengthy trading range following an extended decline. Based on my market analysis, I believed that the Deutsche mark was forming an important price base. I went long within the consolidation, simultaneously placing a good-till-cancelled stop order just below the recent low. I reasoned that if I was right, the market should not fall to new lows. Several days later, the market started falling and I was stopped out of my position at a small loss. The great thing was that after I was stopped out, the market plummeted like a stone. In the past, this type of trade would have wiped me out; instead, I suffered only a minor loss.

Not long thereafter, I became bullish on the Japanese yen, which had formed a technically bullish consolidation, providing a meaningful close point to place a protective stop. While I normally implemented only a one-contract position, the fact that I felt reasonably able to define my risk at only 15 ticks per contract—today, I find it hard to believe that I was able to get away with that close a stop—allowed me to put on a three-contract position. The market never looked back. Although I ended up getting out of that position far too early, I held one of the contracts long enough to triple my small account size. That was the start of my success at trading. Over the next few years, the synthesis of technical and fundamental analysis combined with risk control allowed me to build my small stake into well over $100,000.

Then the streak ended. I found myself trading more impulsively, failing to follow the rules I had learned. In retrospect, I believe I had just become too cocky. In particular, I remember a losing trade in soybeans. Instead of taking my loss when the market moved against me, I was so convinced that the decline was a reaction in a bull market that I substantially increased my position. The mistake was compounded by taking this action in front of an important government crop report. The report came out bearish, and my equity took a dramatic decline. In a matter of days, I had surrendered over one-quarter of my cumulative profits.

After cashing in my chips to buy a house and later taking a year-long sabbatical to write a book,* my savings were sufficiently depleted to defer my reentry into trading for nearly five years. When I began trading again, typical to my usual custom, I started with a small amount: $8,000. Most of this money was lost over the course of a year. I added another $8,000 to the account and, after some further moderate setbacks, eventually scored a few big winning trades. Within about two years, I had once again built my trading account up to over $100,000. I subsequently stalled out, and during the past year, my account equity has fluctuated below this peak.

Although, objectively, my trading has been successful, on an emotional level, I often view it with a sense of failure. Basically, I feel that given my market knowledge and experience, I should have done better. "Why," I ask myself, "have I been able to multiply a sub-$10,000 account more than tenfold on two occasions, yet unable to expand the equity much beyond that level, let alone by any multiples?"

A desire to find the answers was one of my motivations for writing this book. I wanted to ask those traders who had already succeeded: What are the key elements to your success? What approach do you use in the markets? What trading rules do you adhere to? What were your own early trading experiences? What advice would you give to other traders?

While, on one level, my search for answers was a personal quest to help surpass my own barriers, in a broader sense, I saw myself as Everyman, asking the questions I thought others would ask if given the opportunity.

* Jack D. Schwager, *A Complete Guide to the Futures Markets* (John Wiley & Sons, New York, NY, 1984).

Part I

Futures and Currencies

Taking the Mystery
Out of Futures

Of all the markets discussed in this book, the futures market is probably the one least understood by most investors. It is also one of the fastest growing. Trading volume in futures has expanded more than twentyfold during the past twenty years. In 1988, the dollar value of all futures contracts traded in the U.S. exceeded $10 trillion!* Obviously, there is a lot more than pork belly trading involved here.

Today's futures markets encompass all of the world's major market groups: interest rates (e.g., T-bonds), stock indexes (e.g., the S&P 500), currencies (e.g., Japanese yen), precious metals (e.g., gold), energy (e.g., crude oil), and agricultural commodities (e.g., corn). Although the futures markets had their origins in agricultural commodities, this sector now accounts for only about one-fifth of total futures trading. During the past decade, the introduction and spectacular growth of many new contracts has resulted in the financial-type markets (currencies, interest rate instruments, and stock indexes) accounting for approximately 60 percent

*This is a rough but conservative estimate based on 246 million contracts traded and assuming an average contract value well over $40,000. (Excluding short-term interest rate futures, such as Eurodollars, single contract values ranged from about $11,000 for sugar at 10¢/lb. to $150,000 for the S&P 500 at an index value of 300.)

of all futures trading. (Energy and metal markets account for nearly half of the remaining 40 percent.) Thus, while the term commodities is often used to refer to the futures markets, it has increasingly become a misnomer. Many of the most actively traded futures markets, such as those in the financial instruments, are not truly commodities, while many commodity markets have no corresponding futures markets.

The essence of a futures market is in its name: Trading involves a standardized contract for a commodity, such as gold, or a financial instrument, such as T-bonds, for a future delivery date, as opposed to the present time. For example, if an automobile manufacturer needs copper for current operations, it will buy its materials directly from a producer. If, however, the same manufacturer was concerned that copper prices would be much higher in six months, it could approximately lock in its costs at that time by buying copper futures now. (This offset of future price risk is called a hedge.) If copper prices climbed during the interim, the profit on the futures hedge would approximately offset the higher cost of copper at the time of actual purchase. Of course, if copper prices declined instead, the futures hedge would result in a loss, but the manufacturer would end up buying its copper at lower levels than it was willing to lock in.

While hedgers, such as the above automobile manufacturer, participate in futures markets to reduce the risk of an adverse price move, traders participate in an effort to profit from anticipated price changes. In fact, many traders will prefer the futures markets over their cash counterparts as trading vehicles for a variety of reasons:

1. *Standardized contracts*—Futures contracts are standardized (in terms of quantity and quality); thus, the trader does not have to find a specific buyer or seller in order to initiate or liquidate a position.

2. *Liquidity* —All of the major futures markets provide excellent liquidity.

3. *Ease of going short*—The futures markets allow equal ease of going short as well as long. For example, the short seller in the stock market (who is actually borrowing stock to sell) must wait for an uptick before initiating a position; no such restriction exists in the futures markets.

4. *Leverage*—The futures markets offer tremendous leverage. Roughly speaking, initial margin requirements are usually equal to 5 to 10 percent of the contract value. (The use of the term *margin* in the futures market is unfortunate because it leads to tremendous confusion with the concept of margins in stocks. In the futures markets, margins do not imply partial payments, since no actual physical transaction occurs until the expiration date; rather, margins are basically good-faith deposits.) Although high leverage is one of the attributes of futures markets for traders, it should be emphasized that leverage is a two-edged sword. The undisciplined use of leverage is the single most important reason why most traders lose money in the futures markets. In general, futures prices are no more volatile than the underlying cash prices or, for that matter, many stocks. The high-risk reputation of futures is largely a consequence of the leverage factor.

5. *Low transaction costs*—Futures markets provide very low transaction costs. For example, it is far less expensive for a stock portfolio manager to reduce market exposure by selling the equivalent dollar amount of stock index futures contracts than by selling individual stocks.

6. *Ease of offset*—A futures position can be offset at any time during market hours, providing prices are not locked at limit-up or limit-down. (Some futures markets specify daily maximum price changes. In cases in which free market forces would normally seek an equilibrium price outside the range of boundaries implied by price limits, the market will simply move to the limit and virtually cease to trade.)

7. *Guaranteed by exchange*—The futures trader does not have to be concerned about the financial stability of the person on the other side of the trade. All futures transactions are guaranteed by the clearinghouse of the exchange.

Since by their very structure, futures are closely tied to their underlying markets (the activity of arbitrageurs assures that deviations are relatively minor and short lived), price moves in futures will very closely parallel those in the corresponding cash markets. Keeping in mind that the majority of futures trading activity is concentrated in financial instruments, many futures traders are, in reality, traders in stocks, bonds, and currencies. In this context, the comments of futures traders interviewed

in the following chapters have direct relevance even to investors who
have never ventured beyond stocks and bonds.

The Interbank Currency Market Defined

The interbank currency market is a twenty-four-hour market which literally follows the sun around the world, moving from banking centers in the U.S. to Australia, to the Far East, to Europe, and finally back to the U.S. The market exists to fill the need of companies to hedge exchange risk in a world of rapidly fluctuating currency values. For example, if a Japanese electronics manufacturer negotiates an export sale of stereo equipment to the U.S. with payment in dollars to be received six months hence, that manufacturer is vulnerable to a depreciation of the dollar versus the yen during the interim. If the manufacturer wants to assure a fixed price in the local currency (yen) in order to lock in a profit, he can hedge himself by selling the equivalent amount of U.S. dollars in the interbank market for the anticipated date of payment. The banks will quote the manufacturer an exchange rate for the precise amount required, for the specific future date.

Speculators trade in the interbank currency market in an effort to profit from their expectations regarding shifts in exchange rates. For example, a speculator who anticipated a decline in the British pound against the dollar would simply sell forward British pounds. (All transactions in the interbank market are denominated in U.S. dollars.) A speculator who expected the British pound to decline versus the Japanese yen would buy a specific dollar amount of Japanese yen and sell an equivalent dollar amount of British pounds.

Michael Marcus

Blighting Never Strikes Twice

Michael Marcus began his career as a commodity research analyst for a major brokerage house. His near-compulsive attraction to trading led him to abandon his salaried position to pursue full-time trading. After a brief, almost comical, stint as a floor trader, he went to work for Commodities Corporation, a firm that hired professional traders to trade the company's own funds. Marcus became one of their most successful traders. In a number of years, his profits exceeded the combined total profit of all the other traders. Over a ten-year period, he multiplied his company account by an incredible 2,500-fold!

I first met Marcus the day I joined Reynolds Securities as a futures research analyst. Marcus had accepted a similar job at a competing firm, and I was assuming the position he had just vacated. In those early years in both our careers, we met regularly. Although I usually found my own analysis more persuasive when we disagreed, Marcus ultimately proved right about the direction of the market. Eventually, Marcus accepted a job as a trader, became very successful, and moved out to the West Coast.

When I first conceived the idea for this book, Marcus was high on my list of interview candidates. Marcus' initial response to my request was agreeable, but not firm. Several weeks later, he declined, as his desire to maintain anonymity dominated his natural inclination to participate in an endeavor he found appealing. (Marcus knew and respected many of the other traders I was interviewing.) I was very disappointed because

Marcus is one of the finest traders I have been privileged to know. Fortunately, some additional persuasion by a mutual friend helped change his mind.

When I met Marcus for this interview, it had been seven years since we had last seen each other. The interview was conducted in Marcus' home, a two-house complex set on a cliff overlooking a private beach in Southern California. You enter the complex through a massive gate ("amazing gate" as described by an assistant who provided me with driving directions) that would probably have a good chance of holding up through a panzer division attack.

On first greeting, Marcus seemed aloof, almost withdrawn. This quiet side of Marcus' personality makes his description of his short-lived attempt to be a floor trader particularly striking. He became animated, however, as soon as he began talking about his trading experiences. Our conversation focused on his early "roller coaster" years, which he considered to be the most interesting of his career.

How did you first get interested in trading futures?

I was something of a scholar. In 1969, I graduated from Johns Hopkins, Phi Beta Kappa, near the top of my class. I had a Ph.D. fellowship in psychology at Clark University, and fully expected to live the life of a professor. Through a mutual friend, I met this fellow named John, who claimed he could double my money every two weeks, like clockwork. That sounded very appealing [he laughs]. I don't think I even asked John how he could do it. It was such an attractive idea that I didn't want to spoil things by finding out too many facts. I was afraid I would get cold feet.

Weren't you skeptical? Didn't he sound too much like a used car salesman?

No, I had never invested in anything, and I was very naive. I hired John, who was a junior at my school, to be my commodity trading advisor at $30 a week. Occasionally, I threw in free potato chips and soda. He had a theory that you could subsist on that diet.

That's all you paid him? Weren't there any profit incentives—extra potato chips if he did well?

No.

How much money did you allot for trading?

About $1,000 that I had saved up.

Then what happened?

My first trip to a brokerage house was very, very exciting. I got dressed up, putting on my only suit, and we went to the Reynolds Securities office in Baltimore. It was a big, posh office, suggesting a lot of old money. There was mahogany all over the place and a hushed, reverential tone permeated the office. It was all very impressive.

The focal point was a big commodity board at the front of the office, the kind that clicked the old-fashioned way. It was really exciting to hear the click, click, click. They had a gallery from which the traders could watch the board, but it was so far away that we had to use binoculars to see the prices. That was also very exciting, because it was just like watching a horse race.

My first realization that things might become a little scary was when a voice came over the loudspeaker recommending the purchase of soybean meal. I looked at John, expecting to see an expression of confidence and assurance on his face. Instead, he looked at me and asked, "Do you think we should do it?" [he laughs]. It quickly dawned on me that John didn't know anything at all.

I remember soybean meal was trading quietly: 78.30, 78.40, 78.30, 78.40. We put the order in, and as soon as we got the confirmation back, almost mystically, the prices started clicking down. As soon as it knew that I was in, the market took that as a signal to start descending. I guess I had good instincts even then, because I immediately said to John, "We're not doing too well, let's get out!" We lost about $100 on that trade.

The next trade was in corn, and the same thing happened. John asked me whether we should do the trade. I said, "Well all right, let's try corn." The outcome was the same.

Did you know anything at all about what you were doing? Had you read anything about commodities or trading?

No, nothing.

Did you even know the contract sizes?

No, we didn't.

Did you know how much it was costing you per tick?

Yes.

Apparently, that was about the only thing you knew.

Right. Our next trade, in wheat, didn't work either. After that, we went back to corn and that trade worked out better; it took us three days to lose our money. We were measuring success by the number of days it took us to lose.

Were you always getting out after about a $100 loss?

Yes, although one trade lost almost $200. I was down to about $500 when John came up with an idea that was "going to save the day." We would buy August pork bellies and sell February pork bellies because the spread was wider than the *carrying charges* [the total cost of taking delivery in August, storing, and redelivering in February]. He said we couldn't lose on that trade.

I vaguely understood the idea and agreed to the trade. That was the first time we decided to go out to lunch. All the other times we had been too busy scrutinizing the board, but we thought this was a "can't lose" trade, so it was safe to leave. By the time we came back, I was just about wiped out. I remember this feeling of shock, dismay, and incredulity.

I will never forget the image of John—he was a very portly guy with thick, opaque glasses—going up to the quote board, pounding and shaking his fist at it, and shouting, "Doesn't anyone want to make a guaranteed profit!" Later on, I learned that August pork bellies were not deliverable against the February contract. The logic of the trade was flawed in the first place.

Had John ever traded before?

No.

So where did he come up with this story about doubling your money every two weeks?

I don't know, but after that trade, I was wiped out. So I told John that, in light of what happened, I thought I knew as much as he did—which was nothing—and that I was going to fire him. No more potato chips; no more diet soda. I'll never forget his response. He told me, "You are making the greatest mistake of your life!" I asked him what he was going to do. He said, "I am going to Bermuda to wash dishes to make a trading stake. Then I am going to become a millionaire and retire." The thing that amused me was that he didn't say, "I'm going to Bermuda and take a job to make a trading stake." He was very specific; he was going to *wash dishes* to get his trading stake.

What eventually happened to John?

To this day, I have no idea. For all I know, he might be living in Bermuda as a millionaire because he washed dishes.

After that, I managed to rustle up another $500 and placed a few silver trades. I wiped out that stake as well. My first eight trades, five with John and three on my own, were all losers.

Did the thought ever enter your mind that maybe trading was not for you?

No. I had always done well at school, so I figured it was just a question of getting the knack of it. My father, who died when I was fifteen, had left $3,000 in life insurance, which I decided to cash in, despite my mother's objections.

But I knew I really needed to learn something before trading again. I read Chester Keltner's books on wheat and soybeans, and I also subscribed to his market letter, which made trading recommendations. I followed the first recommendation, which was to buy wheat, and it worked. I think I made 4 cents per bushel [$200] on that trade. It was my first win and very exciting.

Then between letters, the market fell back to my original buying price, so I bought it again and made another profit on my own. I felt I was beginning to develop a sense for trading. Even in the beginning, I liked the feeling of doing things on my own. What happened next was just sheer luck. I bought three contracts of December corn in the summer of 1970, based on a Keltner recommendation. That was the summer that blight devastated the corn crop.

Was that your first big win?

Yes, that trade combined with buying some more corn, wheat, and soybeans, partly on recommendations in the letter, and partly on my own intuition. When that glorious summer was over, I had accumulated $30,000, a princely sum to me, having come from a middle class family. I thought it was the best thing in the world.

How did you decide when to take profits?

I took some on the way up and some when the markets started coming down. Overall, I cashed in very well.

So instinctively, you were doing the right thing even then?

Yes. Then that fall I attended graduate school in Worcester, Massachusetts, but I found that I didn't want to think about my thesis. Instead of going to class, I would often sneak down to the Paine Webber office in Worcester to trade.

I was having a great time. I made a little money, not a lot. I was shocked to find myself cutting classes frequently, since I had been a dedicated scholar at Johns Hopkins. I realized that the handwriting was on the wall, and in December 1970 I dropped out of school and moved to New York. I stayed at the Y for a while. When people asked me what I did, I rather pompously told them that I was a speculator. It had a nice ring to it.

In the spring of 1971, the grains started getting interesting again. There was a theory around that the blight had wintered over—that is, it had survived the winter and was going to attack the corn crop again. I decided I would be really positioned for the blight this time.

Was this Keltner's theory, or just a market rumor?

I think Keltner believed it too. I borrowed $20,000 from my mother, added it to my $30,000, and bet everything on the blight. I bought the maximum number of corn and wheat contracts possible for $50,000 in margin. Initially, the markets held steady because there was enough fear of the blight to keep prices up. I wasn't making money, but I wasn't losing it either. Then one day—I will never forget this—there was an article in the *Wall Street Journal* with the headline: "More Blight on the Floor of the Chicago Board of Trade Than in Midwest Cornfields" [he laughs]. The corn market opened sharply lower and fairly quickly went *limit-down*.

[In many futures markets, the maximum daily price change is restricted by a specified limit. Limit-down refers to a decline of this magnitude, while limit-up refers to an equivalent gain. If, as in this case, the equilibrium price that would result from the interaction of free market forces lies below the limit-down price, then the market will *lock* limit-down—i.e., trading will virtually cease. Reason: there will be an abundance of sellers, but virtually no willing buyers at the restricted limit-down price.]

Were you watching the market collapse?

Yes, I was in the brokerage office, watching the board as prices fell.

Did you think of getting out on the way down before the market was locked limit-down?

I felt that I should get out, but I just watched. I was totally paralyzed. I was hoping the market would turn around. I watched and watched and then after it locked limit-down, I couldn't get out. I had all night to think about it, but I really had no choice. I didn't have any more money and had to get out. The next morning, I liquidated my entire position on the opening.

Was the market sharply lower again on the opening?

No, not sharply, just about 2 cents.

How much did you lose on the trade by the time you liquidated?

I lost my own $30,000, plus $12,000 of the $20,000 my mother had lent me. That was my lesson in betting my whole wad.

What did you do then?

I was really upset. I decided I had to go to work. Since there was a recession at the time, I thought I probably couldn't get a really good job and should try to settle for a lesser position. I found that even though I interviewed for positions for which I was unusually well qualified, I couldn't seem to get any job. I finally realized that I couldn't get these jobs because I didn't really want them.

One of the best job openings I found was a commodity research analyst slot at Reynolds Securities. I discovered that it was easier to get this better position because they could tell I really wanted it. I learned that if you shoot for what you want, you stand a much better chance of getting it because you care much more.

Anyway, there was a glass partition between my office and the main office where the brokers sat. I still had the trading bug and it was very painful to watch them trading and whooping it up.

While you were just doing the research?

Right, because the analysts were strictly forbidden to trade. But I decided I wouldn't let that stop me. I borrowed from my mother again, my brother, and my girlfriend and opened an account at another firm. I worked out an intricate code system with my broker to keep people in my office from knowing that I was violating the rules. For example, if I said, "the sun was out," that meant one thing, while if I said, "the weather is cloudy," it meant something else.

While I was trying to write my market reports, I kept peering out through the glass partition to see the prices on the big trading board in the main office. When I was winning, I tried to hide my elation, and when I was losing, I had to make sure not to let it show on my face. I don't think anyone ever caught on, but I was in a manic-depressive state throughout that time. I felt tortured because I wanted to be free to trade without going through this elaborate charade.

Were you making or losing money during this time?

I lost. It was the same old cycle of borrowing money and consistently losing it.

Did you know what you were doing wrong then?

Good question. Basically, I had no real grasp of trading principles; I was doing everything wrong. Then in October 1971, while at my broker's office, I met one of the people to whom I attribute my success.

Who was that?

Ed Seykota. He is a genius and a great trader who has been phenomenally successful. When I first met Ed he had recently graduated from MIT and had developed one of the first computer programs for testing and trading technical systems. I still don't know how Ed amassed so much knowledge about trading at such an early age.

Ed told me, "I think you ought to work here. We are starting a research group and you can trade your own account." It sounded great; the only problem was that the firm's research director refused to hire me.

Why?

I couldn't imagine why since I wrote well and had experience. When I pressed him for a reason, he told me, "I can't hire you because you already know too much and I want to train somebody." I said, "Look, I will do anything you want." Eventually, I convinced him to hire me.

It was really great, because I had Ed to learn from, and he was already a very successful trader. He was basically a trend follower, who utilized classic trading principles. He taught me how to cut my losses, as well as the importance of riding winners.

Ed provided an excellent role model. For example, one time, he was short silver and the market just kept eking down, a half penny a day, a penny a day. Everyone else seemed to be bullish, talking about why silver had to go up because it was so cheap, but Ed just stayed short. Ed said, "The trend is down, and I'm going to stay short until the trend changes." I learned patience from him in the way he followed the trend.

Did Ed's example turn you around as a trader?

Not initially. I continued to lose, even with Ed there.

Do you remember what you were still doing wrong at that time?

I think I wasn't patient enough to wait for a clearly defined situation.

Did you think of just tailcoating Ed, because he was so successful?

No, I couldn't bring myself to do that.

Did you ever think of just giving up on trading?

I would sometimes think that maybe I ought to stop trading because it was very painful to keep losing. In "Fiddler on the Roof," there is a scene where the lead looks up and talks to God. I would look up and say, "Am I really that stupid?" And I seemed to hear a clear answer saying, "No, you are not stupid. You just have to keep at it." So I did.

At the time, I was befriended by a very kind, knowledgeable, and successful semiretired broker at Shearson named Amos Hostetter. He liked my writing, and we used to talk. Amos reinforced a lot of the things Ed taught me. I was getting the same principles from two people.

Were you making recommendations for the firm at the time?

Yes.

And how did the recommendations work out?

They were better because I was more patient. Anyway, I was totally out of money, and out of people who would lend me money. But I still had a kind of stubborn confidence that I could somehow get back on the right track again. I was only making $12,500 a year, but I managed to save $700. Since that wasn't even enough to open an account, I opened a joint account with a friend who also put up $700.

Were you totally directing the trading in this joint account?

Yes, my friend didn't know anything about the markets. This was in July 1972 and, at the time, we were under price controls. The futures market was supposedly also under price controls.

This was Nixon's price freeze?

Yes. As I recall, the plywood price was theoretically frozen at $110 per 1,000 square feet. Plywood was one of the markets I analyzed for the firm. The price had edged up close to $110, and I put out a bearish newsletter saying even though supplies were tight, since prices couldn't go beyond $110, there was nothing to lose by going short at $110.

How did the government keep prices at the set limits? What prevented supply and demand from dictating a higher price?

It was against the law for prices to go higher.

You mean producers couldn't charge more for it?

Right. What was happening though was that the price was being kept artificially low, and there is an economic principle that an artificially low price will create a shortage. So shortages developed in plywood, but supposedly the futures market was also under this guideline. However, no one was sure; it was sort of a gray area. One day, while I was looking at the quote board, the price hit $110. Then it hit $110.10; then $110.20. In other words, the futures price was trading 20 cents over the legal ceiling. So I started calling around to see what was going to happen, but nobody seemed to know.

Was plywood the only market exceeding its price freeze level?

Yes. Anyway, nothing happened. I think the market closed somewhere over $110 that day. The next day it opened at about $110.80. I used the following reasoning: If they let it trade over $110 today, they might let it trade anywhere. So I bought one contract. Well, ultimately, plywood went to $200. After I bought that first contract, and prices rose, it was just a matter of pyramiding and riding the position.

Was that your first really big trade after you had been wiped out in the corn market?

Yes.

Did the cash plywood market stay at $110?

The futures market functioned as a supply of last resort to users who couldn't get supplies elsewhere.

Basically, it created a two-tiered market, a sort of legal black market?

Yes. Those who were frozen out because they didn't have any long-standing relationships with producers could get their plywood at a higher price in the futures market. The producers were fuming at the thought that they had to sell at the legal price ceiling.

Why didn't producers just sell futures and deliver against the contract as opposed to selling in the cash market at the price control level?

The smarter ones were learning that, but it was the infancy of futures trading in plywood and most producers weren't that sophisticated. Some producers probably weren't sure that it was legal to do that. Even if they thought it was, their lawyers might have told them, "Maybe people can buy plywood at any price in the futures market, but we better not sell and deliver above the legal ceiling." There were a lot of questions.

Did the government ever try to interfere with the futures markets?

Well not exactly, but I will get back to that. In just a few months, $700 had grown into $12,000 trading plywood.

Was this the only trade you had on?

Yes. Then I got the bright idea that the same shortage situation was going to occur in lumber. I bet everything on one trade just as I had on the corn/wheat trade, expecting that lumber would also go through the ceiling price.

What was lumber doing at this time?

It did nothing. It just watched plywood go from $110 to $200. Since they were both wood products, and lumber was also in short supply, I reasoned that lumber could go way up—and it should have. However, after I bought lumber at around $130, the government finally woke up to what had happened in plywood, and they were determined not to let the same thing happen in lumber.

The day after I went long, some government official came out with an announcement that they were going to crack down on speculators in lumber who were trying to run up the market like they had plywood. The lumber market crashed just on that statement. I was down to the point where I was close to being wiped out again. There was a two-week period during which they kept issuing these statements. The market stabilized at a level just above where I would have been wiped out. I had just enough money left to hang on to my position.

The market was at $130 when you bought it. Where was it at this time?

About $117.

So even though the magnitude of this decline was much smaller than the price rise in plywood, you lost almost as much money because you had a much larger position in lumber than you had in plywood.

Right. During those two weeks, I was constantly on the verge of being wiped out. It was the worst two weeks in my whole life. I went to the office each day just about ready to give up.

Giving up just to stop the pain, or so that you would at least have something left?

Both. I was so upset that I couldn't stop my hands from shaking.

How close did you come to being wiped out again?

Well, my $12,000 had shrunk to under $4,000.

Did you say to yourself, "I can't believe I have done this again"?

Yes, and I never did it again. That was the last time I bet everything on one trade.

What eventually happened?

I managed to hold on, and the market finally turned around. There was a shortage, and the government didn't seem to have the will to stop the futures market.

Was it insight or courage that gave you the willpower to hold on?

Desperation, mainly, although there was a support point on the charts that the market couldn't seem to take out. So, I held on. At the end of that year, the $700, which I had run up to over $12,000 and back to under $4,000, was now worth $24,000. After that scary experience, I never really overtraded again.

The next year, 1973, the government began lifting the price controls. Because the price controls had created numerous artificial shortages, when they were lifted, there was a tremendous run-up in many commodities. Just about everything went up. Prices doubled in many markets, and I was able to take advantage of the tremendous leverage offered by low futures margins. The lessons I had learned from Seykota about staying in markets with major trends really paid off. In 1973, my account grew from $24,000 to $64,000.

At that time, we were seeing something completely new. I remember those markets. Even after prices had gone up only 10 percent of their eventual advance, historically, it seemed like a very large price move. What made you realize that prices could go so much further?

At the time, I was politically right wing and that fit with being an inflation-alarmist. The theory that the evil government was constantly debasing the currency provided the perfect perspective for trading the inflationary markets of the mid-1970s.

It was the right theory for the right time.

Right. The markets were so fertile for trading then that I could make plenty of mistakes and still do well.

Trading strictly on the long side?

Yes. Everything was going up. Although I was doing very well, I did make one terrible mistake. During the great soybean bull market, the one that went from $3.25 to nearly $12, I impulsively took my profits and got out of everything. I was trying to be fancy instead of staying with the trend. Ed Seykota never would get out of anything unless the trend changed. So Ed was in, while I was out, and I watched in agony as soybeans went limit-up for twelve consecutive days. I was real competitive, and every day I would come into the office knowing he was in and I was out. I dreaded going to work, because I knew soybeans would be bid limit again and I couldn't get in.

Was this experience of not being in a runaway market as aggravating as actually losing money?

Yes, more so. It was so aggravating that one day I felt I couldn't take it anymore and I tried tranquilizers to dull the mental anguish. When that didn't work, somebody said, "Why don't you take something stronger, called thorazine?"

I remember taking this thorazine at home and then getting on the subway to go to work. The subway doors started to close as I was getting on and I started to fall down. At first, I didn't connect it with the thorazine. Anyway, I wandered back home and just fell through the doorway—it was that strong. It knocked me out and I missed work that day. That was the low point in my trading career.

You never threw in the towel and just went back into soybeans at some point?

No, I was afraid of losing.

Despite that mistake, you mentioned before that you built your account up to $64,000 by year-end. What happened next?

Around that time, I would occasionally have to go over to the Cotton Exchange. I would have an adrenalin rush when I heard the traders yelling and screaming. It seemed like the most exciting place in the world. But I learned that I needed to show $100,000 net worth to get in. Since I had virtually no assets outside of my commodity account, I couldn't qualify.

I continued to make money in the markets, and after several months, I had surpassed the $100,000 mark. Around that same time, Ed Seykota recommended that I go long coffee. So I did, but I put a close stop in under the market just in case it went down. The market turned down and I was stopped out quickly. Ed, however, because he was a major trend follower, had no stop in and ended up being locked in a limit-down market for several days in succession.

Each day, Seykota was locked in a losing position while I was out of the market. That was the exact opposite situation of the soybean trade, when he was in a winning trade and I was out. I couldn't help it, but I felt a sense of joy. I asked myself, "What kind of a place is this that one's greatest joy is to be found when somebody else is getting screwed?" That was the point I realized that what I was doing was too competitive, and I decided to become a floor trader at the New York Cotton Exchange

It sounds like the floor would have been even more competitive.

Well, maybe, but it wasn't.

Did you have any concern about being a floor trader—the fact that you were now reducing your field of opportunity down to one market?

I was a little concerned about it. As it turned out, I should have been very worried. However, the thought of trading in the ring was very exciting to me. The truth of the matter was that while I was very good at picking trades, I was a total bust at the execution part. I was very shy, and I was too timid to yell loud enough to make myself heard on the floor. I ended up slipping my orders to a floor trader friend of mine, who handled them for me. That went on for a few months until I realized what I was doing.

Were you still approaching the markets as a position trader even though you were on the floor?

Yes, but it was just out of timidity.

So, I assume that many days you weren't even trading.

Right.

Was there any advantage to being on the floor?

No, not for me. But I did learn a lot from the experience, and I would recommend it to anybody who wants to become a better trader. I used what I learned there for years.

What type of things did you learn?

You develop an almost subconscious sense of the market on the floor. You learn to gauge price movement by the intensity of the voices in the ring. For example, when the market is active and moving, and then gets quiet, that is often a sign that it is not going to go much further. Also, sometimes when the ring is moderately loud and suddenly gets very loud, instead of being a sign that the market is ready to blast off, as you might think, it actually indicates that the market is running into a greater amount of opposing orders.

But how do you use that type of information once you are off the floor? You said that the things you learned on the floor helped you later on.

I learned the importance of intraday chart points, such as earlier daily highs. At key intraday chart points, I could take much larger positions than I could afford to hold, and if it didn't work immediately, I would get out quickly. For example, at a critical intraday point, I would take a twenty-contract position, instead of the three to five contracts I could afford to hold, using an extremely close stop. The market either took off and ran, or I was out. Sometimes I would make 300, 400 points or more, with only a 10-point risk. That was because, by being on the floor, I had become familiar with how the market responded to those intraday points.

My trading in those days was a little bit like being a surfer. I was trying to hit the crest of the wave just at the right moment. But if it didn't work, I just got out. I was getting a shot at making several hundred points and hardly risking anything. I later used that surfing technique as a desk trader. Although that approach worked real well then, I don't think it would work as well in today's markets.

Is that because the markets have become choppier?

Right. In those days, if the market reached an intraday chart point, it might penetrate that point, take off, and never look back. Now it often comes back.

So what is the answer?

I think the secret is cutting down the number of trades you make. The best trades are the ones in which you have all three things going for you: fundamentals, technicals, and market tone. First, the fundamentals should suggest that there is an imbalance of supply and demand, which could result in a major move. Second, the chart must show that the market is moving in the direction that the fundamentals suggest. Third, when news comes out, the market should act in a way that reflects the right psychological tone. For example, a bull market should shrug off bearish news and respond vigorously to bullish news. If you can restrict your activity to only those types of trades, you have to make money, in any market, under any circumstances.

Is that more restrictive trading style the approach you eventually adopted?

No, because basically I enjoyed the game too much. I knew that I should only be in those optimum trades, but trading was a release and hobby for me. It replaced a lot of other things in my life. I placed the fun of the action ahead of my own criteria. However, the thing that saved me was that when a trade met all my criteria, I would enter five to six times the position size I was doing on the other trades.

Were all your profits coming from the trades that met the criteria?

Yes.

Were the other trades breaking even?

The other trades broke even and kept me amused.

Did you keep track of which were which so you knew what was going on?

Just mentally. My goal on the other trades was just to break even. I knew that the big money was going to be made on the trades that met my criteria. There will always be trades that meet those requirements, but there may be fewer of them, so you have to be much more patient.

Why are there fewer such trades? Has the marketplace gotten more sophisticated?

Yes. There are many more professional traders than in my early days. In those years, I had an edge just by knowing the angles that Ed Seykota and Amos Hostetter taught me. Now everybody knows those principles. You have trading rooms filled with bright people and computers.

In those days, you watched the board, and you would buy corn when it moved above a key chart point. An hour later the grain elevator operator would get a call from his broker and he might buy. The next day, the brokerage house would recommend the trade, pushing the market up some more. On the third day, we would get short covering from the people that were wrong, and then some fresh buying from the dentists of the world, who finally got the word that it was the right time to buy. At that time, I was one of the first ones to buy because I was one of the few professional traders playing the game. I would wind up selling out to the dentists several days later.

You're talking about short-term trades. Weren't you trading for the major moves?

I traded some major moves, but many times I would make my profits in two or three days in just that kind of trade.

When did you get back in the market?

Well, the dentists weren't going to keep their positions, since they were buying at the wrong time. So when the market would fall back, I would go back in. Nowadays, the moment the market breaks a key chart point, it is perceived by a whole universe of traders.

So the lagged follow-up trades are no longer there?

Right, the grain elevator operator has already bet. The dentists don't count because their level of trading participation is infinitesimal.

Is that because they now have their money invested with fund managers instead of trading by themselves?

Right, and even if the dentists are still there, they are trading one-lots, which is a meaningless position when the fund managers are trading a thousand at a clip. Now you almost have to be contrary. You have to ask, "Isn't it true that all my fellow professional traders are already in, so who is left to buy?" You didn't have to worry about that before, because there was always somebody left to buy—the people who were getting the information or reacting slower. Now, everybody is just as decisive, just as fast.

Are the markets more prone to false breakouts now?

Yes, much more.

Are trend-following systems then doomed to mediocrity?

I believe so. I believe that the era of trend following is over until and unless there is a particular imbalance in a market that overrides everything else. [The 1988 drought in the grain belt, which developed shortly after this interview, provides a perfect example of the type of exception Marcus is describing.] Another exception would be if we were to enter a major inflationary or deflationary environment.

In other words, unless there is some very powerful force that can overwhelm everything else.

Yes.

Have the markets changed during the past five to ten years because professional money managers now account for a much greater proportion of speculative trading activity, as opposed to the small speculators who tend to make all the mistakes?

The markets have changed. The proof is that Richard Dennis, who has done well for many years, lost over 50 percent on the funds he was managing in 1988. The trend-following systems approach doesn't work anymore. The problem is that once you have defined a trend and taken a position, everyone else has taken a position as well. Since there is no one left to buy, the market swings around in the other direction and gets you out.

One reason we don't have many good trends anymore is that the central banks are preventing currency moves from getting out of hand by taking the other side of the trend.

Haven't they always done that?

I don't think so. If you look at a chart of treasury debt held by foreign central banks, you will see that it has risen astronomically during the last few years. The foreign banks seem to be taking over from private foreign investors in financing our trade debts.

What do you think that means in terms of trading, and has your own trading style changed because of it?

At one time, I traded heavily in currencies. For example, in the years after Reagan was first elected and the dollar was very strong, I would take positions as large as 600 million Deutsche marks between my own account and the company account. At the time, that was about $300 million worth. That was a pretty good line. I was probably one of the bigger currency traders in the world, including the banks.

It was very exhausting because it was a twenty-four-hour market. When I went to sleep, I would have to wake up almost every two hours to check the markets. I would tune in every major center as it opened: Australia, Hong Kong, Zurich, and London. It killed my marriage. Nowadays, I try to avoid the currencies, because I feel it is a totally political situation; you have to determine what the central banks are going to do.

When you were trading the currencies actively, were you getting up through the night because you were worried about getting caught on the wrong side of a major move before the markets opened in the U.S.?

Yes.

Did you always trade that way, or did you get caught enough times so that you started trading around the clock?

It happened enough times to make me leery.

There would be a big gap move that you could have avoided by trading overseas?

That is right. For example, I remember one time, during late 1978, the dollar was getting battered, falling to new lows every day. This was during a period when I was cooperating and trading as a colleague with Bruce Kovner. We used to talk hours every day. One day, we noticed that the dollar got mysteriously strong. There was an intense price movement that couldn't be explained by any known information. We just bailed out of our long currency positions like crazy. That weekend, President Carter announced a dollar support program. If we had waited until the next U.S. trading session, we would have been annihilated.

That situation illustrates one of the principles we believed in— namely, that the big players, including the governments, would always tip their hand. If we saw a surprise price move against us that we didn't understand, we often got out and looked for the reason later.

I remember that market well. The currency futures markets were locked limit-down for several days in a row after that announcement. You must have gotten out right near the top of that market.

We made a great exit on that trade. Anyway, my point is that I believe, as a courtesy, the European central banks are notified about major changes we are going to make, and they often act ahead of U.S. policy announcements. Consequently, the price move shows up in Europe first, even if it is because of something we initiate. If it's an action initiated by the Europeans, the price move is certainly going to occur there first. I think the best hours to trade are often in Europe. If I had a period in which I was going to devote my life to trading, I would want to live in Europe.

Let's go back and fill in some of your trading history. Where did you go after you decided to give up on being a floor trader?

I got a call from Amos Hostetter, who had befriended me at Shearson. At the time, he was also trading some money for Commodities Corporation. Amos told me that I would be well advised to consider joining Commodities Corporation as a trader.

At the time, their theory was that they were going to hire all these great econometricians to be traders. They had people like Paul Samuelson on the board. They brought up the idea of hiring me at a meeting. The first question was, "What articles has he written; in what journals has he been published?" I had a B.A. in liberal arts and that was it. The punch line was, "He just trades." Everybody thought that was very funny.

But weren't they in business to make money trading?

They didn't think it was possible to really make money unless you had a Ph.D. But Amos convinced them to give me a chance. I believe I was the first non-Ph.D. trader they had ever hired. They started me out with $30,000 in August 1974. After about ten years, I had turned that account into $80 million. Those were some very good years.

Did you multiply the original $30,000 into $80 million, or did they add money along the way?

After the first few years, they gave me another $100,000 to trade. After that time, they were always taking money out. In those years, they were

in an expansionary phase, and they taxed the traders 30 percent a year
to pay for their expenses.

**So you had to make 30 percent a year to keep your account level.
You must have had some incredible return years, given the growth
of your account—particularly under that handicap.**

I was making at least 100 percent a year for years and years.

What was your best year?

My best year must have been 1979. It was an incredible year. I caught
gold when it went up to over $800.

You caught the whole move?

I was in and out, but I remember catching big chunks of it—$100 per
ounce at a time. It was a wild time. In those days, I would buy gold in
Australia, Hong Kong would push it up $10 higher, it would go up
another $10 in London, and by the time New York opened, I was able
to sell out at a $30 profit.

**It sounds like there was an enormous advantage to buying gold in
the overseas markets rather than in the United States.**

In those days, I had an advantage by being in California, because I was
up trading in Hong Kong when my New York colleagues were asleep. I
remember when I heard about the invasion of Afghanistan on the
television news. I called Hong Kong to see if anybody knew about it,
and nobody seemed to; the price wasn't changing. I was able to buy
200,000 ounces of gold before anybody knew what was happening.

**That's 2,000 contracts! Did you have any liquidity problems with
their taking on that size position in Hong Kong?**

No, they gave me the stuff, but of course, they got fried by doing it. I
was told on my last visit to Hong Kong that I shouldn't visit the

gold floor. Some of the people still remember that episode.

They knew who was on the other side of the trade?

Yes, they knew.

Did they think that you knew something?

No, they probably thought I was just crazy, coming in and buying all that gold. Then, when the news broke about five to ten minutes later, everybody started scrambling. I had an immediate $10 per ounce profit on 200,000 ounces.

It's hard to believe you could trade off the television news.

I know. I had never done it before. That was the first, last, and only time, but I did do it.

That particular gold market ended in a near-vertical rise and fall. Did you get out in time?

Yes, I got out around $750 on the way up. I felt sick, when I saw gold go up to nearly $900. But later when it was back down to $400, I felt much better about it.

All in all, you got out very well. What tipped you off that we were near a top?

At that time, we had many wild markets. One of my rules was to get out when the volatility and the momentum became absolutely insane. One way I had of measuring that was with limit days. In those days, we used to have a lot of situations when a market would go limit-up for a number of consecutive days. On the third straight limit-up day, I would begin to be very, very cautious. I would almost always get out on the fourth limit-up day. And, if I had somehow survived with any part of my position that long, I had a mandatory rule to get out on the fifth limit-up day. I just forced myself out of the market on that kind of volatility.

Your transition from being a losing trader to being very successful coincided with the big bull phase in the commodity markets during the early to mid-1970s. How much of your early success was due to your skills as a trader and how much was just the markets?

Honestly, I think the markets were so good, that by buying and holding you just couldn't lose. There were a lot of other success stories. Fortunes were being made.

But a lot of those people didn't keep their fortunes.

That's true. But, I was very fortunate. By the time the markets got difficult again, I was a good trader. By then, I had really learned my craft.

Also, by that time, I had the advantage of having become very knowledgeable in one market: cocoa. For almost two years, I traded almost nothing but cocoa, because of the information and help I got from Helmut Weymar [the founder of Commodities Corporation]. Helmut was an incredible expert on cocoa. He wrote a book that was so deep I couldn't understand the cover. Also, he had all kinds of friends in the business. With the knowledge and information I got from Helmut and his friends, I felt that I knew the universe of cocoa in a way that I had never known any market before.

That phase of almost exclusive cocoa trading obviously came to an end. What happened?

Helmut retired from cocoa trading.

I assume Helmut was not nearly as successful a trader as you were.

Let's just say that I traded much better on Helmut's information than he did.

Excluding the early losing years, were there any trades that stand out as being particularly traumatic?

Well, I would never let myself get caught up in potentially intimidating disasters. The worst situation occurred during my heavy currency trading period. I was doing well and could afford to hold large positions. One time, I had a really large position in Deutsche marks when the Bundesbank came in and decided to punish the speculators. I called in just around the time that all this was happening and found out that I was out $2½ million in about five minutes. So I got out, rather than see the $2½ million loss go to $10 million. Then I had to endure the disturbing experience of watching the market recover its entire fall.

How long after you got out?

About half an hour.

Did you go back in?

No, they had taken the starch out of me by that point.

In retrospect, do you feel you did the right thing by getting out of that trade?

Yes, but it still hurt to realize that if I had sat it out and done nothing, I would have been OK instead of losing $2½ million.

Did you invest any of the money you were making in your trading, or did you keep plowing it back into your own account?

I made a number of bad investments and lost a fairly large chunk of the money I had made trading. When I was trading big, I wanted to have a reason to keep doing it, so I just spent money wildly. At one time, I owned about ten houses and ended up losing money on all of them. Some I sold before I had even spent a single night in them. I had a plane charter service and lost a lot of money on that. At one point, I figured out that for every dollar I made trading, 30 percent was going to the government, 30 percent was going to support my planes, and 20 percent was going to support my real estate. So I finally decided to sell everything.

It sounds like as wise as you were as a trader, you were naive as an investor.

Yes, I was incredibly naive. Out of a fairly large number of real estate transactions—many in California—I lost money on all but one of them. I am probably the only person alive that can claim that dubious distinction.

Why do you think you did so poorly on your investments?

I would do everything emotionally. I didn't analyze anything.

In a sense, you were repeating the mistake of your early trading experience: getting involved in something you knew nothing about and then losing money. Didn't any bells go off? It almost sounds like you had a self-destructive instinct in losing your money elsewhere.

Yes, absolutely. I probably lost more than half the money I made.

During this period when you were doing all these unwise things, didn't anybody try to grab you by the shoulders and say, "Do you realize what you're doing?"

Yes, but any time someone on my staff did, I would fire them. At one time, I was employing sixty or seventy people. In addition to all my money-losing businesses, I had a huge nut to make to just support the payroll. Frankly, a lot of the money I made just went down the drain.

Did these losses have any of the emotional impact of losses in the market? The reason I ask is that you seem to talk about these investment losses very dispassionately.

Yes, it hurt to realize what a fool I had been, but I have learned not to be as attached to material things. I accepted it as a life lesson. I learned I don't have to own a house in every beautiful place in the world; I can stay at a hotel and walk on the beach or climb a trail there. Or, if I really feel like spoiling myself, I can charter a plane; I don't have to own one.

Right, that certainly makes sense, but what I am getting at is that I suspect that if you had lost the same amount of money trading, it would have been a much more traumatic experience. Is that because your ego wasn't attached to these other ventures?

Yes, I'm sure that's true. I always felt that, at least, I was smart at one thing. I feel like trading is the only thing I am really good at. If not for that, I probably would have wound up shining shoes.

Do you think being a great trader is an innate skill?

I think to be in the upper echelon of successful traders requires an innate skill, a gift. It's just like being a great violinist. But to be a competent trader and make money is a skill you can learn.

Having been through the whole trading experience from failure to extreme success, what basic advice could you give a beginning trader or a losing trader?

The first thing I would say is always bet less than 5 percent of your money on any one idea. That way you can be wrong more than twenty times; it will take you a long time to lose your money. I would emphasize that the 5 percent applies to one idea. If you take a long position in two different related grain markets, that is still one idea.

The next thing I would advise is to always use stops. I mean actually put them in, because that commits you to get out at a certain point.

Do you always pick a point where you will get out before you get in?

Yes, I have always done that. You have to.

I would imagine in your case you can't actually put a stop in because your orders are too large.

Yes, but my broker can hold it.

When you place an order to get into a position, is it accompanied by an order to get out?

That's right. Another thing is that if a position doesn't feel right as soon as you put it on, don't be embarrassed to change your mind and get right out.

So, if you put the trade on and five minutes later it doesn't feel right, don't think to yourself, "If I get out this quickly, my broker will think that I'm an idiot."

Yes, exactly. If you become unsure about a position, and you don't know what to do, just get out. You can always come back in. When in doubt, get out and get a good night's sleep. I've done that lots of times and the next day everything was clear.

Do you sometimes go back in right after you get out?

Yes, often the next day. While you are in, you can't think. When you get out, then you can think clearly again.

What other advice would you give the novice trader?

Perhaps the most important rule is to hold on to your winners and cut your losers. Both are equally important. If you don't stay with your winners, you are not going to be able to pay for the losers.

You also have to follow your own light. Because I have so many friends who are talented traders, I often have to remind myself that if I try to trade their way, or on their ideas, I am going to lose. Every trader has strengths and weaknesses. Some are good holders of winners, but may hold their losers a little too long. Others may cut their winners a little short, but are quick to take their losses. As long as you stick to your own style, you get the good and bad in your own approach. When you try to incorporate someone else's style, you often wind up with the worst of both styles. I've done that a lot.

Is it a problem because you don't have the same type of confidence in a trade that isn't yours?

Exactly. In the final analysis, you need to have the courage to hold the position and take the risk. If it comes down to "I'm in this trade because Bruce is in it," then you are not going to have the courage to stick with it. So you might as well not be in it in the first place.

Do you still talk to other traders about markets?

Not too much. Over the years, it has mostly cost me money. When I talk to other traders, I try to keep very conscious of the idea that I have to listen to myself. I try to take their information without getting overly influenced by their opinion.

I assume that we are talking about very talented traders, and it still doesn't make a difference. If it is not your own idea, it messes up your trading?

Right. You need to be aware that the world is very sophisticated and always ask yourself: "How many people are left to act on this particular idea?" You have to consider whether the market has already discounted your idea.

How can you possibly evaluate that?

By using the classic momentum-type indicators and observing market tone. How many days has the market been down or up in a row? What is the reading on the sentiment indexes?

Can you think of any good examples of market tone tipping you off on a trade?

The most classic illustration I can think of is one of the soybean bull markets in the late 1970s. At the time, soybeans were in extreme shortage. One of the things pushing the market up was the weekly government reports indicating strong export commitments and sales. I was holding a heavy long position in soybeans and someone from Commodities Corporation called me with the latest export figures. He said, "I have good news and I have bad news." I said, "OK, what is the good news?" "The good news is that the export commitment figure was fantastic. The bad news is that you don't have a *limit position* [the maximum permissible speculative position size]." They were expecting the market to be limit-up for the next three days.

Actually, I wound up being a little depressed that I didn't have a larger position. The next morning, I entered an order to buy some more contracts on the opening, just in case I got lucky and the market traded before locking limit-up. I sat back to watch the fun. The market opened limit-up as expected. Shortly after the opening, I noticed a lot of ticks being recorded, as if the market was trading at the limit-up. Then prices eased off limit-up just as my broker called to report my fills. The market started trading down. I said to myself, "Soybeans were supposed to be limit-up for three days, and they can't even hold limit-up the first morning." I immediately called my broker and frantically told him to sell, sell, sell!

Did you get out of your whole position?

Not only that, but I was so excited that I lost count of how much I was selling. I accidentally wound up being short a substantial amount of soybeans, which I bought back 40 to 50 cents lower. That was the only time I made a lot of money on an error.

I remember a situation just like that. It was the cotton bull market when prices almost reached $1 a pound. To this day, I recall I was long cotton and the week's export figure came out showing a half million bales of exports to China. It was the most bullish cotton export figure I had ever seen. But instead of opening limit-up the next day, the market opened only about 150 points higher and then started trading off. That proved to be the exact high.

Another interesting example, I remember, occurred when we were in a very inflationary period and all the commodity markets were trading in lockstep fashion. On one particularly powerful day, almost all the markets went limit-up. On that day, cotton opened limit-up, fell back, and finished only marginally higher for the day. That was the market peak. Everything else stayed locked limit-up, but cotton never saw the light of day again.

Is the implied rule that if you find a common behavior between markets, you want to sell the one that is lagging as soon as it starts heading down?

You absolutely want to put down a bet when a market acts terribly relative to everything else. When the news is wonderful and a market can't go up, then you want to be sure to be short.

What kinds of misconceptions about the markets get people into trouble?

Well, I think the leading cause of financial disablement is the belief that you can rely on the experts to help you. It might, if you know the right expert. For example, if you happen to be Paul Tudor Jones' barber, and he is talking about the market, it might not be a bad idea to listen. Typically, however, these so-called "experts" are not traders. Your average broker couldn't be a trader in a million years. More money is lost listening to brokers than any other way. Trading requires an intense personal involvement. You have to do your own homework, and that is what I advise people to do.

Any other misconceptions?

The foolish belief that there is conspiracy in the markets. I have known many of the great traders in the world, and I can say that 99 percent of the time, the market is bigger than anybody and, sooner or later, it goes where it wants to go. There are exceptions, but they don't last too long.

You have attributed a lot of your success to Ed and Amos who taught you the principles of trading. Have you, in turn, taught other traders?

Yes. My best result, in terms of his becoming the best trader I ever worked with, as well as being a close friend, is Bruce Kovner.

How much of his success do you attribute to your training, and how much of it was just his own talent?

When I first met Bruce, he was a writer and a professor; in his spare time, he was doing some trading. I was staggered by the breadth of trading knowledge he had accumulated in such a short time. I remember the first day I met Bruce I tried to impress him with complicated concepts. Here I was, a professional trader who, in those days, spent fifteen hours a day trading and analyzing the markets, and I couldn't come up with anything that he couldn't understand. I recognized his talent immediately.

That relates to his intellect, but was there something about him that told you that he was going to be a good trader?

Yes, his objectivity. A good trader can't be rigid. If you can find somebody who is really open to seeing anything, then you have found the raw ingredient of a good trader—and I saw that in Bruce right away. I knew from the moment I first met him that he was going to be a great trader.

What I tried to do was convey to Bruce the principles that Ed and Amos had taught me, along with some of my acquired skills. My best trading occurred when Bruce and I were collaborating; we did some phenomenal trading. There were years when I was up 300 percent and he was up 1,000 percent. He had a very great gift.

Do you feel you get ground down as a trader?

Absolutely. Around 1983, I began to taper off in my trading. I felt that I needed to recharge my batteries.

How important is gut feel in trading?

Gut feel is very important. I don't know of any great professional trader that doesn't have it. Being a successful trader also takes courage: the courage to try, the courage to fail, the courage to succeed, and the courage to keep on going when the going gets tough.

Do you have any goals aside from trading at this point?

I have taken karate for many years. I am already at a high level, but I would like to get the black belt. Also, I have made a study of spiritual traditions and there is a bit more work I would like to do with that.

You sound very vague about it. Do you want to be vague?

It is very hard to talk about this. Let me see how I can put it. Albert Einstein said that the single most important question is whether the universe is friendly. I think it is important for everybody to come to a point where they feel inside that the universe is friendly.

Are you there now?

I'm a lot closer.

But that's not where you started off?

No. I started off with the feeling that it was an unfriendly place.

Do you see yourself trading ten or twenty years from now?

Yes, it's too much fun to give up. I don't want to make a lot more money. I would probably just end up losing it in real estate again.

Is the fun aspect still there if you are doing it thirteen hours a day?

No. If trading is your life, it is a torturous kind of excitement. But if you are keeping your life in balance, then it is fun. All the successful traders I've seen that lasted in the business sooner or later got to that point. They have a balanced life; they have fun outside of trading. You can't sustain it if you don't have some other focus. Eventually, you wind up over-trading or getting excessively disturbed about temporary failures.

When you do hit a losing streak, how do you handle it?

In the past, I've sometimes tried to fight back by trading even heavier after I start losing, but that usually doesn't work. Then I start cutting down very fast to the point of stopping completely if it gets bad enough. But usually it never gets that bad.

Do you sometimes manage to fight your way out of it?

Sometimes, but most of the time I would have been better off if I had just stopped. I've had trouble bringing myself to do that, because I am a natural fighter. The typical pattern is: Lose, fight like hell, lose again, then cut back, or sometimes stop, until I get on a winning track.

How long have you stopped for?

Usually three, four weeks.

When you are in a losing streak, is it because you are out of sync with the markets, or is there a better way to describe it?

I think that, in the end, losing begets losing. When you start losing, it touches off negative elements in your psychology; it leads to pessimism.

There are very few traders who have been as successful as you. What do you think makes you different?

I am very open-minded. I am willing to take in information that is difficult to accept emotionally, but which I still recognize to be true. For example, I have seen others make money much faster than I have only to wind up giving everything back, because when they started losing, they couldn't stop. When I have had a bad losing streak, I have been able to say to myself, "You just can't trade anymore." When a market moves counter to my expectations, I have always been able to say, "I had hoped to make a lot of money in this position, but it isn't working, so I'm getting out."

Do you keep track of your equity on a day-to-day basis? Do you actually plot it?

I have done that a lot in the past.

Is that helpful? Do you think it's a good idea for traders to plot their equity?

I think so. If the trend in your equity is down, that is a sign to cut back and reevaluate. Or if you see that you are losing money a lot faster than you made it, that would be a warning.

Are there any advisors you pay attention to?

My favorite market letter in terms of readability, imagination, and knowledge of the subject is the *California Technology Stock Letter* (CTSL Publishing Partners, 155 Montgomery Street, Suite 1401, San Francisco, CA 94104). I also like the market letters put out by Marty Zweig *(The Zweig Letter*, The Zweig Forecast, P.O. Box 360, Bellmore, NY 11710) and Richard Russell *(Dow Theory Letters*, Dow Theory Letters Inc., P.O. Box 1759, LaJolla, CA 92038).

Of the traders I have interviewed, Zweig is probably the one most mentioned.

You always get something of value out of Marty Zweig. He is very solid.

Judging by the letters you have mentioned, I take it that you trade stocks as well. How long have you been trading stocks?

For about the last two years.

Do you trade stocks differently than you trade futures?

I'm more patient.

Is the selection process different?

No, I look for confirmation from the chart, the fundamentals, and the market action. I think you can trade anything in the world that way.

Do you focus on any particular types of stock?

I don't trade the Dow stocks. I prefer the little ones, because they are not dominated by the big professional traders who are like sharks eating each other. The basic principle is that it is better to trade the Australian dollar than the Deutsche mark, and the small OTC stock than the big Dow stock.

What are the fundamentals you look for in a stock?

I like to use something I found in *Investor's Daily*: the *earnings per share* (EPS). [The EPS ranking is based on comparing the earnings per share growth of a stock relative to all other stocks. For more details on the EPS, see the William O'Neil and David Ryan interviews.] I combine the EPS with my own sense of market share potential. If a company has already saturated their little niche in the world, a high EPS is not that important. But, in those issues where the EPS is growing, and there is still plenty of pie out there, the situation is much more attractive.

I also like to look at the price/earnings (P/E) ratio in conjunction with the EPS. In other words, while I like to see a company with a strong earnings growth pattern, I also want to know how much the market is paying for that earnings growth pattern.

So you like seeing a high EPS with a low P/E.

Yes. That's the best combination. I am sure there is a way of combining the two on a computer and coming up with a very good system.

How about the *relative strength* [a measure of a stock's price performance relative to all other stocks], which is another key indicator in *Investor's Daily*?

I don't think that helps that much. Relative strength tells you what a stock has already done. Frequently, by the time you get a high relative strength figure, the stock has exhausted itself.

Is there anything else you look for in a stock?

I look at the basic industry. For example, right now [May 1988], I happen to be bullish on tanker rates and, therefore, the shipping business.

For what reasons?

Supply and demand. Tanker rates are like commodity prices; they follow a classic cyclical pattern. Prices get high and everyone makes a lot of money, so they build a lot of ships and prices go down. Eventually the ships are scrapped and prices go back up again. We have had very low rates for many years and have scrapped a lot of tankers annually. So we are entering that part of the cycle where prices go back up again.

Does trading become more difficult as the size of the account gets bigger?

Yes, because you are forced to compete in fewer and fewer markets that are being traded by other big professionals.

How much common behavior is there between different markets? For example, can you trade bonds in the same way you trade corn?

I really feel that if you can trade one market, you can trade them all. The principles are the same. Trading is emotion. It is mass psychology, greed, and fear. It is all the same in every situation.

For most great traders, early failure is more the rule than the exception. Despite an incredible long-term performance record, Michael Marcus began his trading career with an unbroken string of trading losses. Moreover, he wiped out not just once, but several times. The moral is: Early trading failure is a sign that you are doing something wrong; it is not necessarily a good predictor of ultimate potential failure or success.

I found it particularly interesting that, despite a number of painful trading losses, Marcus' most devastating experience was actually a profitable trade in which he got out prematurely. Taking advantage of potential major winning trades is not only important to the mental health of the trader, but is also critical to winning. In the interview, Marcus stressed that letting winners ride is every bit as important as cutting losses short. In his own words, "If you don't stay with your winners, you are not going to be able to pay for the losers."

Marcus learned about the dangers of overtrading the hard way. In one instance (the grain trade in the nonexistent corn blight year), an account he had built up from a very small stake to $30,000 was wiped out by betting all his money on a single trade. He made the same mistake a second time in the lumber market, coming to the brink of disaster before narrowly escaping. These experiences had a dramatic impact on Marcus' trading philosophy. It is no accident that the first rule he cites when asked to give advice to the average trader is: Never commit more than 5 percent of your money to a single trade idea.

In addition to not overtrading, Marcus stresses the importance of committing to an exit point on every trade. He feels that protective stops are very important because they force this commitment on the trader. He also recommends liquidating positions to achieve mental clarity when one is losing money and is confused regarding market decisions.

Marcus also emphasizes the necessity of following your own mind as a trader. He suggests that following the advice of others, even when they are good traders, often leads to problems as it combines the worst elements of both traders.

Finally, despite being an aggressive trader, Marcus strongly believes in being restrictive in selecting trades. He advises waiting for those trades in which all the key elements line up in one direction. By doing so you greatly enhance the probability of success on each trade. Making lots of trades when the conditions appear to be only marginally in favor of the trade idea has more to do with entertainment than trading success.

Bruce Kovner

The World Trader

Today, Bruce Kovner may well be the world's largest trader in the interbank currency and futures markets. In 1987 alone, he scored profits in excess of $300 million for himself and the fortunate investors in his funds. During the past ten years, Kovner has realized a remarkable 87 percent averaged annual compounded return. Two thousand dollars invested with Kovner in early 1978 would have been worth over $1,000,000 ten years later.

Despite his incredible track record and huge trading size, Kovner has managed to keep a surprisingly low profile. He has assiduously pursued his privacy by steadfastly refusing all interview requests. "You might be wondering why I consented to this interview," he said. As a matter of fact, I was, but I did not want to raise the question. I had assumed that his agreement reflected a vote of confidence and trust. Seven years earlier, our paths had crossed briefly when we both worked at Commodities Corporation—he as one of the firm's principal traders, I as an analyst.

Kovner continued, "It seems like I can't avoid some publicity, and the stories are usually distorted and fanciful. I thought that this interview would help establish at least one accurate record."

Kovner hardly fits the intuitive image of a trader who typically holds positions with a total face value measured in billions of dollars. With his incisive intellect and easygoing manner, he reminds one more of a professor than a giant-scale trader in the highly leveraged currency and futures markets. Indeed, Kovner started out as an academic.

After graduating from Harvard, Kovner taught political science courses at Harvard and the University of Pennsylvania. Although he liked teaching, he was not enthused with the academic life. "I didn't enjoy the process of always confronting a blank page in the morning and thinking of something brilliant to write."

In the early 1970s, Kovner managed a number of political campaigns, with the idea of eventually running for office himself. He abandoned politics because he didn't have the financial resources, or the desire to work his way up the political ladder from committee jobs. During this time he also worked as a consultant for various state and federal agencies.

Still searching for a career direction, Kovner shifted his attention to the financial markets in the mid-1970s. He believed that his economics and political science education provided the right background, and he found the idea of analyzing the world to make trading judgments tremendously appealing. For about a year, Kovner immersed himself in studying markets and the related economic theory. He read everything he could get his hands on.

One subject he studied intensively was interest rate theory. "I fell in love with the *yield curve*." [The yield curve is the relationship between the yield on government securities and their time to maturity. For example, if each successively longer-term maturity provided a higher yield than a shorter-term maturity—for example, five-year T-notes at a higher yield than one-year T-bills—the yield curve would reflect a continually rising slope on a graph.]

Kovner's study of the interest rate markets coincided with the initial years of trading in interest rate futures. At that time, the interest rate futures market was relatively unsophisticated and price distortions, which would be quickly eradicated by arbitrageurs today, persisted over time. As Kovner explains it, "The market hadn't become important enough for CitiBank or Solomon Brothers, but it was important enough for me."

One of the primary anomalies Kovner discovered was related to the price spread (difference) between different futures contracts. Futures are traded for specific months (for example, March, June, September, and December). Given the prevailing phase of the business cycle, interest rate theory predicted that the nearby contract (for example, March) should trade at a higher price (lower yield) than the next contract (for example, June). Although the nearest two contracts did indeed tend to reflect this relationship, Kovner found that the price difference between more forward contracts often started trading at near-zero levels. His first trade involved buying a forward interest rate contract and selling a more forward contract, in the expectation that, as the purchased contract became the nearby contract with the passage of time, the price spread between the two contracts would widen.

That first trade worked just according to textbook theory and Kovner was hooked as a trader. His second trade also involved an *intra-market spread* [the purchase of one contract against the sale of another contract in the same market]. In this case, he bought the nearby copper contract and sold a more forward contract, in the expectation that supply tightness would cause the nearby copper contract to gain relative to the forward position. Although his idea eventually proved right, he was too early and lost money on that trade. At the end of these two trades, Kovner was still ahead, with his original $3,000 stake having grown to about $4,000.

My third trade is what really put me in the business. In early 1977, an apparent shortage was developing in the soybean market. It was a demand driven market. Every week the *crush* was higher than expected and nobody believed the figures. [The crush is the amount of soybeans processed for use as soybean meal and soybean oil.] I was watching the July/November *spread* [the price difference between the old crop July contract and the new crop November contract]. Since it looked like we were going to run out of soybeans, I thought that the old crop July contract would expand its premium to the new crop November contract. This spread had been trading in a narrow consolidation near 60-cents premium July. I figured I could easily stop myself out just below the consolidation at around a 45-cents premium. At the time, I didn't realize how volatile the spread could be. I put on one spread [that is, bought July soybeans and simultaneously sold November soybeans] near 60 cents and it widened to 70 cents. Then I put on another spread. I kept on pyramiding.

How big of a position did you build up?

I eventually built up to a position of about fifteen contracts, but not before I had to switch brokerage firms. When I started out, I was trading at a small brokerage house. The head of the company, who was an old floor trader, went over the trades every day and spotted what I was doing. By that time, I had built my position up to about ten or fifteen contracts. The margin on a single outright contract was $2,000, while the spread margin was only $400.

He told me, "The spread position you have on trades like an *outright long position*. I am going to raise your margins from $400 to $2,000 per contract." [Spread margins are lower than outright margins, reflecting the assumption that a net long or short position will be considerably more volatile than a spread position. Reason: In a spread, the long contract portion of the position is likely to at least partially offset price movement in the short contract position. In a shortage situation, however, an intercrop spread, such as long July soybeans/short November soybeans can prove to be nearly as volatile as a net long or short position.]

He was obviously quite concerned with the risk in your position.

Yes. He was concerned that I had only put up $400 margin per spread, on a spread which behaved like a net long position.

Actually, he wasn't that far off.

He was right, but I was furious. So I moved my account to another brokerage firm, which shall remain nameless, for reasons that will soon become clear.

You were furious because you felt he was being unfair, or—

Well, I am not sure I thought he was being unfair, but I certainly knew he was an obstacle to my objective. I moved my account to a major brokerage house, and got a broker who was not very competent. The market kept moving up and I kept adding to my position. I had put on my first spread on February 25; by April 12, my account was up to $35,000.

Were you just adding to your position as the market went up, or did you have some plan?

I had a plan. I would wait until the market moved up to a certain level and then retraced by a specified amount before adding another unit. My pyramiding did not turn out to be the problem.

The market had entered a string of limit-up moves. On April 13, the market hit a new record high. The commotion was tremendous. My broker called me at home and said, "Soybeans are going to the moon. It looks like July is going limit-up, and November is sure to follow. You are a fool to stay short the November contracts. Let me lift your November shorts for you, and when the market goes limit-up for the next few days, you will make more money." I agreed, and we covered my November short position.

All of it?!

All of it [he laughs loudly].

Was this a spur of the moment decision?

It was a moment of insanity. Fifteen minutes later, my broker calls me back, and he sounds frantic. "I don't know how to tell you this, but the market is *limit-down*! I don't know if I can get you out." I went into shock. I yelled at him to get me out. The market moved off of limit-down by a little bit and I got out.

Did you end up getting out at limit-down?

I got out between limit-down and slightly above limit-down. I can tell you the dimensions of the loss. At the moment I covered my short November position leaving myself net long July, I was up about $45,000. By the end of the day, I had $22,000 in my account. I went into emotional shock. I could not believe how stupid I had been—how badly I had failed to understand the market, in spite of having studied the markets for years. I was sick to my stomach, and I didn't eat for days. I thought that I had blown my career as a trader.

**But you still had $22,000 compared to your original stake of only
$3,000. Keeping things in perspective, you were still in pretty good
shape.**

Absolutely. I was in good shape, but—

**Was it the stupidity of the mistake or was it the money that you had
given back that caused such emotional pain?**

No, it wasn't the money at all. I think it was the realization that there
really was "fire" there. Until then, I had ridden $3,000 to $45,000 without
a moment of pain.

On the way up, did you think, "This is easy"?

It *was* easy.

**Did you give any thought to the possibility that the market streak
could eventually go the other way?**

No, but clearly, my decision to lift the short side of my spread position
in the middle of a panic showed a complete disregard for risk. I think
what bothered me so much was the realization that I had lost a process
of rationality that I thought I had. At that moment, I realized that the
markets were truly capable of taking money away every bit as fast as
they gave it to you. That made a very strong impression on me. Actually, I was very lucky to get out with $22,000.

**I assume that your quick action that day probably averted a com-
plete disaster.**

Absolutely. After that day, the market went straight down as fast as it
had gone up. Perhaps, if I hadn't made my stupid mistake, I might have
made the mistake of riding the market down.

What eventually happened to the spread?

The spread collapsed. Eventually, it went below the level that I had first begun buying it at.

Since you liquidated your position on the day the market and the spread topped, you would have given back a portion of the profits even if it wasn't for the disastrous decision that forced you out of the market.

That may be true, but for me, that was my "going bust" trade. It was the closest I ever came to going bust and, psychologically, it felt as if I had.

Was that your most painful trade?

Yes. Far and away.

Even though you actually ended up making a substantial amount of money on the trade?

I multiplied my money by nearly sixfold on that trade. I was, of course, insanely leveraged, and I didn't understand how risky my position was.

Was getting out of your entire position immediately after your broker called to tell you the market was limit-down a matter of panic, or do you think you had some instinctive common sense about controlling risk?

I'm not sure. At that moment, I was confronted with the realization that I had blown a great deal of what I thought I knew about discipline. To this day, when something happens to disturb my emotional equilibrium and my sense of what the world is like, I close out all positions related to that event.

Do you have a recent example?

October 19, 1987—the week of the stock market crash. I closed out all
my positions on October 19 and 20 because I felt there was something
happening in the world that I didn't understand. The first rule of trading—there are probably many first rules—is don't get caught in a situation in which you can lose a great deal of money for reasons you don't
understand.

**Let's get back to the period after your soybean trade. When did you
start trading again?**

About a month later. After a few months I had my account back to about
$40,000. Around that time, I answered an ad for a trading assistant po-
sition at Commodities Corporation. I was interviewed by Michael Marcus in his usual idiosyncratic manner. He had me return to Commodities
Corporation several weeks later. "Well," he said, "I have some good
news and some bad news. The bad news is that we are not hiring you as
a trading assistant; the good news is that we are hiring you as a trader."

How much money did Commodities Corporation give you to trade?

Thirty-five thousand dollars.

Were you trading your own money, as well, at the same time?

Yes, and that is something I am very glad about. Commodities Corporation had a policy that allowed you to trade your personal account, as
well as the company account, and Michael and I were very aggressive
traders.

Were you influenced by Michael?

Oh, yes, very much. Michael taught me one thing that was incredibly
important [pause].

That is a great lead-in. What is the punch line?

He taught me that you *could* make a million dollars. He showed me that
if you applied yourself, great things could happen. It is very easy to
miss the point that you really can do it. He showed me that if you take
a position and use discipline, you can actually make it.

It sounds like he gave you confidence.

Right. He also taught me one other thing that is absolutely critical: You
have to be willing to make mistakes regularly; there is nothing wrong
with it. Michael taught me about making your best judgment, being
wrong, making your next best judgment, being wrong, making your third
best judgment, and then doubling your money.

**You are one of the most successful traders in the world. There are
only a small number of traders of your caliber. What makes you
different from the average guy?**

I'm not sure one can really define why some traders make it, while others
do not. For myself, I can think of two important elements. First, I have
the ability to imagine configurations of the world different from today
and really believe it can happen. I can imagine that soybean prices can
double or that the dollar can fall to 100 yen. Second, I stay rational and
disciplined under pressure.

Can trading skills be taught?

Only to a limited extent. Over the years, I have tried to train perhaps
thirty people, and only four or five of those have turned out to be good
traders.

What happened to the other twenty-five?

They are out of the business—and it had nothing to do with intelligence.

When you compare the trainees that made it to the majority that did not, do you find any distinguishing traits?

They are strong, independent, and contrary in the extreme. They are able to take positions others are unwilling to take. They are disciplined enough to take the right size positions. A greedy trader always blows out. I know some really inspired traders who never managed to keep the money they made. One trader at Commodities Corporation—I don't want to mention his name—always struck me as a brilliant trader. The ideas he came up with were wonderful; the markets he picked were often the right markets. Intellectually, he knew markets much better than I did, yet I was keeping money, and he was not.

So where was he going wrong?

Position size. He traded much too big. For every one contract I traded, he traded ten. He would double his money on two different occasions each year, but still end up flat.

Do you always use fundamental analysis in forming your trading decisions?

I almost always trade on a market view; I don't trade simply on technical information. I use technical analysis a great deal and it is terrific, but I can't hold a position unless I understand why the market should move.

Is that to say that virtually every position you take has a fundamental reason behind it?

I think that is a fair statement. But I would add that technical analysis can often clarify the fundamental picture. I will give you an example. During the past six months, I had good arguments for the Canadian dollar going down, and good arguments for the Canadian dollar going up. It was unclear to me which interpretation was correct. If you had put a gun to my head and forced me to choose a market direction, I probably would have said "down."

Then the U.S./Canadian trade pact was announced, which changed the entire picture. In fact, the market had broken out on the upside a few days earlier, as the negotiations were finishing up. At that instant, I felt completely comfortable saying that one of the major pieces in the valuation of the Canadian dollar had just changed, and the market had already voted.

Prior to the agreement, I felt the Canadian dollar was at the top of a hill, and I wasn't sure whether it was going to roll backwards or forwards. When the market moved, I was prepared to go with that movement because we had a conjunction of two important elements: a major change in fundamentals (although, I wasn't smart enough to know in which direction it would impact the market), and a technical price breakout on the upside.

What do you mean you weren't smart enough to know in which direction the trade pact announcement would move the market? Since U.S./Canadian trade is so much a larger component of Canadian trade than it is of U.S. trade, wouldn't it have been logical to assume that the trade pact would be bullish for the Canadian dollar?

It didn't have to happen that way. I could just as easily have argued that the trade pact was negative for the Canadian dollar because the elimination of the trade barriers would allow imports from the U.S. to submerge Canadian interests. There are still some analysts who adhere to that argument. My point is that there are well-informed traders who know much more than I do. I simply put things together. They knew which way to go, and they voted in the marketplace by buying Canadian dollars.

Is the generalization of that example that when an important fundamental development occurs, the initial direction of the market move is often a good tip-off of the longer-term trend?

Exactly. The market usually leads because there are people who know more than you do. For example, the Soviet Union is a very good trader.

Good trader in which markets?

In currencies, and grains to some degree.

How does one know what the Soviets are doing?

Because the Soviets act through commercial banks and dealers, and you hear about it.

It seems rather contradictory to me that a country that is so poor in running its own economy should be a good trader.

Yes, but if you ask people in the business, you will find out that they are.

Why, or how?

It is a joke, but perhaps they do read some of our mail. The Soviets (and other governments) occasionally have advance information. Why shouldn't they? They have the best developed intelligence service in the world. It is a well known fact in the intelligence community that the Soviets (and others) are capable of eavesdropping on commercial communication. That is why the large commodity trading firms sometimes use scramblers when they are making very sensitive calls.

My point is that there are thousands of difficult-to-understand mechanisms that lead the market, which come into play before the news reaches some poor trader sitting at his desk. But the one thing that does hit the market is a huge sale or purchase.

Isn't that the basic rationalization for technical analysis?

Technical analysis, I think, has a great deal that is right and a great deal that is mumbo jumbo.

That's an interesting statement. What's right and what's black magic?

There is a great deal of hype attached to technical analysis by some technicians who claim that it predicts the future. Technical analysis tracks the past; it does not predict the future. You have to use your own intelligence to draw conclusions about what the past activity of some traders may say about the future activity of other traders.

For me, technical analysis is like a thermometer. Fundamentalists who say they are not going to pay any attention to the charts are like a doctor who says he's not going to take a patient's temperature. But, of course, that would be sheer folly. If you are a responsible participant in the market, you always want to know where the market is—whether it is hot and excitable, or cold and stagnant. You want to know everything you can about the market to give you an edge.

Technical analysis reflects the vote of the entire marketplace and, therefore, does pick up unusual behavior. By definition, anything that creates a new chart pattern is something unusual. It is very important for me to study the details of price action to see if I can observe something about how everybody is voting. Studying the charts is absolutely crucial and alerts me to existing disequilibria and potential changes.

Do you sometimes put on a trade because you look at a chart and say, "I've seen this pattern before, and it is often a forerunner of a market advance." That is, even though you may not have any fundamental reasons?

Yes, I will do that sometimes. I would only add that, as a trader who has seen a great deal and been in a lot of markets, there is nothing disconcerting to me about a price move out of a trading range that nobody understands.

Does that imply you usually go with breakouts?

Sure.

But the markets are often prone to false breakouts. There has to be more to it than that.

Tight congestions in which a breakout occurs for reasons that nobody understands are usually good risk/reward trades.

How about breakouts that occur because there is a story in the *Wall Street Journal* that day?

That would be much less relevant. The Heisenberg principle in physics provides an analogy for the markets. If something is closely observed, the odds are it is going to be altered in the process. If corn is in a tight consolidation and then breaks out the day the *Wall Street Journal* carries a story about a potential shortage of corn, the odds of the price move being sustained are much smaller. If everybody believes there is no reason for corn to break out, and it suddenly does, the chances that there is an important underlying cause are much greater.

It sounds like you are saying that the less explanation there is for a price move occurring, the better it looks.

Well, I do think that. The more a price pattern is observed by speculators, the more prone you are to have false signals. The more a market is the product of nonspeculative activity, the greater the significance of technical breakouts.

Has the greatly increased use of computerized trend-following systems increased the frequency of false technical signals?

I think so. The fact that there are billions of dollars out there trading on technical systems that use moving averages or other simple pattern recognition approaches helps produce many more false signals. I have developed similar systems myself, so that I can tell when the other systems are going to kick in. If it is clear that prices are moving because these billions are kicking into the market, it is a lot less interesting than if a breakout occurs because the Russians are buying.

Let's say you do buy a market on an upside breakout from a consolidation phase, and the price starts to move against you—that is, back into the range. How do you know when to get out? How do you tell the difference between a small pullback and a bad trade?

Whenever I enter a position, I have a predetermined stop. That is the only way I can sleep. I know where I'm getting out before I get in. The position size on a trade is determined by the stop, and the stop is determined on a technical basis. For example, if the market is in the midst of a trading range, it makes no sense to put your stop within that range, since you are likely to be taken out. I always place my stop beyond some technical barrier.

Don't you run into the problem that a lot of other people may be using the same stop point, and the market may be drawn to that stop level?

I never think about that, because the point about a technical barrier—and I've studied the technical aspects of the market for a long time—is that the market shouldn't go there if you are right. I try to avoid a point that floor traders can get at easily. Sometimes I may place my stop at an obvious point, if I believe that it is too far away or too difficult to reach easily.

To take an actual example, on a recent Friday afternoon, the bonds witnessed a high-velocity breakdown out of an extended trading range. As far as I could tell, this price move came as a complete surprise. I felt very comfortable selling the bonds on the premise that if I was right about the trade, the market should not make it back through a certain amount of a previous overhead consolidation. That was my stop. I slept easily in that position, because I knew that I would be out of the trade if that happened.

Talking about stops, I assume because of the size that you trade, your stops are always mental stops, or is that not necessarily true?

Let's put it this way: I've organized my life so that the stops get taken care of. They are never on the floor, but they are not mental.

What eventually tells you that you are wrong on a major position trade? Your stop point will limit your initial loss, but if you still believe in the fundamental analysis underlying the trade, I assume that you will try it again. If you are wrong about the general direction of the market, won't you take a series of losses? At what point do you throw in the towel on the trade idea?

First of all, a loss of money itself slows me down, so I reduce my positions. Secondly, in the situation you described, the change in the technical picture will give me second thoughts. For example, if I am bearish on the dollar and a major intermediate high has been penetrated, I would have to reevaluate my view.

Earlier you mentioned that you had developed your own trend-following systems to provide an indicator of where the large amount of money managed under such systems could be expected to hit the market. Do you use your own trend-following systems to trade any portion of the money you manage?

Yes, about 5 percent.

Is that the level of your confidence? I guess it is not negative 5 percent, so it could be worse.

Overall, my systems make money, but they have volatility characteristics, and problems related to risk control that I don't like. But, since they offer diversification from my other trading, I use them to a small degree.

Do you feel it is possible to ever develop a system that would do as well as a good trader?

I think it is unlikely because the learning features of such a system would have to be very highly developed. Computers are good at "learning" only when there are clear hierarchies of information and precedent. For example, expert systems for medical diagnostics are very good because the rules are very clear. The problem with developing expert systems for trading is that the "rules" of the trading and investment game keep changing. I have spent some time working with expert system developers, and we concluded that trading was a poor candidate for this approach, because trading decisions encompass too many types of knowledge, and the rules for interpreting the information keep changing.

Does the fact that you are trading so much greater size than you did in your early years make it more difficult?

There are far fewer markets with sufficient liquidity for the optimum size of my trades.

How much money are you currently managing?

Over $650 million.

I assume more than half of that is due to capital appreciation.

Yes, last year's profits alone were about $300 million.

What are some markets that you really have trouble trading because of insufficient liquidity?

An example of a market I like a great deal, but in which the liquidity is often poor, is copper. In copper, I am now the elephant.

What kind of size can be moved comfortably in a market like copper before it becomes a problem?

I would say, in a day, you can comfortably move 500 to 800 contracts; uncomfortably, somewhat more than that. But the daily volume of copper is currently only 7,000 to 10,000 contracts and a lot of that is local trading or spreads. In contrast, in the T-bond market, you can move 5,000 contracts without a problem. You can also move very large size, in the interbank currency market.

Can you trade a market like coffee, which doesn't have deep liquidity, but sometimes can develop enormous trends?

Yes, I did trade coffee last year and made a few million dollars in it. Now, if I am managing $600 million, and I kick in $2 million in profits on coffee trades, it doesn't really matter that much. In fact, it could even be counterproductive, since the time and energy I spend concentrating on coffee diminishes my focus on the currency markets, which I trade far more heavily.

It would appear that you have reached a size level that impedes your trading performance. Since you have substantial personal funds, did you ever consider just trading your own money and avoiding all the related headaches in managing money?

Yes, but there are several reasons why I don't. Although I invest a great deal of my own money in my funds, the portion of my funds that is managed money represents a *call*. [Analogy to an option that has unlimited profit potential in the event of a price rise, but risk limited to its cost in the event of a decline.] I don't say this to be flippant, since my reputation among my investors is extremely important to me, but a call is a much better position than a symmetrical win/lose position.

Is there a practical limit to the amount of money you can manage?

In most commodity futures markets, there certainly is. However, in currencies, interest rates, and a few commodities such as crude oil, there are limits, but they are very high. I plan to very carefully manage the future growth in the size of funds I am managing.

When you put in orders in markets that are not among the most liquid—in other words, not T-bonds or the major currencies—do you find your orders actually moving the market?

They can, but I never bully a market.

Talking about that, one often hears stories about very large traders trying to push the markets up or down. Does that work?

I don't think so. It can be done for the short term, but eventually it will lead to serious mistakes. It usually results in arrogance and a loss of touch with the underlying market structure, both fundamentally and technically. The traders that I know who thought too highly of their ability and tried to bully the market, ultimately made the mistake of overtrading and went under.

Without mentioning any names, can you provide an example?

There is a recent example of a British trading organization getting into serious trouble after they tried to corner the crude oil market. At first they succeeded, but then they lost control and crude oil prices fell by $4.

What was the end result?

They lost about $40 million and the organization is in trouble.

You are probably managing more money than any other futures trader in the world. How do you handle the emotional strain when you hit a losing period?

The emotional burden of trading is substantial; on any given day, I could lose millions of dollars. If you personalize these losses, you can't trade.

Do the losses bother you at all anymore?

The only thing that disturbs me is poor money management. Every so
often, I take a loss that is significantly too large. But I never had a lot of
difficulty with the process of losing money, as long as losses were the
outcome of sound trading techniques. Lifting the short side of the
July/November soybean spread was an example that scared me. I learned
a lot about risk control from that experience. But as a day-in, day-out
process, taking losses does not bother me.

Did you have any losing years?

Yes, in 1981 I lost about 16 percent.

Was that due to errors *you* made, or the nature of the markets?

It was a combination of the two. My main problem was that it was the
first major bear market in commodities I had experienced, and bear
markets have different characteristics than bull markets.

**Was it a matter of becoming complacent about markets always being
in an uptrend?**

No, the problem was that the principal characteristic of a bear market is
very sharp down movements followed by quick retracements. I would
always sell too late and then get stopped out in what subsequently proved
to be part of a wide-swinging congestion pattern. In a bear market, you
have to use sharp countertrend rallies to enter positions.

What other mistakes did you make that year?

My money management was poor. I had too many correlated trades.

Was your confidence shaken at all that year? Did you go back to the drawing board?

I went back and designed a lot of risk management systems. I paid strict attention to the correlations of all my positions. From that point on, I measured my total risk in the market every day.

When you trade currencies, do you use the interbank market or the futures market?

I only use the interbank market, unless I am doing an arbitrage trade against the *IMM*. [The International Monetary Market (IMM) is a subsidiary of the Chicago Mercantile Exchange and the world's foremost currency futures exchange.] The liquidity is enormously better, the transaction costs are much lower, and it is a twenty-four-hour market, which is important to us because we literally trade twenty-four hours a day.

What portion of your trading is in currencies?

On average, about 50 to 60 percent of our profits come from currency trading.

I assume you are also trading currencies beyond the five that are currently actively traded on the IMM.

We trade any currency that is highly liquid. Virtually all the European currencies (including those of the Scandinavian countries), all the major Asian currencies and the Mideast currencies. *Crosses* are probably the most important trading vehicle that we use that you can't trade on the IMM. [Crosses are a trade involving two foreign countries. For example, buying British pounds and selling an equal dollar amount of Deutsche marks is a cross.] You can't trade crosses on the IMM because they have fixed contract sizes.

But you could do a cross on the IMM by adjusting the ratio of the number of contracts between the two currencies to equalize the dollar value of each position.

But it is much more exact and direct to use the interbank market. For example, Deutsche mark/British pound and Deutsche mark/Japanese yen crosses are highly traded and very active.

I assume that when you do a mark/yen cross, you price it in dollars, not in terms of one of the two currencies.

That's right. You simply say: Buy $100 [million] worth of marks and sell $100 [million] worth of yen. In the interbank market, the dollar is the unit of exchange all over the world.

In situations where a surprise news development or the release of an economic statistic out of line with expectations causes a sharp price response in currencies, does the interbank market react less violently than the futures market, or do the arbitrageurs keep the two markets tightly linked?

The two markets are well arbitraged, but those are the moments when a very swift arbitrageur will make some money. The markets do get a little bit out of line, but not a lot.

Will the interbank market price response to such events be less extreme?

Yes, because what happens on the futures market is that the locals back away and let the stops run. The only thing that pulls the markets back is the arbitrageurs who have the bank on the other side.

What percentage of bank market trading represents commercial activity, or hedging, vis-à-vis speculative trades?

The Fed has done a study on that. I don't have the figures on hand, but it is basically a hedging market. The banks are the principal speculators, as well as a few players like myself.

Is there a reason why the futures market hasn't been able to capture a larger percentage of world currency trading?

The currency futures market is not efficient in several of the most important respects. First, hedging usually has a specific dollar and date requirement. For example, if I need to hedge $3.6 million for April 12, the bank just takes it. The futures market, however, trades only for specific dates and fixed contract sizes, so the hedger is not precisely covered.

So actually there is no way the futures market can compete, because the interbank market can tailor a hedge for any customer.

That's right. In addition, the activity takes place within normal commercial banking relations. That is, very often, the hedger wants to show his banking interest that he has a locked-in profit so he can borrow against it.

Can you talk about your fundamental analysis methodology? How do you determine what the right price for a market should be?

I assume that the price for a market on any given day is the correct price, then I try to figure out what changes are occurring that will alter that price.

One of the jobs of a good trader is to imagine alternative scenarios. I try to form many different mental pictures of what the world should be like and wait for one of them to be confirmed. You keep trying them on one at a time. Inevitably, most of these pictures will turn out to be wrong—that is, only a few elements of the picture may prove correct. But then, all of a sudden, you will find that in one picture, nine out of ten elements click. That scenario then becomes your image of the world reality.

Let me give you an example. The Friday after the October 19 stock market crash, I had trouble sleeping, which is very unusual for me. But I am sure I wasn't the only trader to lie awake that night. All week long, I struggled with how the events of that week were going to impact the dollar. I was trying on different visions of the world. One of these pictures was total panic—the world coming to an end, financially.

In this scenario, the dollar becomes the safest political haven, and as a result, there could be a tremendous rise in the dollar. In fact, on Tuesday of that week, the dollar did rise dramatically as many people withdrew their money from other places. During the next three days, there was tremendous confusion. By the end of the week, the dollar had started to give ground again.

It was then that it all coalesced in my mind. It became absolutely clear to me that given the combination of a need for stimulative action, dictated by the tremendous worldwide financial panic, the reluctance of the Bank of Japan and German Bundesbank to adopt potentially inflationary measures, and the continuing wide U.S. trade deficits, the only solution was for Treasury Secretary Baker to let the dollar go. Someone had to play the stimulative role, and that someone would be the United States.

As a result, the dollar would drop and it would not be in the interest of the other central banks to defend it. I was absolutely convinced that was the only thing that Baker could do.

You realized all this late Friday. Was it too late to take action in the markets?

Yes, and it was a very tense weekend because I realized that the dollar might open sharply lower. I waited for the Far East markets to open Sunday night.

Do you do a lot of your trading outside of U.S. hours?

Yes. First, I have monitors everywhere I go—in my home, in my country home. Second, I have a staff on duty twenty-four hours a day.

Is your staff instructed to alert you immediately in case something big happens?

Absolutely. First of all, we have call levels in every currency. If a currency breaks out of a range that we have previously identified, my staff is under instructions to call.

How often do you get calls in the middle of the night?

I have an assistant trader, and the joke is that he is allowed to wake me up at home twice a year. But it really isn't necessary very often. Whenever the markets are busy, I know what is going on all the time. My home is fully equipped with trading monitors and direct lines. Also, my assistant's job is to be up and get the calls. He probably gets called three or four times a night.

Are you saying that you delegate the nighttime decision making?

We create a scenario for every currency at least once a week. We define the ranges we expect for each currency and what we will do if it breaks out of these ranges.

So your assistant knows that if currency X gets to 135—

He should buy it or sell it. Those decisions have been made beforehand. But they are under instruction to call me if the Prime Minister resigns, or if there is a major unexpected currency revaluation, or something else happens to invalidate the recent scenario.

Are there times you end up trading at night?

Yes, a lot.

You obviously can't trade round the clock. How do you structure your time to balance your work versus your personal life?

I generally try to keep my trading confined between 8 A.M. and 6 or 7 P.M. The Far East is very important, and if the currency markets are very active, I will trade the Far East, which opens at 8 P.M. The A.M. session in Tokyo trades until 12 P.M. If the markets are in a period of tremendous movement, I will go to bed for a couple of hours and get up to catch the next market opening. It is tremendously interesting and exciting.

To see the wave roll from country to country?

Absolutely. When you are really involved, the screen almost reaches out
and grabs you. The way the quotes are made changes: They get wider;
they get wilder. I have contacts all over the world in each of these markets
and I know what is going on. It is a tremendously exciting game. There
are opportunities all the time. Forgetting trading for a minute, one of the
reasons I am in this business is that I find the analysis of worldwide political and economic events extraordinarily fascinating.

**The way you describe it, you make the whole process sound like a
constant game, rather than work. Do you really look at it that way?**

It doesn't feel like work, except when you lose—then it feels like work
[he laughs]. For me, market analysis is like a tremendous multidimen-
sional chess board. The pleasure of it is purely intellectual. For example, it is trying to figure out the problems the finance minister of New
Zealand faces and how he may try to solve them. A lot of people will
think that sounds ridiculously exotic. But to me, it isn't exotic at all.
Here is a guy running this tiny country and he has a real set of problems.
He has to figure how to cope with Australia, the U.S., and the labor
unions that are driving him crazy. My job is to do the puzzle with him
and figure out what he is going to decide, and what the consequences of
his actions will be that he or the market doesn't anticipate. That to me,
in itself, is tremendous fun.

**In following all these varied world markets, I know you read a
tremendous amount of economic literature. Do you also pay any
attention to the various market advisory letters?**

I get a "guru report" every day.

Who is on that list?

All the newsletter writers who have a large following. People like Prechter, Zweig, Davis, Eliades, and so on.

Do you use your guru report as a measure of contrary opinion?

I try not to be too much of a wise guy because during major price moves, they will be right for a portion of it. What I am really looking for is a consensus that the market is not confirming. I like to know that there are a lot of people who are going to be wrong.

So if you see that most of the members on your guru list are bullish at a time when the market is not moving up, and you have some fundamental reason to be bearish, you will feel stronger about the trade?

Yes, much stronger.

Do you think people can trade profitably by just following the gurus?

Probably, but my impression is that to make money, you have to hold a position with conviction. That is very difficult when you are following someone else. There are some good gurus, however. For example, in the stock market, I like Marty Zweig. He uses excellent risk control. Unlike some other gurus, he doesn't believe he is predicting the future; he is simply observing what is happening and making rational bets.

You talk about both the importance of risk control and the necessity of having the conviction to hold a position. How much risk do you typically take on a trade?

First of all, I try very hard not to risk more than 1 percent of my portfolio on any single trade. Second, I study the correlation of my trades to reduce my exposure. We do a daily computer analysis to see how correlated our positions are. Through bitter experience, I have learned that a mistake in position correlation is the root of some of the most serious problems in trading. If you have eight highly correlated positions, then you are really trading one position that is eight times as large.

Does that mean if you are bullish in both the Deutsche mark and Swiss franc, then you decide which one you like better and place your entire long position in that currency?

Yes, that is definitely true. But even more important is the idea of trading a long in one market against a short in a related market. For example, right now, although I am net short the dollar, I am long the yen and short the Deutsche mark. In all my trading, if I am long something, I like to be short something else.

Do the cross rates like the Deutsche mark/Japanese yen move slower than the individual currencies themselves?

Not necessarily. For example, recently the sterling/mark cross rate was in a yearlong congestion between approximately 2.96 and 3.00. It finally broke out about a month ago. The day it broke out, it challenged the top of the range about twenty times. The Bank of England kept on defending it. Finally the Bank of England gave in. As soon as the cross rate pierced the 3.01 level, there were no trades. In fact, there were no trades until it hit 3.0350. So it moved virtually a full 1 percent without trading.

Is that unusual for the interbank market?

Very unusual. It meant everybody was watching the 3.00 level. Once everyone realized the Bank of England was not stepping in, no one wanted to be a seller.

Is that type of breakout—a violent and quick one—much more reliable than a typical breakout?

Yes, it is much more reliable.

Even though your fills are worse?

Terrible fills. The worse the fills are, the better your trade. In that case, after trading for a couple of hours between 3.04 and 3.02, the rate went straight up to 3.11.

Do you believe that the cross rates provide better trading opportunities in currencies than net short or long positions against the dollar?

Yes, because there are a lot fewer people paying attention to the cross rates. The general rule is: The less observed, the better the trade.

Your trading style involves a synthesis of fundamental and technical analysis. But if I were to say to you, Bruce, we are going to put you in a room and you can have either all the fundamental information you want, or all the charts and technical input you want, but only one, which would you choose?

That is like asking a doctor whether he would prefer treating a patient with diagnostics or with a chart monitoring his condition. You need both. But, if anything, the fundamentals are more important now. In the 1970s, it was a lot easier to make money using technical analysis alone. There were far fewer false breakouts. Nowadays, everybody is a chartist, and there are a huge number of technical trading systems. I think that change has made it much harder for the technical trader.

Do you think that the trend-following system approach will eventually self-destruct under the weight of its own size and the fact that most of these systems are using similar approaches?

I think that is true. The only thing that will save those technical systems is a period of high inflation, when simple trend-following methodologies will work again. However, there is no question in my mind that if we have stable, moderate rates of inflation, the technical trading systems will kill each other off.

Let's shift our conversation to the stock market. Do you believe that the stock market behaves differently from other markets, and if so, how?

The stock market has far more short-term countertrends. After the market has gone up, it always wants to come down. The commodity markets are driven by supply and demand for physical goods; if there is a true shortage, prices will tend to keep trending higher.

So if the stock index market is much choppier, are there any technical approaches that can work?

Perhaps, but they keep changing. I have found that very long-term decision-making systems will catch the bigger stock market advances, but you need to use very wide stops.

So you have to be very long term to filter out the noise.

Much longer than most traders can handle because that strategy involves riding out large retracements. As an alternative approach, one of the traders I know does very well in the stock index markets by trying to figure out how the stock market can hurt the most traders. It seems to work for him.

How can he quantify that?

He looks at market sentiment numbers, but basically it is a matter of gut feel.

Some critics have attributed the October 1987 crash to program trading. What are your own feelings?

I think two different elements were involved. First, overly high prices left the stock market vulnerable to a decline, which was triggered by rising interest rates and other fundamental causes. Second, that decline was accentuated by heavy selling from pension funds who were involved in so-called portfolio insurance.

Are we talking about *portfolio insurance* as opposed to arbitrage-type *program trading*? [Portfolio insurance involves systematically selling stock index futures as stock prices decline (and covering those shorts when prices rise) in order to reduce portfolio risk. Program trading normally refers to buying and selling stock index futures against an opposite position in a basket of stocks when the prices of the two are out of line.]

Right. The only way in which arbitrage could be said to have contributed to the problem, rather than helped it, is that if it weren't for program trading arbitrage, portfolio insurance may never have been developed.

So the arbitrageurs are only to be blamed for the market decline insofar as they made portfolio insurance possible?

Yes. If you read the Brady report, you will see that the portfolio insurers came into the market with billions of dollars worth of sales in a few hours. The market was unable to absorb it. Portfolio insurance was a terrible idea; it was insurance in name only. In fact, it was nothing more than a massive stop-loss order. If it were not for portfolio insurance selling, the market would still have gone down sharply, but nothing like the 500-point decline we witnessed.

Do you feel great traders have a special talent?

In a sense. By definition, there can only be a relatively small group of superior traders, since trading is a zero-sum game.

What is the balance of trading success between talent and hard work?

If you don't work very hard, it is extremely unlikely that you will be a good trader.

Are there some traders who can just coast by on innate skills?

You can do that for a while. There are a lot of one-year wonders in trading. It is quite common to find somebody who has a strong feeling that
sugar is going to 40 cents, or that the copper spreads are going to widen
dramatically, and that one idea turns out right. For example, recently I
heard about a trader who made $27 million trading copper spreads this
past year, and then lost virtually all of it.

What advice would you give the novice trader?

First, I would say that risk management is the most important thing to
be well understood. Undertrade, undertrade, undertrade is my second
piece of advice. Whatever you think your position ought to be, cut it at
least in half. My experience with novice traders is that they trade three
to five times too big. They are taking 5 to 10 percent risks on a trade
when they should be taking 1 to 2 percent risks.

**Besides overtrading, what other mistakes do novice traders typi-
cally make?**

They personalize the market. A common mistake is to think of the market
as a personal nemesis. The market, of course, is totally impersonal; it
doesn't care whether you make money or not. Whenever a trader says,
"I wish," or "I hope," he is engaging in a destructive way of thinking
because it takes attention away from the diagnostic process.

In my conversation with Kovner, I was struck by the immense complexity and scope of his analysis. I still can't figure out how he can find
the time to follow and analyze intricately the economies of so many different countries, let alone integrate these various analyses into a single
picture. Clearly, Kovner's unique synthesis of worldwide fundamental
and technical analysis is hardly translatable to the average trader. Never-
theless, there are key elements in Kovner's trading approach that have
direct relevance to the more mundane trader.

Kovner lists risk management as the key to successful trading; he
always decides on an exit point before he puts on a trade. He also stresses

the need for evaluating risk on a portfolio basis rather than viewing the risk of each trade independently. This is absolutely critical when one holds positions that are highly correlated, since the overall portfolio risk is likely to be much greater than the trader realizes.

One statement by Kovner, which made a particularly strong impression on me, concerned his approach in placing stops: "I place my stop at a point that is too far away or too difficult to reach easily." In this manner, Kovner maximizes the chances that he will not be stopped out of a trade that proves correct, while at the same time maintaining rigid money management discipline. The philosophy behind this approach is that it is better to allocate the predetermined maximum dollar risk in a trade to a smaller number of contracts, while using a wider stop. This is the exact reverse of the typical trader, who will try to limit the loss per contract, but trade as many contracts as possible—an approach which usually results in many good trades being stopped out before the market moves in the anticipated direction. The moral is: Place your stops at a point that, if reached, will reasonably indicate that the trade is wrong, not at a point determined primarily by the maximum dollar amount you are willing to lose per contract. If the meaningful stop point implies an uncomfortably large loss per contract, trade a smaller number of contracts.

Kovner's worst trading mistake—his "going bust trade," as he terms it—resulted from a spur of the moment decision. My own personal experience underscores that there is probably no class of trades with a higher failure rate than impulsive (not to be confused with intuitive) trades. Regardless of the approach used, once a strategy is selected, the trader should stick to his or her game plan and avoid impulsive trading decisions (for example, putting on an unplanned trade because a friend has just recommended it; liquidating a position before the predetermined stop point is reached because of an adverse price movement).

Finally, Kovner views a good trader as "strong, independent, and contrary in the extreme," and points to discipline and a willingness to make (and accept) mistakes as significant traits of the winning trader.

Richard Dennis

A Legend Retires

Richard Dennis became intrigued by commodity trading during the late 1960s, while earning the minimum wage as a runner on the exchange floor. In the summer of 1970, he decided to take a crack at trading on his own, and with $1,600 borrowed from his family, he purchased a seat on the Mid America Exchange.

The Mid Am, as it is called, is a kind of minor league exchange because it trades pint-sized versions of the contracts traded on the major exchanges. The Mid Am tends to attract the business of small hedgers and speculators for whom a single regular-sized contract represents too large a position. As a fledgling trader with little risk capital, the Mid Am was well suited to Dennis—it was also the only exchange on which he could afford a seat.

The seat cost Dennis $1,200, leaving him a scant $400 for trading. Incredible as it may seem, he eventually transformed that tiny stake into a fortune, which has been estimated by some to approach $200 million. As his father is reported to have said, in what must be one of the grand understatements of all time, "Let's just say Richie ran that four hundred bucks up pretty good."

Although Dennis has been exceptionally successful over the long haul, he has withstood a few dramatic setbacks. He was in the midst of one such downturn at the time of our interview. Several of the public funds managed by Dennis lost enough during the late 1987–early 1988 period to trigger the 50 percent loss cutoff point for the cessation of trading. Dennis' personal account witnessed a similar fate. As he expressed in a letter to investors, "These results parallel immense losses in my own personal trading."

Perhaps one of Dennis' most impressive traits as a trader is his ability to weather such hard times with little emotional impact. Apparently, he has learned to accept such sporadic large losses as part of the game. His confidence during such periods remains unshaken, as he believes he will eventually rebound if he stays true to his basic trading strategy. Had I not known, judging by the mood and confidence of the man I interviewed, I would sooner have guessed that he had just made a small fortune rather than lost one.

Whatever the stereotype image of a centimillionaire may be, Dennis does not fit it. His low-spending lifestyle is legendary. In fact, his only real extravagances are his sizable political and charitable contributions. His political views also do not mesh with the popular image of the very rich. Dennis is the founder of the Roosevelt Center for American Policy Studies, a liberal think tank, and he supports the concept of higher tax rates for wealthy Americans. In recent years, he has taken an increasingly active role in the political sphere, supporting a variety of liberal candidates. Unlike trading, his win-loss ratio in politics has been disappointing. In the 1988 presidential race, Dennis was the national cochairman for the Babbitt campaign.

In drawing up a list of candidates to be interviewed for this project, Dennis was an essential name. He is one of the foremost trading legends of our time—a trader that a number of others interviewed in this book cited with the phrase, "I'm not in his league."

In setting up the interview, I dealt with one of Dennis' assistants. After explaining the project to him, he told me he would talk to Dennis and get back to me. About one week later, I received a call informing me that Dennis could see me on a date about one month forward for exactly one hour. I explained that I was coming to Chicago for the primary purpose of interviewing Dennis and that one hour was hardly enough time to cover all the essential areas. The response essentially was: that was all the time allotted; the implicit message: Take it or leave it. I agreed, hoping that I would get some more time if the interview was going well.

I arrived about five minutes before the appointed time and was ushered into a large but decidedly unpretentious office. Dennis arrived precisely on the hour, shook hands politely, and sat down at his desk. He apologized in advance if, in the course of the interview, he occasionally glanced at the quote screen, explaining that he could keep his mind on the interview at the same time, and would signal me if he had to put in any orders. Having the experience of trading myself (albeit on an infinitesimally smaller scale), I explained that I understood.

As the interview began, there was an element of unease on both our parts. In my case, I had a sense of a ticking clock with not enough time to accomplish the task at hand. In the case of Dennis, I believe it was a matter of a genuinely shy personality, at least in terms of a first meeting. After five to ten minutes, the tension was gone, the atmosphere became relaxed, and the conversation flowed smoothly.

Forty-five minutes into the interview, I began to think that things were going so well that Dennis would continue our conversation beyond the allotted hour. At exactly ten minutes before the end of the hour, my illusion was shattered. "I've only got about ten more minutes," he said, "so if there's still stuff that's important you may want to get to it." I shuffled through my index cards and quickly tried to identify some of the key questions I had not yet covered. Precisely at the end of the hour, Dennis said, "That's about all the time I have, thank you."

One segment of questions I did not get to dealt with the political side of Dennis' experiences. These topics included the Senate hearings on alleged manipulation of the soybean market by Dennis, the Roosevelt Institute, and the various political figures Dennis had known. Although these subjects were certainly areas of interest and color, they were not pertinent to the primary focus of this book. Consequently, I chose questions related to trading before attempting to turn to anything politically oriented.

At the end of the interview, I played my final card by saying, "I didn't even get to any questions related to the political side." "They're not interested in that anyway," Dennis replied as he politely said goodbye and left the office.

About six weeks later, I requested and obtained a follow-up interview with Dennis. The portion of the interview dealing with the budget deficit problem and Dennis' large losses in his public fund trading at that time came from this second meeting.

A month after our last conversation, Dennis announced that he was retiring from trading to concentrate on his political interests full-time. Will Dennis never trade again? Maybe, but don't bet on it.

How did you first get involved in commodity trading?

After graduating high school, I got a summer job as a runner on the floor and I dabbled in trading a little bit. With my minimum-wage salary, I was making $40 a week, and losing $40 an hour trading. I didn't know what I was doing. The advantage was that at least I got to do it with small amounts of money. I like to say the tuition was small for what I learned.

I heard the story that before you turned twenty-one, you had your father stand in the ring, while you stood on the sidelines signaling trades to him.

That was in 1968 and 1969. My father had the membership but he didn't know much about trading. He was just going along with it because I was underage and wanted to do it. When I turned twenty-one, it was one of the happiest days in his life because he said, "I really hate this. I have no idea what I'm doing. It's yours!"

Were you at a disadvantage trading one step removed, with your father filling the orders?

Sure. We consistently lost.

But you couldn't have lost very much because you were trading very small.

I probably lost a couple of thousand dollars during that period.

Do you consider that period worthwhile, nonetheless, because of the lessons learned?

Yes, in retrospect, I would say this to new traders—although it may not be a reassuring thought—when you start, you ought to be as bad a trader as you are ever going to be.

Because it is less expensive at that time?

Right. You shouldn't be too surprised if you really screw up.

Do you know traders for whom early success proved to be their undoing?

I have noticed variations of that. There are a lot of people who get imprinted like ducks. You can teach them that a warship is their mother if you get them young enough. For a lot of traders, it doesn't matter so much whether their first big trade is successful or not, but whether their first big profit is on the long or short side. Those people tend to be perennial bulls or bears, and that is very bad. Both sides have to be equally OK. There can't be anything psychologically more satisfying about one than the other. If there is, your trading is going to go askew.

    I think that's what happened to a lot of people in the 1973 runaway bull market in soybeans. Even if they didn't make money themselves, but were just present to witness the market mania and see a few people make a lot of money, they were imprinted with it.

You're talking about a subsequent bias to the bullish side because of that experience?

Yes.

What gave you confidence when you first started trading on the Mid America Exchange with such a small stake? After all, one mistake and you were out of the game.

Well, no, the advantage of the Mid America Exchange was that they traded minicontracts. I had a few mistakes in me, and I made most, but not all of them. I don't know that I had any confidence. I just had what a lot of people have when they get in this business: a need to try to succeed. I mean, if you were betting on this sort of thing before the fact, you should have bet that it wouldn't work. There is no doubt about that.

Most traders are not successful in the first year. What were you doing differently?

I was doing enough things right that I didn't capsize even with that small capitalization. I was lucky enough to stagger into having the right positions on before the big corn blight in 1970.

Was that luck or foresight?

I think it was more foresight. I had very pale ideas, rules, and attitudes about the market then. But a few that I learned were right, like go with the trend.

One Friday, the grain markets all closed at their highs for the year. I believed—and I still believe—that you go with the trend, and the stronger the trend, the better. I remember getting in on the close and just buying a couple of minicontracts in corn, wheat, and beans. The next Monday morning they all opened up the limit because of the corn blight news.

Sure that didn't have to happen, and if it didn't, it would have set me back. It might have taken a lot longer to get to about $2,000, which compared to $400 was a real grubstake. But, it wasn't like I threw a dart and decided what to do. I did something that should work in the long run—I went with the trend.

Is this particular pattern—a very strong close on a Friday—a market characteristic that you find useful as an indicator of the following week's price action?

Yes, at a minimum, it is important not to have a short position with a loss on Friday if the market closes at a high, or a long position if it closes at a low.

I was curious about your going to graduate school despite your initial trading success.

I signed up for graduate school before the summer of 1970, which was when I traded in the pit for the first time. I had just planned to trade over the summer, but the three months and $3,000 in profits made a big impression on me. I went to Tulane in New Orleans and lasted for about one week. I used my laundromat quarters phoning trades into Chicago. Once I used up all the quarters and had nothing but dirty clothes, I had no choice but to come back to Chicago.

Since then you have been a full-time commodity trader?

Yes.

What comes to mind as your most dramatic or most emotional trading experience?

There was one in the first year. I had just quit graduate school to trade. One day, I made a particularly bad trade and lost about $300. Since I only had about $3,000, that was a very big loss and it was destabilizing. I then compounded the error by reversing my original position and losing again. To top things off, I then reversed back to my original position and lost a third time. By the end of the day, I had lost $1,000, or one-third of my entire capitalization.

Since then, I have learned that when you have a destabilizing loss, get out, go home, take a nap, do something, but put a little time between that and your next decision. When you are getting beat to death, get your head out of the mixer. Looking back, I realized that if I had had a trading rule about losses, I wouldn't have had that traumatic experience.

In retrospect, would you say that was one of your best trades because you were so imprinted with that experience that you didn't make a mistake of that magnitude, percentagewise, again?

Absolutely. I learned to avoid trying to catch up or double up to recoup losses. I also learned that a certain amount of loss will affect your judgment, so you have to put some time between that loss and the next trade.

I guess a corollary of that would be: When things aren't going right, don't push, don't press.

Yes. After all is said and done, you have to minimize your losses and try to preserve capital for those few instances when you can make a lot in a very short period of time. What you can't afford to do is throw away your capital on suboptimal trades. If you do, you will be too debilitated to trade when the right position comes along. Even if you put the trade on, it will be relatively small because your capital will have been depleted by the other trades.

Was the 1973 soybean market your first really big market?

I made enough money in that market to go to the Chicago Board of Trade the next year. I didn't make my money by just going long soybeans. I was basically a pit trader, who traded in and out a lot. The markets were very good, because there was excellent order flow. It was a great time to be in the pit.

So it wasn't so much catching the trend. It was more a matter of scalping the market successfully.

Also, so many people would make incredibly bad trades just to take a profit. They would get out even though the market was locked limit-up and almost sure to go up the next day. They couldn't stand the profits burning a hole in their pocket. I would try to get in when they were getting out.

It sounds like easy pickings.

There was some amount of risk, but if you were disposed to going with a strong trend, it was a deal. They were giving you an edge to do it.

Giving you a high probability that the next day you would be ahead?

You have to remember some of these markets went up the limit ten days in a row. Most people thought that even four or five consecutive limit-up days was impossible.

In situations where a market goes limit-up, limit-up, limit-up, at some point, the market may open limit-down. How do you recognize or sense when not to buy at limit bid?

It's just an odds play. There is a lot of volatility in the outcome, but you know the odds are in your favor when you go long at limit bid.

In all the years you have traded, have there been any really bad years? Was there a particular market or two that you were dead wrong about and that caused it to be a bad year?

When we have had bad trading periods, it is really not one market that does it. In those situations, almost all the markets are going sideways and making lots of false breakouts. If one of the markets is decent, that is usually enough to avoid a bad situation.

Is there any year that stands out?

1978 was not a good year for trading. I compounded losses unnecessarily because I was in the process of making the transition from floor trader to off-the-floor trader and had no idea how different they were.

Was 1978 the year that you started trading from an office?

In 1977, I was mostly a floor trader, and by 1978 I had made the full-time transition.

Did that switch cause you to become more of a long-term position trader?

Ultimately, what I learned from 1978 is that you have to be longer term

as a desk trader. In the pit, if it looked like soybeans were going to break
3 cents, I would sell, and if it didn't break, I would get out. You don't
have that luxury off the floor, because you lose the edge when putting
in the orders. Also, the judgments you make looking at prices on the
screen aren't as good as those made in the pit watching what is going on.
In the pit, there are indicators that you learn subconsciously, like "these
three guys are never right at market turns," and if they all do the same
thing at the same time, a light clicks on. It took me a long time to realize that those tools weren't going to be available anymore.

**Why did you make the change? You were doing really well on the
floor. Why switch to a desk?**

When I started in 1970, there were no futures markets in currencies,
interest rates, or gold. By 1978, these markets had been listed on the
board long enough to be viable. The currencies started in 1974, but it
took several years to get enough volume.

**So, it was the desire to trade more markets than you physically could
in a single location that motivated your move?**

And the opportunity didn't exist five years earlier.

**I understand that you initiated a trader-trainee program. What
year was that?**

We hired a group at the beginning of 1984 and another group at the beginning of 1985.

What was the motivation for this program?

I have a partner who has been a friend since high school. We have had
philosophical disagreements about everything you could imagine. One
of these arguments was whether the skills of a successful trader could be
reduced to a set of rules—that was my point of view—or whether there
was something ineffable, mystical, subjective, or intuitive that made
someone a good trader. This argument had been going on for a long time,
and I guess I was getting a little frustrated with idle speculation. Final-

ly, I said, "Here is a way we can definitely resolve this argument. Let's hire and train some people and see what happens." He agreed.

It was an intellectual experiment. We trained them as well as we could. That was the way to do the experiment right, I thought. I tried to codify all the things I knew about the markets. We taught them a little bit about probability, money management, and trading. It turned out I was right. I don't say that to pat myself on the back, but even I am surprised how well it worked. It's frightening how well it worked.

Is your basic contention that you can take almost any reasonably intelligent individual and turn him into a successful trader?

No. We screened for people we thought would be right. We received 1,000 applications and narrowed it down to forty people whom we interviewed. Then we picked ten.

What qualities were you looking for?

I don't like to discuss that because if I told you one of the things we looked for was chess players, and we ever do it again, we would be inundated by résumés from chess players.

Was intelligence one of the key items?

It was one of the traits, but it wasn't the essential item. To find the things that we were looking for, we could choose from intelligent or extremely intelligent people. We picked the ones with extreme intelligence just because they were available.

Didn't you have any reluctance about giving away trade secrets?

Sure, but I don't think trading strategies are as vulnerable to not working if people know about them, as most traders believe. If what you are doing is right, it will work even if people have a general idea about it. I always say that you could publish trading rules in the newspaper and no one would follow them. The key is consistency and discipline. Almost anybody can make up a list of rules that are 80 percent as good as what we taught our people. What they couldn't do is give them the confidence to stick to those rules even when things are going bad.

How long was the training process?

Shockingly short. In the first year, it took two weeks. Then we had them trade for a month and keep a log indicating why they made their trades. We wanted to see if they were consistent in doing what they had been taught. We really got good at it in the second year—the course took just one week.

How many trainees were there?

Twenty-three in total.

What were the results?

We dropped three people who didn't do well. The other twenty, however, have averaged about 100 percent profit per year.

When you train people, you tell them your basic approach to the markets. Isn't there a risk of creating twenty clones of Richard Dennis? Wouldn't their trading results be highly correlated with what you are doing?

There was a huge spread. One of the things that we repeatedly told the class was: "We are going to teach you what we think works, but you are expected to add your own personal flair, feeling, or judgment."

How large are the stakes these traders are using?

It has increased over the years as they have made money. I would say on average about $2 million each.

What did they start out with?

One hundred thousand dollars each.

I've heard this group of traders referred to as the "turtles." I found that term somewhat amusing. What is the origin of the name?

When I decided to do the trader-trainee program, I had just returned from a trip to the Far East. In telling someone about the program I said, "We are going to grow traders just like they grow turtles in Singapore." I had visited a farm there and seen a huge vat with thousands of squirming turtles; that became my image of growing traders.

How much of a role does luck play in trading?

In the long run, zero. Absolutely zero. I don't think anybody winds up making money in this business because they started out lucky.

But on individual trades, obviously, it makes a difference?

That is where the confusion lies. On any individual trade it is almost all luck. It is just a matter of statistics. If you take something that has a 53 percent chance of working each time, over the long run there is a 100 percent chance of it working. If I review the results of two different traders, looking at anything less than one year doesn't make any sense. It might be a couple of years before you can determine if one is better than the other.

You are one of the few people who is both a discretionary trader and a systems trader. How would you compare the two approaches?

Professional traders may do some very intelligent things, but they have a tendency not to think systematically about what they are doing. For example, most traders who do a trade that works will not think: Why did it work? What did I do here that I might be able to do in another market, at another time? There is not a lot of reflection on the process of trading. In contrast, I think I always have been analytical about trading, even before I ever researched a mechanical system.

On the opposite extreme, you have the academic types who research before they have ever traded. They lack the seat-of-the-pants knowledge necessary to develop good trading systems. Mercifully, I did the trading first. Therefore, the research we do is more applicable to the real world.

Can you give me an example of how the lack of real world experience would hurt the researcher?

As an example, assume I develop a mechanical system that often signals placement of stops at points where I know there will tend to be a lot of stops. In the real world, it is not too wise to have your stop where everyone else has their stop. Also, that system is going to have above-average skids. If you don't understand that and adjust the results accordingly, you are going to get a system that looks great on paper, but is going to do consistently poorer in the real world.

You mentioned that before you developed a mechanical trading system, you paid close attention to the trading process. Did you keep a log of what you did right and wrong, or was it a matter of memory?

Yes, I would write down observations and think about them. I thought about everything I was doing.

Is that something you would advise other traders to do to improve— that is, keep track of what they are doing right and what they are doing wrong?

Sure. The trading experience is so intense that there is a natural tendency to want to avoid thinking about it once the day is over. I am that way when things are working. But, when they are not, it spurs me to want to think about what I'm doing and how I might do better. When things go bad, traders shouldn't stick their heads in the sand and just hope it gets better.

What you are saying is that the times when it is most tempting to avoid thinking about the markets at all are the times when you should be thinking about them the most.

Right. I don't have any problem with that because I am obsessive about the markets.

What do you do in a situation where your feelings as a trader tell you to do one thing and your systems point in the other direction?

If they are absolutely opposed, you do nothing until you can resolve that conflict.

Are most of your systems trend oriented in nature?

Yes.

So, by definition, they will never be in the right direction at market turns. Yet you, as an experienced trader, may sense when a market may be prone for a turn. In a situation like that, would you be willing to buy because of what you see as a trader even though your system is short?

I would probably want to be flat, since I tend to weigh the psychological, opinion-oriented segment of trading about equal with the technical and trend-following element.

So you want to see the market display some signs of turning around before you'll commit?

What is more likely is that I will be positioned in the right direction of a trend and decide to liquidate faster than a trend-following system would because of the intuitive factor.

What about entering a new trade counter to a prevailing trend?

I've certainly done it—that is, made countertrend initiations. However, as a rule of thumb, I don't think you should do it.

Do those type of trades do more poorly than other trades?

Generally, yes, although every now and then they may give you a great story like going short sugar at 60 cents, which I did. [Sugar plummeted from a high of 66 cents in November 1974 to a relative low under 12 cents only seven months later. Each 1-cent move in sugar is worth $1,120 per contract. A large trader like Dennis will often trade positions measured in thousands of contracts.] I've got ten stories like that. But I have to tell you, in all honesty, I don't think the broad class of trades I have done like that have been profitable.

The short sugar trade is a great example because the market had witnessed an incredibly explosive upmove and it took a lot of courage to step in as a seller at 60 cents. But take the flip side when sugar is in a real bear market and is down to 5 cents; every trend-following system in the world is going to be short. Yet, if conditions are such that the fundamentals are in transition and the market price is only a little over the cost of the bag it's packed in, would you make an exception?

Actually, I've lost more money in situations like that because all the market has to do is go down one more cent and you are out of there. I made a lot of money going short sugar at 60 cents, but I lost much more going long sugar at 6 cents.

When you do a trade like that, that is, buying a market because the downside is so-called " limited, " do you just ride it out, or do you eventually throw in the towel?

You throw it in. Because how do you know? Maybe it is going to 2 cents; maybe it is going to 1 cent.

I guess a main concern is that you are constantly giving up the premium in the forward months. [In a bear market, the more forward contracts tend to trade at a premium. For example, May sugar might be at 6 cents, July at 6½, and October at 7. Even if cash prices remained stable, a holder of October futures would lose 1 cent between May and October.]

Sure, you are forced out at 3 and get back in at 5. Then it falls to 3 again.

Otherwise, there wouldn't be that much risk in the trade.

Right. The idea that one side of the market is much more likely to work in the absence of anything else is an illusion. The market just wouldn't be there if that was true. There were plenty of guys who went short soybeans at $4 in 1973, because just like sugar at 4 cents couldn't go any lower, beans at $4 couldn't go any higher. Well, not only did they go higher, they went to a high of $12.97 in a matter of four or five months.

There is another point that I think is as important: You should expect the unexpected in this business; expect the extreme. Don't think in terms of boundaries that limit what the market might do. If there is any lesson I have learned in the nearly twenty years that I've been in this business, it is that the unexpected and the impossible happen every now and then.

So don't be too tied to history?

Right.

And yet, all your rules are based on history. Is there a contradiction there?

No, because a good trend-following system will keep you in the market until there is evidence that the trend has changed. If you had been doing your historical research on soybeans in 1972, you would have concluded that any time soybeans advance by 50 cents, you might as well get out, because the market had never moved up or down by significantly more than that. Obviously, that was the wrong conclusion because it went up another $8. A good trend-following system, however, would have kept you in for most of the move.

So you don't want to draw boundaries from history over market behavior?

Right. The correct approach is to say: This structure means up, and this structure means up no more, but never that this structure means up this much and no more.

When you trade a system, do you go with the version of the system that tested out best for the past, or do other factors command consideration?

One of the toughest problems in deciding how to trade is whether you just go with what is optimal for the data base, or whether you start from some other premise. You might deliberately trade something other than the *optimal parameter set* [version of the system with the best past performance] because you think the future is going to be unlike the past in a specific way. By definition, any other parameter set is going to have a poorer past performance than the optimal set. But if the difference in performance is only 10 percent, it might well be worth that 10 percent difference if you believe the suboptimal set, as measured by past data, will fit the future better.

You have gone from being a very small trader to a very large trader, especially now that you are managing outside money. Do you find that order size gets in the way? Does it become substantially more difficult to be successful when you are trading size?

At some level it would. I don't think we have reached that point yet, although we may not be tremendously far away from it. I think about three times the amount we are handling now would be just about it. We currently have about $120 million in customer funds.

In other words, you haven't hit the wall yet?

No.

Is that because you are using many different approaches and, therefore, don't have all your orders going in at one point?

Yes. You have to think about diversification. If you had one method, or one person, making all the decisions, you couldn't handle amounts that large. But if you use different strategies and have a diversity in decision makers, you can handle several hundred million dollars without any major problem.

Could that have been a subliminal reason for developing your training program—to try to diversify the decision-making process?

Actually, we hadn't thought of it that way, but it did work to our advantage. In fact, we are going to try to market some of the traders we have trained for trading customer money.

Is *slippage* a problem in your trading? [Slippage is the difference between the theoretical execution price assumed by a computer program and the actual fill price.]

No. We try to make a hard-nosed estimate when building the cost of trading into a system. Also, we reduce our costs significantly by having our own brokers.

When you hold a major position, at what point do you know you are wrong? What tells you to get out of the position?

If you have a loss on a trade after a week or two, you are clearly wrong. Even when you are around breakeven, but a significant amount of time has passed, you are probably wrong there too.

Do you define your maximum risk point when you get into a trade?

You should always have a worst case point. The only choice should be to get out quicker.

Are you largely a self-taught trader, or did other traders teach you lessons that were worthwhile?

I would say I am self-taught. What is really amazing is how little published literature there is on trading.

Is there anything you can recommend to people who are interested in trading?

I think Edwin Lefevre's *Reminiscences of a Stock Operator* [reputedly a semifictionalized biography of Jesse Livermore, the legendary stock trader] is interesting and captures the feel of trading pretty well, but that book was written sixty-five years ago.

Are there some key trading strategies that you can talk about without revealing any secrets?

The market being in a trend is the main thing that eventually gets us in a trade. That is a pretty simple idea. Being consistent and making sure you do that all the time is probably more important than the particular characteristics you use to define the trend. Whatever method you use to enter trades, the most critical thing is that if there is a major trend, your approach should assure that you get in that trend.

A trend could easily be defined using a simple system. Is there something special that you look for to define a trend?

No. If I see a trend developing, I know eventually I'll have to get in. The question is whether I get in earlier or later, and that might depend on how I see the market reacting to news. If a market goes up when it should go up, I might buy earlier. If it goes down when it should go up, I'll wait until the trend is better defined.

How much common behavior is there between markets? Are the patterns of beans similar to the patterns of bonds, or do markets have their own personalities?

I could trade without knowing the name of the market.

So, what you are saying is that patterns in different markets are very similar.

Yes. In our research, if a system doesn't work for both bonds and beans, we don't care about it.

Would you say the stock market is an exception? That is, does the stock market also behave like other markets, or does the stock market have its own behavior pattern?

I think it is probably separate.

Why would you say that is true?

Well, my research on individual stocks shows that price fluctuations are closer to random than they are in commodities. Demonstrably, commodities are trending and, arguably, stocks are random.

Do you have an explanation for that phenomenon?

I believe that there is not enough fundamental information per stock to create sufficient trends to move them from their random character. There aren't as many commodities as there are stocks.

In other words, there is not the same flow of information as in the commodity markets?

There is not enough information, not enough fundamentals. Just nothing going on.

In the commodity markets, technical information is basically confined to price, volume, and open interest. Since there is so much more technical information available for stock indexes—advance/decline ratios, various sentiment indicators, relationships between different groups of stocks, etc.—do ordinary trend-following systems start off at a big disadvantage because they don't use enough information?

I'm not sure that is the disadvantage. I think the disadvantage is that stock index prices are too close to random to develop enough clear-cut trends because the inputs—the individual stocks—are mostly random.

What are your thoughts on the recent attacks against program trading?

The people that are complaining ought to be ashamed of themselves.

Do you mean people in the financial community?

Yes. They should have enough sophistication to understand the inanity of what they are complaining about.

Do you see program trading as a convenient scapegoat for a declining market?

Sure. It is a good excuse for doing a lousy job for yourself and your clients. The claim is that program traders are taking money out of the pockets of the people who are investing in the stock market. Nothing could be further from the truth. Program trading may move the stock market around a bit, but not in any systematic way. If program trading caused prices to go too high or too low, that should provide better opportunities for the value investor. Of course, it's bad for those people who pretend they are value investors, but are really traders.

How do you handle a losing streak?

Cut back. If it is really bad, stop and get out.

Do you sometimes need to get away from the markets for a few days?

Generally, it just takes a day or two, but you do need to stop for a period of time. It is almost like a pitcher not balking. Before he throws the ball, he has to stop at least for that second. That is what I try to do—at least have a pause. It could be for just one day.

What is the biggest public fallacy about market behavior?

That markets are supposed to make sense.

How about fallacies regarding technical analysis?

The belief that technical factors are not as important as the fundamentals.

Are there any analysts whose work you respect?

There are a lot of them. Zweig, for example, is good.

Would you consider the work of outside analysts as an input in a trade?

No. When we taught our people to trade, I had a hypothetical question: Suppose everything you know about the markets indicates a "buy." Then you call the floor and they tell you that I'm selling. Do you: (a) buy, (b) go short, (c) do nothing? If they didn't eventually understand that (a) was correct because they have to make their own market decisions, then they didn't fit into the program.

Why do you handle other people's money? You are doing very well on your own.

Well, there is one big advantage: managed money offers potential return with no risk. For ten years, people have been asking me if I'm getting tired of all the risk. Do I think I'm going to burn out? Do I think I'm going to stop? For the longest time I didn't understand what they were talking about. But I have to admit, at this point, I understand the value of cutting down your own risk. I could have traded smaller and had a smaller profit and smaller risk. But if customer money comes in, I could use that to supplement the profitability and still keep my risk lower. It just gives you a better deal.

In a later interview, Dennis changed his mind on this subject, possibly influenced by the aggravation related to large losses in his public funds. Dennis decided to extricate himself gradually from the money management business, saying: "I found that it was more trouble than it was worth. The costs were not financial; they were psychological." The material that follows is from that second interview.

I know this is not going to be your favorite subject, but I've got to ask you about it. Some of the public funds you managed ceased trading in April 1988. Is that because they reached the automatic 50 percent loss cutoff point?

Actually, they were down just under 49 percent when we stopped trading. Rather than trigger the automatic termination point, we liquidated all positions and resolicited the investors to allow a lower cutoff point.

Would you do anything differently in the future because of this particular experience?

I would cut back a little faster than I did, but the trades would still be the same. Someone said to me, "You claim the markets were bad. Well, since you could have done the exact opposite and made a lot of money, weren't they really good?" I told him that the last thing I would have wanted to do was to be on the opposite side of those trades. In the long run, that is a way to lose an infinite amount of money.

The short side of the interest rate markets in October 1987 resulted in one of your worst losses. What went wrong there?

A large part of that loss was due to the fact that the market gapped way past our point for covering our short position. For example, on October 20, we would normally have been out of our short Eurodollar position about 40 to 50 points higher, but the market opened 240 points higher that day. We blew 190 points in a skid that was absolutely unavoidable.

If the market is that much out of line, do you still get out of your position right away?

Sure. If you have any doubt about getting out as fast as possible in a situation like that, then you are really in big trouble.

Do you think the sharp losses you suffered were due to any change in the markets?

That's hard to say. The only factor I can objectively identify is the tendency toward more false breakouts.

Do you feel the recent prevalence of false breakouts is related to the tremendous increase in computerized trend-following trading during the past five to ten years? Are there just too many people doing the same thing, getting in each other's way?

Yes, there is no doubt about it. In a perverse sort of way, it represents the ultimate triumph of technical trading over fundamental trading. I say perverse because it is a victory that devalues technical trading.

Do you think we may see the day when trend-following systems no longer work?

There will come a day when easily discovered and lightly conceived trend-following systems no longer work. It is going to be harder to develop good systems.

Given that, can the approaches you were using before still work with the same efficacy?

Actually, I believe that if you view the problem correctly, you can make the fact that there are many other trend followers in the market work to your advantage. I can't get too specific about the solution, because if we are right, that is pretty valuable information. To be successful you always have to be one step ahead of everyone else.

It sounds like you started working on this problem well before your performance problems began in late 1987.

That's right. During the past ten years, there has been a virtual bandwagon-effect of people using trend-following approaches. We have been thinking about this problem for a long time. Half the work in solving a problem is finding the right way to conceptualize it. It took us years before we figured out the right questions to ask.

When did you finally arrive at what you considered a satisfactory solution?

Ironically, right around the time we closed down the public funds.

I know you can't be specific, but does your solution to false breakouts involve being far more short-term oriented, so that you can respond more quickly to those situations?

The secret is being as short term or as long term as you can stand, depending on your trading style. It is the intermediate term that picks up the vast majority of trend followers. The best strategy is to avoid the middle like the plague.

When you talk about the experience of managing well over $100 million and losing roughly 50 percent, not to mention your personal large losses, you discuss it with great emotional detachment. Do you really take it that calmly? Isn't there an emotional side to it?

I try for there not to be. It is totally counterproductive to get wrapped up in the results. Trading decisions should be made as unemotionally as possible.

Yes, but how do you do that?

You have to maintain your perspective. There is more to life than trading. Also, to me, being emotionally deflated would mean lacking confidence in what I am doing. I avoid that because I have always felt that it is misleading to focus on short-term results.

So you are able to avoid the emotional trap?

Yes, but the flip side is that I also avoid the emotional elation when things are going well. There is no way to play just one side of that street. If you feel too good when things are going well, then inevitably you will feel too bad when they are going poorly. I wouldn't claim that I realized that after three years of trading, but after you've done it for twenty years, it either drives you crazy, or you learn to put it into perspective.

Does it become easier after twenty years?

Not necessarily [he laughs]. It gets easier to put it into perspective, but everyone has shock absorbers that deteriorate over time. Being a trader is like being a boxer: Every now and then, the market gives you a good wallop. After twenty years you get a bit punch-drunk.

Is there any advice you can give to other traders on how to stay emotionally calm during periods of trading losses?

It is a little bit like playing golf: You can throw your clubs around after making a bad shot, but while you are making the next shot you should keep your head down and your eye on the ball.

Do you use long-term scenarios about economic growth, inflation, and the dollar in making your trading decisions?

I have mental pictures, but I try not to use them when I'm trading. Trading to me is like betting on independent roles of the dice that you think are loaded a little bit in your favor, because you know some statistical things about the market. Long-term scenarios can prove to be right or wrong, but even if they are right, on balance, I'm not convinced that they make much difference over the term of any individual trade.

Even if you think the dollar is going to collapse, that doesn't affect your basic trading pattern?

I would like to say it doesn't, and I don't think it should, but it probably has in the past. The worst thing you can do is miss a profit opportunity (assuming you are already disciplined enough to cut your losses short). And if you think about it, rigid long-term views are the kind of thing most likely to lead you to that mistake. For example, if I believe the dollar is going to weaken, and because of this I ignore a sell signal in the foreign currencies, I might risk missing a large profit. What is my reward if my view was right? Avoiding a small loss. Therefore, the risk/reward is all wrong for my type of trading.

Acknowledging that caveat, as a long-time market observer, what major trends do you see shaping up over the coming years?

I bet we will be at record levels of inflation by the end of 1990. [This interview was conducted in mid-1988.]

What is going to be the driving force behind that inflation?

It is going to be driven by trying to avoid a deep recession. The recession is going to be caused by the federal budget deficit as investors require higher and higher levels of real interest rates to buy the debt. The government will try to avoid the recession by stimulating the economy, a tactic which essentially doesn't work.

In other words, fear of a recession will cause tremendous monetary easing, which in turn will lead to inflation?

It is, unfortunately, a very Republican idea, but I think it is right. Whether you like it or not, the financial markets are in conservative hands. People who lend money to the government and business will not buy monetary easing as a solution to a recession.

Are you implying that the deficit problem is just a time bomb, which will eventually shatter the economy?

Sure. We tend to think that since it is not a problem now, that means it won't be. We expect continuity in our lives, but the economy, and certainly the markets, are more discontinuous than continuous.

And you are saying that people look at the deficit year after year and think, "Well, it can't be so bad, the economy is strong," and one day everybody wakes up—

It is like having termites in the foundation of your house. You may not notice them until one day they gnaw away a big chunk and the house collapses. I don't think anybody should take a large amount of comfort in the fact that things appear to be holding together.

Hypothetically, if you were President and could influence change, would the deficit be the first thing you would change?

Sure. I think it is especially important for Democrats, since they were the first ones to pick up the banner of *Keynesianism* [the advocacy of government programs to increase employment], to admit that while it may be a great theory, it doesn't work in the real world.

I don't think Keynes ever proposed using deficit spending in strong economic times.

No, that's true. He proposed surpluses that were supposed to be counter-cyclical to deficits. Surpluses in good times; deficits in bad times. The trouble is that we have only one side of that equation because of the lack of political will to create the surpluses when times are good. So what we really ought to do is admit that Keynesian economics is just an excuse for easy money, overspending, and overconsuming. We ought to just admit that the government is a debt junkie and the whole concept of deficit spending is flawed in practice.

You mean Keynesianism as it is being applied, not Keynesian economics as he himself purported it?

The theory is fine, it just doesn't work in the real world. Therefore, we shouldn't use it. Besides, Keynesian economics was a solution to the problem of oversaving and underconsumption, which was a fair enough attempt to pull us out of the Great Depression. The problem now is the exact opposite: undersaving and overconsumption. Even if Keynesianism were politically tenable, you still need a different solution because you have the exact opposite problem.

Is there an economic theory that you feel fits the times and makes sense?

We have to get rid of deficit spending. We need to retire the deficit in some orderly way, and the federal government should have to balance its budget just as the states do. At that point, Milton Friedman's proposal for a constant money supply adjusted by a growth factor would probably be a good idea.

What is the most important advice you could give the novice trader?

Trade small because that's when you are as bad as you are ever going to be. Learn from your mistakes. Don't be misled by the day-to-day fluctuations in your equity. Focus on whether what you are doing is right, not on the random nature of any single trade's outcome.

After Dennis announced his retirement from trading to pursue his political interests full time, I called with some follow-up questions. I spoke to an aide who took down the questions. Several days later, he called back with Dennis' replies. These questions and answers follow.

Individuals who invested in your funds during your final year as a money manager fared poorly. How would an investor have done if he started on your first day as a money manager and kept his money fully invested until your last day in that role?

Each $1,000 invested would have been worth $3,833 when the accounts were closed. [This works out to approximately a 25 percent annual compounded return. The figure would have been more than double that at the equity peak about one year earlier.]

You are rumored to have lost a very substantial portion of your own net worth during your final year of trading. Are these stories true or exaggerated?

I lost about 10 percent of the money I had made in the markets. Of course, measured as a percentage of my net worth, the figure is much higher because of my charitable and political contributions over the years.

Did your poor trading results during the past year speed your career transitions?

It made no difference.

Have you really gone cold turkey, or are you still trading lightly?

I am not trading at all.

Richard Dennis is one of the legendary commodity traders of our time. He is the type of trader you might visualize implementing large long positions near market bottoms and large short positions near market tops. It is thus surprising that Dennis downplays the value of trying to pick major turning points. In fact, he claims that such trades have done little, if anything, to contribute to his trading success.

Dennis believes that one of the worst mistakes a trader can make is to miss a major profit opportunity. According to his own estimate, 95 percent of his profits have come from only 5 percent of his trades. Missing only a few such profit opportunities could have a dramatic negative impact on performance. As a corollary, you need to guard against holding too rigid an opinion on a market, since such an opinion could easily lead to missing a major trend.

One particularly useful piece of advice offered by Dennis is that the times when you least want to think about trading—the losing periods—are precisely the times when you need to focus most on trading.

Paul Tudor Jones

The Art of Aggressive Trading

October 1987 was a devastating month for most investors as the world stock markets witnessed a collapse that rivaled 1929. That same month, the Tudor Futures Fund, managed by Paul Tudor Jones, registered an incredible 62 percent return. Jones has always been a maverick trader. His trading style is unique and his performance is uncorrelated with other money managers. Perhaps most important, he has done what many thought impossible: combine five consecutive, triple-digit return years with very low equity retracements. (I am fudging slightly; in 1986, Paul's fund realized only a 99.2 percent gain!)

Jones has succeeded in every major venture he has tried. He started out in the business as a broker and in his second year grossed over $1 million in commissions. In fall 1980, Jones went to the New York Cotton Exchange as an independent floor trader. Again he was spectacularly successful, making millions during the next few years. His really impressive achievement though was not the magnitude of his winnings, but the consistency of his performance: During his three and a half years as a floor trader, he witnessed only one losing month.

In 1984, partially out of boredom, and partially out of fear of eventually losing his voice—an occupational hazard for a pit trader—Jones again abandoned his successful career for a new venture: money management. He launched the Tudor Futures Fund in September 1984 with $1.5 million under management. At the end of October 1988, each

$1,000 invested in this fund was worth $17,482, while the total amount of money he managed had grown to $330 million. In fact, the amount under management would have been higher, but Jones stopped accepting new investment funds in October 1987 and has also made cash disbursements since that time.

If one believes in cycles—as Jones does—it appears that he is due for another career change. It is hard to imagine what he can do for an encore.

Jones is a compendium of contrasts. In private conversation he is relaxed, but as a trader he shouts his orders with the ferocity of a drill sergeant. His public image is one of a swaggering, egotistical trader, but one-on-one he is easygoing and unassuming. The media usually dramatizes the flamboyant elements of his lifestyle—Chesapeake Bay Mansion, private 3,000-acre wildlife preserve, beautiful women, fine restaurants—but he has also made helping the poor a second avocation.

Jones has emulated New York businessman Eugene Lang by setting up a fund to finance the college education of eighty-five elementary school graduates in Brooklyn's economically depressed Bedford-Stuyvesant section. This is not merely a matter of donating money; Jones has become personally involved by meeting with his adopted students weekly. More recently, he started the Robin Hood Foundation, whose endowment has grown to $5 million. This organization, true to its name, raises money from the rich and distributes it to private groups and individuals working to aid the poor.

Jones had arranged our interview for 3:15 P.M., a time by which all the futures markets are closed, except for the stock indexes. Even with only one market trading, I was a little concerned about the practicality of starting the interview at that time, since I knew that the S&P stock index futures contract was one of Jones' primary trading vehicles. In fact, when I arrived he was in the midst of trading the S&P.

I waited until he finished shouting orders over the speakerphone and explained that I did not want to interrupt his trading. "Maybe we should delay the interview until the market closes," I suggested. "No problem," he answered, "let's go."

As it turned out, Jones was not merely trading the S&P that afternoon, he was building up a major position in anticipation of a huge break in the stock market. There is an intensity in Jones' placement of an order that is reminiscent of a tennis player aggressively returning a volley.

("Buy 300 at even! Go, go, go! Are we in? Speak to me!") Yet, he shifted easily between trading and our conversation.

Jones speaks with admiration about his first tutor in the business, the legendary cotton trader, Eli Tullis. Perhaps the one trait of Tullis that made the greatest impression on Jones was his steel-hard emotional control. He recalls how Tullis could carry on a polite, relaxed conversation with visitors, without blinking an eye, at the same time his positions were getting decimated in the market.

Jones' casualness in seeing visitors, talking to his staff, and participating in this interview at the same time he was trading a heavy S&P position reflected the same trait. A rally in stock index futures in the closing minutes of trading that day caused over a $1 million loss in Jones' position. Yet, he was so composed that I didn't realize the market had moved against him until I checked the closing prices later that day.

There was insufficient time to complete the interview at our first meeting. I returned about two weeks later. Two things were notable about this second meeting. First, whereas he had been strongly bearish and heavily short the stock market at the time of our first conversation, Jones' short-term opinion on the stock market had shifted to bullish in the interim. The failure of the stock market to follow through on the downside at the price and time he had anticipated convinced him that the market was headed higher for the short term.

"This market is sold out," he emphasized at our second meeting. This 180-degree shift in opinion within a short time span exemplified the extreme flexibility that underlies Jones' trading success. He not only quickly abandoned his original position, but was willing to join the other side once the evidence indicated his initial projection was wrong. (Yes, his change of heart proved well timed.)

Second, Jones had suddenly adopted a very cautious tone regarding projections p rtaining to the stock market and the economy. He was concerned that a second major selling wave in the stock market—the first being October 1987—could lead to a type of financial McCarthyism. Indeed, there is historical precedence for such concern: During the Senate hearings held in the 1930s, committee members were so desperate to find villains responsible for the 1929 stock crash that they dragged up New York Stock Exchange officials who had held long positions during the price collapse.

Jones feared that, as a prominent speculator and forecaster of economic trends, he might make a convenient target for any future governmental witch-hunts. Jones had been particularly rattled by a call from a prominent government official regarding his trading. "You wouldn't believe how high-placed this person was," he explained to me in a voice tinged with incredulity, taking particular care not to divulge anything specific.

Although Jones remained friendly, the directness of the first interview was replaced by an almost prerecorded quality in his replies. For example, a question about trading strategy was met with a response about front-running—an illegal practice in which a broker places his own order in front of a large customer order. This reply virtually bordered on the absurd since Jones handles no customer orders. It made as much sense as a football fan, who bets in his office pool, denying that he took a bribe to throw the game. It sounded as if Jones was using the interview as a forum for making an official statement, perhaps to be used as evidence in some hypothetical future congressional hearing. I thought that Jones was being overly cautious—if not paranoid—but then again, the expectation that a true economic crisis would lead to "killing the messengers of bad news" does not really seem that far-fetched.

When did you first get interested in trading?

When I was in college I read an article on Richard Dennis, which made a big impression on me. I thought that Dennis had the greatest job in the world. I already had an appreciation for trading because my uncle, Billy Dunavant, was a very successful cotton trader. In 1976, after I finished college, I went to my uncle and asked him if he could help me get started as a trader. He sent me to Eli Tullis, a famous cotton trader, who lived in New Orleans. "Eli is the best trader I know," he told me. I went down to see Eli and he offered me a job on the floor of the New York Cotton Exchange.

How come you went to work for Eli instead of your uncle?

Because my uncle was primarily involved in the cash side of the business, merchandising cotton. I was interested in becoming a trader straightaway.

How long did you work on the floor of the exchange? What was your job there?

I was a floor clerk; that is how everybody begins. But I also did a lot of analytical work, watching the market to try to figure out what made it tick. I clerked in New York for about six months and then returned to New Orleans to work for Eli.

Did you learn a lot about trading from Eli?

Absolutely. Working with Eli was a fabulous experience. He would trade position sizes of 3,000 contracts when the entire market open interest was only 30,000. He would trade more volume than any cotton trader off the floor. He was a true sight to behold.

Was he trading futures against cash or just speculating?

He was a pure speculator. The amazing thing was that since he used his own broker on the floor, everyone always knew exactly what his position was. He was very easy to tag. Eli's attitude was, "The hell with it, I'm going to take them head on."

So everyone knew his hand?

Definitely.

But, apparently, it didn't hurt him?

No.

Is that an exception? Do you try to hide your positions?

I try. But, realistically, the guys in the pit who have been there for five or ten years know it is me. Everyone knows when I trade. The one thing I learned from Eli is that, ultimately, the market is going to go where it is going to go.

So you don't think it is important to hide your positions?

I think it is important to make an effort. For instance, my orders used to be particularly easy to read because I traded in multiples of 300 contracts. Now I break my orders up; I might give one broker an order for 116 and another broker an order for 184. I have at least four brokers in every pit.

What else did you learn from Tullis?

He was the toughest son of a bitch I ever knew. He taught me that trading is very competitive and you have to be able to handle getting your butt kicked. No matter how you cut it, there are enormous emotional ups and downs involved.

That sounds like a general character-building lesson. What about specifics regarding trading?

Tullis taught me about moving volume. When you are trading size, you have to get out when the market lets you out, not when you want to get out. He taught me that if you want to move a large position, you don't wait until the market is in new high or low ground because very little volume may trade there if it is a turning point.

One thing I learned as a floor trader was that if, for example, the old high was at 56.80, there are probably going to be a lot of buy stops at 56.85. If the market is trading 70 bid, 75 offered, the whole trading ring has a vested interest in buying the market, touching off those stops, and liquidating into the stops—that is a very common ring practice. As an upstairs trader, I put that together with what Eli taught me. If I want to cover a position in that type of situation, I will liquidate half at 75, so that I won't have to worry about getting out of the entire position at the point where the stops are being hit. I will always liquidate half my position below new highs or lows and the remaining half beyond that point.

Any other lessons you can attribute to Tullis?

By watching Eli, I learned that even though markets look their very best when they are setting new highs, that is often the best time to sell. He instilled in me the idea that, to some extent, to be a good trader, you have to be a contrarian.

You have done tens of thousands of trades. Is there any single trade that stands out?

Yes, the 1979 cotton market. One learns the most from mistakes, not successes. I was a broker back then. We had lots of speculative accounts and I was long about 400 contracts of July cotton. The market had been trading in a range between 82 and 86 cents, and I was buying it every time it came down to the low end of that range.

One day, the market broke to new lows, took out the stops, and immediately rebounded about 30 or 40 points. I thought the reason the market had been acting so poorly was because of the price vulnerability implied by the proximity of those well-known stops. Now that the stops had been touched off, I thought the market was ready to rally.

I was standing outside the ring at the time. In an act of bravado, I told my floor broker to bid 82.90 for 100 July, which at the time was a very big order. He bid 90 for 100, and I remember the Refco broker came running across the pit screaming, "Sold!" Refco owned most of the certificated stock at that time [the type of cotton available for delivery against the contract]. In an instant I realized that they intended to deliver against the July contract, which then was trading at about a 4-cent premium to the October contract. It also dawned on me that the whole congestion pattern that had formed between 82 and 86 cents was going to be a market measurement for the next move down [the break from 82 cents was going to equal the width of the prior 4-cent trading range].

So you knew you were wrong immediately?

I saw immediately that the market was going straight down to 78 cents, and that it was my blood that was going to carry it there. I had come in long 400 contracts, entered another 100 as a day trade, and a final 100 on that macho-type bid that I should never have made.

So you realized instantly that you wanted to be out.

No, I realized instantly that I wanted to be short.

How fast did you react?

Almost immediately. When the Refco broker shouted, "Sold," everyone in the ring turned around and looked at me, because they knew what I was trying to do. The guy standing next to me said, "If you want to go to the bathroom, do it right here." He said I looked three shades of white. I remember turning around, walking out, getting a drink of water, and then telling my broker to sell as much as he could. The market was limit-down in sixty seconds, and I was only able to sell 220 contracts.

When did you get out of the rest of your position?

The next morning the market opened 100 points lower and I started selling from the opening bell. I sold only about 150 contracts before the market locked limit-down again. By the time it was all over, I ended up selling some contracts as much as 4 cents below the point I first knew the position was no good.

Even though you reacted fairly quickly, you still took a big hit. In retrospect, what should you have done?

First of all, never play macho man with the market. Second, never overtrade. My major problem was not the number of points I lost on the trade, but that I was trading far too many contracts relative to the equity in the accounts that I handled. My accounts lost something like 60 to

70 percent of their equity in that single trade.

Did that particular trade change your whole trading style in terms of risk?

Absolutely. I was totally demoralized. I said, "I am not cut out for this business; I don't think I can hack it much longer." I was so depressed that I nearly quit.

How many years had you been in the business at that time?

Only about three and a half years.

Had you been successful up to that point?

Relatively. Most of my clients had made money, and I was an important producer for my company.

How about someone who had given you $10,000 at the beginning of the three-year period?

They were probably up about threefold.

So everyone who was with you for a long time was still ahead of the game?

Yes, but I had to suffer some intense drawdowns during the interim. That cotton trade was almost the deal-breaker for me. It was at that point that I said, "Mr. Stupid, why risk everything on one trade? Why not make your life a pursuit of happiness rather than pain?"

  That was when I first decided I had to learn discipline and money management. It was a cathartic experience for me, in the sense that I went to the edge, questioned my very ability as a trader, and decided that I was not going to quit. I was determined to come back and fight. I decided that I was going to become very disciplined and businesslike about my trading.

Did your trading style change radically from that point on?

Yes. Now I spend my day trying to make myself as happy and relaxed as I can be. If I have positions going against me, I get right out; if they are going for me, I keep them.

I guess you not only started trading smaller, but also quicker?

Quicker and more defensive. I am always thinking about losing money as opposed to making money. Back then, in that cotton trade, I had a vision of July going to 89 cents and I thought about all the money I was going to make on 400 contracts. I didn't think about what I could lose.

Do you always know where you are getting out before you put a trade on?

I have a mental stop. If it hits that number, I am out no matter what.

How much do you risk on any single trade?

I don't break it down trade by trade. All the trades I have on are interrelated. I look at it in terms of what my equity is each morning. My goal is to finish each day with more than I started. Tomorrow morning I will not walk in and say, "I am short the S&P from 264 and it closed at 257 yesterday; therefore, I can stand a rally." I always think of it in terms of being short from the previous night's close.

Risk control is the most important thing in trading. For example, right now I am down about 6½ percent for the month. I have a 3½ percent stop on my equity for the rest of the month. I want to make sure that I never have a double-digit loss in any month.

One aspect of your trading style is a contrarian attempt to buy and sell turning points. Let's say you are looking for a top and go short with a close stop when the market reaches a new high. You then get stopped out. On a single trade idea, how many times will you try to pick a turning point before you give up?

Until I change my mind, fundamentally. Otherwise, I will keep cutting my position size down as I have losing trades. When I am trading poorly, I keep reducing my position size. That way, I will be trading my smallest position size when my trading is worst.

What are the trading rules you live by?

Don't ever average losers. Decrease your trading volume when you are trading poorly; increase your volume when you are trading well. Never trade in situations where you don't have control. For example, I don't risk significant amounts of money in front of key reports, since that is gambling, not trading.

If you have a losing position that is making you uncomfortable, the solution is very simple: Get out, because you can always get back in. There is nothing better than a fresh start.

Don't be too concerned about where you got into a position. The only relevant question is whether you are bullish or bearish on the position that day. Always think of your entry point as last night's close. I can always tell a rookie trader because he will ask me, "Are you short or long?" Whether I am long or short should have no bearing on his market opinion. Next he will ask (assuming I have told him I am long), "Where are you long from?" Who cares where I am long from. That has no relevance to whether the market environment is bullish or bearish right now, or to the risk/reward balance of a long position at that moment.

The most important rule of trading is to play great defense, not great offense. Every day I assume every position I have is wrong. I know where my stop risk points are going to be. I do that so I can define my maximum possible drawdown. Hopefully, I spend the rest of the day enjoying positions that are going in my direction. If they are going against me, then I have a game plan for getting out.

Don't be a hero. Don't have an ego. Always question yourself and your ability. Don't ever feel that you are very good. The second you do, you are dead.

Jesse Livermore, one of the greatest speculators of all time, reportedly said that, in the long run, you can't ever win trading markets. That was a devastating quote for someone like me, just getting into the business. The idea that you can't beat the markets is a frightening prospect. That is why my guiding philosophy is playing great defense. If you make a good trade, don't think it is because you have some uncanny foresight. Always maintain your sense of confidence, but keep it in check.

But you have been very successful for years. Aren't you more confident now than you were before?

I am more scared now than I was at any point since I began trading, because I recognize how ephemeral success can be in this business. I know that to be successful, I have to be frightened. My biggest hits have always come after I have had a great period and I started to think that I knew something.

My impression is that you often implement positions near market turns. Sometimes your precision has been uncanny. What is it about your decision-making process that allows you to get in so close to the turns?

I have very strong views of the long-run direction of all markets. I also have a very short-term horizon for pain. As a result, frequently, I may try repeated trades from the long side over a period of weeks in a market which continues to move lower.

Is it a matter of doing a series of probes until you finally hit it?

Exactly. I consider myself a premier market opportunist. That means I develop an idea on the market and pursue it from a very-low-risk standpoint until I have repeatedly been proven wrong, or until I change my viewpoint.

In other words, it makes a better story to say, "Paul Jones buys the T-bond market 2 ticks from the low," rather than, "On his fifth try, Paul Jones buys the T-bond market 2 ticks from its low."

I think that is certainly part of it. The other part is that I have always been a swing trader, meaning that I believe the very best money is to be made at the market turns. Everyone says you get killed trying to pick tops and bottoms and you make all the money by catching the trends in the middle. Well, for twelve years, I have often been missing the meat in the middle, but I have caught a lot of bottoms and tops.

If you are a trend follower trying to catch the profits in the middle of a move, you have to use very wide stops. I'm not comfortable doing that. Also, markets trend only about 15 percent of the time; the rest of the time they move sideways.

What is the most prominent fallacy in the public's perception about markets?

That markets can be manipulated. That there is some group on Wall Street that controls price action in the markets. I can go into any market and create a stir for a day or two, maybe even a week. If I go into a market at just the right moment, by giving it a little gas on the upside, I can create the illusion of a bull market. But, unless the market is really sound, the second I stop buying, the price is going to come right down. You can open the most beautiful Saks Fifth Avenue in Anchorage, Alaska, with a wonderful summer menswear department, but unless somebody wants to buy the clothes, you will go broke.

What other misconceptions do people have about the markets?

The idea that people affiliated with Wall Street know something. My mother is a classic example. She watches "Wall Street Week" and she takes everything they say with almost a religious fervor. I would bet that you could probably fade "Wall Street Week."

I know you talk to traders in virtually every major market on an almost daily basis. Are you uncomfortable about being on the opposite side of the fence from these people?

Yes. Who wants to fade a winner? I want to be with them because I make a point of talking to the people who have the best track records.

How do you keep all these other opinions from confusing your own vision? Let's say you are bearish on a market and 75 percent of the people you talk to about that market are bullish. What do you do?

I wait. I will give you a perfect example. Until last Wednesday, I had been bearish on crude oil, while it was in the midst of a $2 advance. The best crude oil trader I know was bullish during that period. Because he was bullish, I never went short. Then the market started to stall and one day he said, "I think I am going to go flat here." I knew that instant—particularly, given the fact that bullish news was coming out of OPEC right at that time—that crude oil was a low-risk short. I sold the hell out of it, and it turned out to be a great trade.

Are there any market advisors that you pay attention to?

Marty Zweig and Ned Davis are great; Bob Prechter is the champion. Prechter is the best because he is the ultimate market opportunist.

What do you mean by opportunist?

The reason he has been so successful is that the Elliott Wave theory allows one to create incredibly favorable risk/reward opportunities. That is the same reason I attribute a lot of my own success to the Elliott Wave approach.

Any advisor you consider underrated?

I think Ned Davis does the best research on the stock market that I have seen. Although he is well known, I don't think he has received the recognition he deserves.

Any analysts you consider overrated?

Judge not, least you be judged.

Very few traders have reached your level of achievement. What makes you different?

I think one of my strengths is that I view anything that has happened up to the present point in time as history. I really don't care about the mistake I made three seconds ago in the market. What I care about is what I am going to do from the next moment on. I try to avoid any emotional attachment to a market. I avoid letting my trading opinions be influenced by comments I may have made on the record about a market.

No loyalty to positions is obviously an important element in your trading.

It is important because it gives you a wide open intellectual horizon to figure out what is really happening. It allows you to come in with a completely clean slate in choosing the correct forecast for that particular market.

Has the tremendous growth of the money you are managing made it more difficult to trade at the same level of profitability?

It has made it tremendously more difficult.

Do you think you could make a substantially higher percentage return if you were trading smaller amounts of money?

Without question.

Do you ever question whether the detrimental impact of size on your performance outweighs profit incentive fees you earn from managing money?

I think about that question every day. It is going to be interesting to see what happens by the time your book is published.

Have you stopped accepting new investment funds?

Yes, a long time ago.

You have been both a broker and a money manager. How do you compare the relative advantages and disadvantages of these two jobs?

I got out of the brokerage business because I felt there was a gross conflict of interest: If you are charging a client commissions and he loses money, you aren't penalized. I went into the money management business because if I lost money, I wanted to be able to say that I had not gotten compensated for it. In fact, it would probably cost me a bundle because I have an overhead that would knock out the Bronx Zoo. I never apologize to anybody, because I don't get paid unless I win.

Do you keep your money in your own funds?

I would say that 85 percent of my net worth is invested in my own funds, primarily because I believe that is the safest place in the world for it. I really believe that I am going to be so defensive and conservative that I will get my money back.

You did extraordinarily well during October 1987, a month which was a disaster for many other traders. Could you fill in some of the details?

The week of the crash was one of the most exciting periods of my life.

We had been expecting a major stock market collapse since mid-1986 and had contingency plans drawn up because of the possibility we foresaw for a financial meltdown. When we came in on Monday, October 19, we knew that the market was going to crash that day.

What made you so sure?

Because the previous Friday was a record volume day on the downside. The exact same thing happened in 1929, two days before the crash. Our *analog model* to 1929 had the collapse perfectly nailed. [Paul Jones' analog model, developed by his research director, Peter Borish, superimposed the 1980s market over the 1920s market. The two markets demonstrated a remarkable degree of correlation. This model was a key tool in Jones' stock index trading during 1987.] Treasury Secretary Baker's weekend statement that the U.S. would no longer support the dollar because of its disagreements with West Germany was the kiss of death for the market.

When did you cover your short position?

We actually covered our shorts and went somewhat long on the close of the day of the crash itself [October 19].

Were most of your profits in October due to your short stock index position?

No, we also had an extremely profitable bond position. The day of the crash we put on the biggest bond position we ever had. The bond market had been acting terrible all day long on October 19. During the day, I was very concerned about the financial safety of our clients' and our own assets. We had our assets with various commission houses on the street, and I thought those funds could be in jeopardy. It was an intolerable situation for me.

I kept on thinking: What is the Fed reaction going to be? I thought that they would have to add massive amounts of liquidity to create a very

rosy environment, instantaneously. However, since bonds had been acting poorly all day, I couldn't bring myself to pull the trigger on a long
bond position. During the last half hour of trading, bonds suddenly
started to turn up, and it clicked in my mind that the Fed was going to
take actions that would create a tremendous upsurge in bond prices. As
soon as I saw the bond market act right for a moment, I went wild.

**Do you believe that October 1987 was an early warning signal of
more negative times ahead?**

I think the financial community, particularly Wall Street, was dealt a life-
threatening blow on October 19, but they are in shock and don't realize
it. I remember the time I got run over by a boat, and my backside was
chewed up by the propeller. My first thought was, "Dammit, I just ruined
my Sunday afternoon because I have to get stitched up." Because I was
in shock, I didn't even realize how badly cut up I was until I saw the
faces of my friends.

   Everything gets destroyed a hundred times faster than it is built up.
It takes one day to tear down something that might have taken ten years
to build. If the economy starts to go with the kind of leverage that is in
it, it will deteriorate so fast that people's heads will spin. I hate to believe
it, but in my gut that is what I think is going to happen.

   I know from studying history that credit eventually kills all great
societies. We have essentially taken out our American Express card and
said we are going to have a great time. Reagan made sure that the
economy would be great during his term in office by borrowing our way
into prosperity. We borrowed against the future, and soon we will have
to pay.

Are you blaming the current situation on Reaganomics?

I think Reagan made us feel good as a country—and that is wonderful—
but, in terms of economics, he was the biggest disaster that ever struck.
I think he basically hoodwinked us by promising to cut the deficit, and
then went on the biggest spending binge in the history of this country. I
don't think a Democrat could have gotten away with it, because everyone
would have been very vigilant about a $150–180 billion deficit.

Do you see any way in which we can solve our current problems before we go into a deep recession, or even depression?

That is what scares me so much. I don't see any blueprint out of our current dilemma. Maybe there are macroeconomic forces at work that are part of a larger super cycle that we don't have any control over. Perhaps we are simply responding to the same type of cycles that most advanced civilizations fell prey to, whether it was the Romans, sixteenth-century Spain, eighteenth-century France, or nineteenth-century Britain. I think that we are going to be in for a period of pain. We are going to relearn what financial discipline is all about.

Do you use trading systems at all?

We have tested every system under the sun and, amazingly, we have found one that actually works well. It is a very good system, but for obvious reasons, I can't tell you much more about it.

What type of realm does it fall into: contrarian? trend following?

Trend following. The basic premise of the system is that markets move sharply when they move. If there is a sudden range expansion in a market that has been trading narrowly, human nature is to try to fade that price move. When you get a range expansion, the market is sending you a very loud, clear signal that the market is getting ready to move in the direction of that expansion.

Are you trading a portion of your funds on that system at the present time?

We just started trading the system about six months ago, and so far it is doing very well.

Do you feel a good system can compete with a good trader?

A good system may be able to trade more markets effectively than a good trader because it has the advantage of unlimited computing power. After all, every trade decision is the product of some problem-solving process—human or otherwise. However, because of the complexity in defining interacting and changing market patterns, a good trader will usually be able to outperform a good system.

But a good system can help diversify?

Unequivocally. A good system will catch ten times as much of the price move as I will, during the 15 percent of the time a market is in a major trending phase.

The following section of the interview was conducted two weeks later. During the interim, Jones had reversed his trading bias on the stock market from bearish to bullish.

Two weeks ago you were very bearish. What made you change your mind?

You mean besides the *Wall Street Journal* article that publicized to the world that I was short 2,000 S&P contracts? The market didn't go down. The first thing I do is put my ear to the railroad tracks. I always believe that prices move first and fundamentals come second.

Do you mean that if you were right, prices should have gone down and they didn't?

One of the things that Tullis taught me was the importance of time. When I trade, I don't just use a price stop, I also use a time stop. If I think a market should break, and it doesn't, I will often get out even if I am not losing any money. According to the 1929 analog model, the market should have gone down—it didn't. This was the first time during the past three years that we had a serious divergence. I think the strength of the economy is going to delay the stock market break.

I believe one reason why we are diverging from the 1929 model is because of the much easier availability of credit today. Volvo is giving out 120-month car loans. Think about that! Who owns a car for ten years? Twenty years ago, the average length of a car loan was twenty-four months; today it is fifty-five months. I think the final bottom line will be the same, but the ease of credit will delay the process relative to the 1920s, when we had a cash economy.

Some of your preliminary comments before the start of our interview today make it sound like you are paranoid because of your success.

If the misery in this country gets deep enough, the perception is going to be that we did well as a trading firm, while other people were hurt, because we had some knowledge. It is not that we had any unfair knowledge that other people didn't have, it is just that we did our homework. People just don't want to believe that anyone can break away from the crowd and rise above mediocrity.

I understand that, similar to a number of other traders I have interviewed, you have trained a group of apprentice traders. What was your motivation?

When I was twenty-one years old, a guy took me under his wing and it was the greatest thing that ever happened to me. I felt an obligation to do the same thing for other people.

How did you find the people you trained?

Countless interviews. We have been deluged by applicants.

How many traders have you hired?

About thirty-five.

Have they been successful?

Some have done very well, but overall we have had mixed success.

Do you believe that is because it takes talent to be a good trader?

I never thought that before, but I am starting to believe that now. One of my weaknesses is that I always tend to be too optimistic, particularly about the ability of other people to succeed.

Was your I Have a Dream Program, in which you have pledged to sponsor the education of a group of kids from a poverty sticken area, inspired by the "60 Minutes" show about Eugene Lang?

Right. I went to talk to him the week after the show, and within three months we had set up our own program. I have always been a big believer in leverage. The thing that really turned me on about the program was the potential for its multiplicative impact. By helping one kid, you can have an impact on his family and other kids.

    We have also recently set up a new program called the Robin Hood Foundation. We are trying to seek out and fund people who are on the frontlines in providing food and shelter to the poor. We are seeking out the people who are used to working with virtually no budget at all, rather than the bureaucracies, which often do not deploy the money effectively.

Has this become a major part of your life?

I would say so. The markets have been so good to me that I feel I should give back something in return. I can't say that I have been successful because I am better than anybody else. By the grace of God, I was in the right place at the right time, so I feel a tremendous obligation to share.

Is the positive intensity of winning as strong as the pain of losing?

There is nothing worse than a bad trading day. You feel so low that it is difficult to hold your head up. But, if I knew that I could also have a similar experience in the exhilaration of winning, I would take the combination of winning and losing days any time because you feel that much more alive. Trading gives you an incredibly intense feeling of what life is all about. Emotionally, you live on the extremes.

What is the most important advice you could give the average trader?

Don't focus on making money; focus on protecting what you have.

Do you still see yourself trading ten or fifteen years down the road?

I wouldn't have it any other way.

Paul Jones was a winning trader from his start in the business, but, in the early years, his performance was volatile. It took a traumatic trading experience to permanently forge the importance of risk control into his mind. Since that gut-wrenching cotton trade in 1979, Jones has managed to maintain excellent net profitability, while bringing his risk way down.

Today, risk control is the essence of Jones' trading style and success. He never thinks about what he might make on a given trade, but only on what he could lose. He mentally marks each of his positions to the market. No matter how large a profit he may have in a position, in Jones' mind his entry price was the previous night's close. Since this approach assures that there is never a cushion in his trades, Jones never gets complacent about any of his positions. He not only watches the risk of each position, but he closely monitors the performance of his entire portfolio in real-time. If his total equity drops 1 to 2 percent during a single trading session, he might well liquidate all of his positions instantaneously to cut his risk. "It is always easier to get back in than to get out," he says.

If Jones' trading starts going poorly, he will continually reduce his position size until he is on track again. That way, when he is trading his worst, he is also trading his smallest. In any month with net trading losses, Jones will automatically reduce his risk exposure to make sure he never registers a double-digit loss in a single month. After big winning streaks, he is particularly cautious about getting overconfident.

In short, Jones maintains risk control in a dozen different ways. As he puts it, "The most important rule in trading is: Play great defense, not great offense."

Gary Bielfeldt

Yes, They Do Trade T-Bonds in Peoria

For years, I have heard the name BLH mentioned as one of the major players in the futures markets, particularly T-bonds, the world's largest futures market. I assumed BLH was a huge trading corporation, but in seeking out the country's best traders, I discovered that BLH was basically a single individual: Gary Bielfeldt.

Who is Gary Bielfeldt? Where did he get the capital to rival the primary Wall Street institutions as a major force in the T-bond futures market? Bielfeldt began his trading career twenty-five years ago, with a mere $1,000 investment. At first, his capital was so limited he confined himself to trading a single corn contract—one of the smallest futures contracts at a time of relative stagnation in agricultural prices. From this extremely modest start, Bielfeldt eventually built his account up to staggering proportions.

How did he do it? Bielfeldt does not believe in diversification. His trading philosophy is that you pick one area and become expert at it. For much of his trading career, the soybean complex and, to a more minor extent, the related grain markets provided that focal point of attention.

Although Bielfeldt had the desire to become a full-time trader from the beginning, his tiny capital base restricted his trading to a part-time endeavor. In those early years, he earned his living running a small brokerage office. The problem he faced was how he, a trader without any independent funds, could develop a sufficient capital base to become a professional trader. Bielfeldt's strong desire to make this leap in his capital base prompted him to take a large, if not imprudent, risk.

By 1965, Bielfeldt had painstakingly built up his initial $1,000 stake to $10,000. Based on his fundamental evaluation of the soybean market, as well as the concurring opinion by his former agricultural economics professor, Thomas Hieronymus, Bielfeldt strongly believed that prices would go higher. In an all-or-nothing play, he bought twenty soybean contracts, an extremely high-leverage position given his $10,000 account size. A mere 10-cent price decline would have completely wiped out his account, while a considerably smaller decline would have been sufficient to generate a forced-liquidation margin call. Initially, prices did move lower, and Bielfeldt came perilously close to that damaging margin call. But he held on, and prices eventually reversed to the upside. By the time he liquidated the position, he had more than doubled his equity on that single trade. That trade launched Bielfeldt toward his much sought after goal of becoming a full-time trader.

Bielfeldt built his account with unerring consistency. By the early 1980s, Bielfeldt's trading size had grown to the point that government-established speculative position limits in the soybean and grain markets were becoming an impediment. This factor, aided by a particularly bad trade in the soybean market in 1983, prompted Bielfeldt to shift his focus to the T-bond futures market, which at the time had no position limit. (Although a position limit was eventually implemented in the T-bond market, the 10,000 contract limit dwarfed the 600-contract limit in soybeans.)

The 1983 soybean loss may have been the best thing that ever happened to Bielfeldt. His shift to T-bonds coincided with an evolving major bottom in that market. He became very bullish and built up a huge long T-bond position at the right time. When the T-bond market exploded during the mid-1984 to early 1986 period, Bielfeldt was perfectly positioned to garner huge profits. His ability to stay with a major position for a long-term move allowed him to leverage his well-timed trade to a much greater degree than would have been achieved by most professional traders with the same initial position. This long T-bond position was Bielfeldt's best trade ever and catapulted him into a new echelon. That, in short, is the story of how a one-lot corn trader became a T-bond futures trader in the same league as the most prominent institutional market participants.

Bielfeldt could not be further removed from the popular image of a large-scale trader in the highly leveraged sphere of futures trading. One would hardly expect to find one of the world's largest bond traders in Peoria. Bielfeldt's attachment to his home town is so strong that he refused to consider becoming a trader on the floor of the Chicago Board of Trade because it would have meant giving up his cherished lifestyle. He is the epitome of the small town model American citizen: honest, hard working, devoted to family and community. One of Bielfeldt's major goals has been to plow back a portion of his trading-derived wealth into projects benefiting his home town.

I interviewed Bielfeldt in his large, comfortably furnished office. The huge, wraparound desk configuration was flanked by ten quote screens. Despite this vast array of electronics, Bielfeldt was low keyed. He rarely glanced at the screens during the afternoon I spent in his office, and it is hard to visualize him trading frantically at any time, the vast array of quote machines notwithstanding.

Bielfeldt is a soft-spoken man of few words. He is also a very modest man who consistently hesitated talking about his achievements, lest it sound like bragging. His very conservative nature led him to avoid even seemingly innocuous subjects. For example, at one point in discussing the reasons for his net trading losses in a given year, he asked me to turn off my tape recorder. I could hardly imagine what he might say that necessitated this precautionary measure. The off-the-record comments proved far from shocking. It turned out that his trading losses in that year were influenced by an overextension into other commitments, including his membership on the Chicago Board of Trade Board of Directors, a position which required frequent travel to Chicago. Apparently, he was reluctant to be quoted because he did not want to make it seem that he was blaming his other responsibilities—which he deemed part of his natural obligations—for his trading losses.

The combination of Bielfeldt's laconic nature, modesty, and conservatism made this a very difficult interview. In fact, this was the only interview I conducted in which the average length of the questions was longer than the average length of the responses. I considered deleting the interview from the book—a tempting choice since I had an excess of material. However, I found Bielfeldt's story so compelling and his character so strong that I was reluctant to take the easy way out. As a compromise, I weighted this chapter to the narrative side and limited the interview section to a few excerpts.

What is your basic approach in analyzing and trading the markets?

I always try to lean primarily on fundamental analysis. However, since I found it was very difficult to know all the fundamentals—usually you are doing pretty well if you have 80 percent of the pieces—I thought it was important to have something to fall back on in case my fundamental analysis was wrong.

I assume you are referring to technical analysis as a supplement.

Right. I developed my own trend-following system.

Do you trade this system in any consistent way?

I use the system primarily as a backup to tell me when to get out of a position.

Can you think of an example?

At the start of 1988, I was long the bond market primarily because I was expecting a weaker economy. Everything seemed to be on target until early March when the bond market started edging down. At some point, you have to say you are wrong. In this case, my system provided me with the rationale for getting out of my losing position.

What went wrong with that trade?

Basically, the economy was a lot stronger than I had anticipated. I thought that there would be a bigger fear factor left over from the October 1987 stock market crash than actually materialized.

What is your opinion of trend-following systems?

The best thing anyone can do when starting out is to learn how a trend system works. Trading a trend system for a while will teach a new trader the principle of letting profits run and cutting losses short. If you can just learn discipline by using a trend-following system, even temporarily, it will increase your odds of being successful as a trader.

Do you have an opinion about systems sold to the public?

I looked at some of these systems a few years ago and found that they generally made too many trades. If a system trades too frequently, the transaction costs will be too high, a factor that will significantly reduce the probability of the system working. I think to be viable, a trend-following system has to be medium to longer term. The more sensitive systems just generate too much commission.

Besides providing a training vehicle for learning good trading habits, do you feel that trend-following systems can provide an effective trading approach?

I would advise anyone who develops a system to combine it with their own judgment. In other words, they should trade half the money on a system and the other half using their own judgment, just in case the system isn't working.

Is that the way you trade?

I used to pay more attention to systems than I do now. Basically, I just focus on my own judgment.

Is that because your own judgment is more reliable, or because systems haven't been working as well as they used to?

They haven't worked as well as they used to because there are too many people using them. Whenever too many people are doing the same thing, the market will go through a period of adjustment.

What are the key factors you focus on in fundamentally evaluating the T-bond market?

The economy is definitely the single most important factor. Four other important elements are inflation expectations, the dollar, the trade balance, and the budget deficit.

You have been trading for over twenty-five years—a much longer time period than most other traders. Is there any single trade that stands out as the most dramatic?

There are quite a few trades that would qualify as dramatic, but the one that stands out most prominently was my attempt to pick the bottom of the bond market in 1983 and 1984.

When did you start trying to buy the bonds?

I started trying to pick a bottom when the bonds were trading in the 63–66 area.

How much risk did you allow when putting on a trade?

Generally anywhere from ½ to 1½ points. [One point in T-bond futures is equal to 32 ticks. A 1-point move is equal to $1,000 per contract.]

So if you tried to pick a spot that looked good and it didn't work, you would bail out and try again at another spot?

Right.

Since bonds eventually declined into the 50s, I guess you must have had a few strikes against you before you finally went long in the right place.

Yes, there were several losses over a period of time.

Do you remember when you finally got positioned at a point where you didn't have to get out?

I turned really bullish in May 1984, when they auctioned off five-year notes at a 13.93 yield. I had been involved in banking since 1974, and at the time, we couldn't find any qualified borrowers for three-year loans at 13 percent. Yet here were government five-year notes selling at nearly a full percentage point above that level. Moreover, this was at a time when we were at the height of a recession in Peoria: Unemployment was approaching 20 percent and the farm crisis was worsening. I felt that interest rates had probably gone high enough. From that point on through April 1986, I traded T-bonds heavily from the long side. There is no question that that was my best trade and longest trend ever.

What are the elements of good trading?

The most important thing is to have a method for staying with your winners and getting rid of your losers.

What do you do to make sure that you stay with a winning position to exploit the longer-term trend? How do you avoid the temptation of taking profits prematurely?

The best way I know to learn discipline and patience is to think through a trade thoroughly before putting it on. You need to develop a plan of your strategies for various contingencies. That way, you won't get swayed by every news item that hits the market and causes prices to move up or down. Also, it helps greatly to have a long-term objective that you have derived by really doing your homework. You combine that long-term objective with a protective stop that you move as the position goes your way. Alternatively, you could use a trend-following system to signal when you should get out of the trade. By having thought out your objective and having a strategy for getting out in case the market trend changes, you greatly increase the potential for staying in your winning positions.

Why do most traders lose?

They overtrade, which means that they have to be right a lot just to cover commissions.

What are the traits of a successful trader?

The most important is discipline—I am sure everyone tells you that. Second, you have to have patience; if you have a good trade on, you have to be able to stay with it. Third, you need courage to go into the market, and courage comes from adequate capitalization. Fourth, you must have a willingness to lose; that is also related to adequate capitalization. Fifth, you need a strong desire to win.

Those elements seem fairly straightforward, except for the willingness to lose. Can you expound on that?

You should have the attitude that if a trade loses, you can handle it without any problem and come back to do the next trade. You can't let a losing trade get to you emotionally.

Can you talk more about what you mean by courage?

If a 260-pound fullback is running through the line and a 175-pound linebacker has to stop him, he has to have the courage to go into him. You need that kind of courage to be able to participate in the markets. If everyone is bullish the dollar, and the yen is sharply lower, it takes courage to fade that major consensus and buy the yen.

How do you judge success?

Most people will judge success by how well they do in their field. A teacher would judge success by how well the students do and how they go through life. A trader would probably judge success by whether he wins or loses in the market.

Speaking personally, how do you judge success?

I judge success by what I do with the money I accumulate. One of the things that my wife and I have done is to establish a foundation so that we could share some of our success with the community by supporting various programs.

Is this foundation one that you just fund, or do you have a hands-on relationship in running it?

My family and I are directly involved in evaluating different projects and deciding which ones to fund.

When did you set up this foundation?

In 1985. But I had thought about the idea as far back as the early 1970s. I had always planned that if I were to become successful, I would set up a foundation to help the community.

Do you think this long-term goal was an important motivation leading to your success as a trader?

Yes, I think it helped.

What advice do you have for the beginning trader?

When you are starting out, it is very important not to get too far behind because it is very difficult to fight back. Most traders have a tendency to take risks that are too large at the beginning. They tend not to be selective enough about when they take risks.

At this point, Bielfeldt asked me to turn off the tape recorder. He talked about the relevance and application of poker strategy to trading. His reason for keeping the comments off-the-record was that he didn't want to contribute to the image of trading as a form of gambling. I found his analogy particularly apropos and finally persuaded him to put it on the record.

Could you explain your analogy between trading and poker?

I learned how to play poker at a very young age. My father taught me the concept of playing the percentage hands. You don't just play every hand and stay through every card, because if you do, you will have a much higher probability of losing. You should play the good hands, and drop out of the poor hands, forfeiting the ante. When more of the cards are on the table and you have a very strong hand—in other words, when you feel the percentages are skewed in your favor—you raise and play that hand to the hilt.

If you apply the same principles of poker strategy to trading, it increases your odds of winning significantly. I have always tried to keep the concept of patience in mind by waiting for the right trade, just like you wait for the percentage hand in poker. If a trade doesn't look right, you get out and take a small loss; it's precisely equivalent to forfeiting the ante by dropping out of a poor hand in poker. On the other hand, when the percentages seem to be strongly in your favor, you should be aggressive and really try to leverage the trade similar to the way you raise on the good hands in poker.

Bielfeldt's story provides an inspiring example of what is attainable given patience on the one hand and an aggressive trading style on the other. Here is an individual who, starting with a minuscule amount of money, working independently, and without benefit of staff or elaborate technology, became one of the world's most successful traders. Moreover, because of his long-term goals and actions, his ultimate success positively impacted an entire community.

The portion of Gary Bielfeldt's interview that I found most insightful was his analogy between poker and trading. It is also interesting to compare Bielfeldt's key point in this analogy to the similar advice offered by James Rogers: Have the patience to wait for the right trade to come along.

Ed Seykota

Everybody Gets What They Want

Although completely unknown, not only to the public, but to most of the financial community as well, Ed Seykota's achievements must certainly rank him as one of the best traders of our time. In the early 1970s, Seykota was hired by a major brokerage firm. He conceived and developed the first commercial computerized trading system for managing clients' money in the futures markets. His system proved quite profitable, but interference and second-guessing by management significantly impeded its performance. This experience provided the catalyst for Seykota going out on his own.

In the ensuing years, Seykota applied his systematized approach to trading a handful of accounts and his own money. During that period, the accounts Seykota managed have witnessed an absolutely astounding rate of return. For example, as of mid-1988, one of his customer accounts, which started with $5,000 in 1972, was up over 250,000 percent on a cash-on-cash basis. (Normalized for withdrawals, the account theoretically was up several million percent.) I know of no other trader who has matched this track record over the same length of time.

I had never heard of Seykota when I first began working on this book. Seykota's name had come up several times during my interview of Michael Marcus as the person who was most influential in transforming him into a successful trader. After our interview, Marcus said reflectively, "You know, you really should interview Ed Seykota. He is not only a great trader; he is a mind."

Marcus provided an introduction over the phone, and I briefly outlined the concept of my book to Seykota. Since I was already out West, it was most convenient for me to interview Seykota on the same trip by rerouting my return to New York via Reno. Seykota was agreeable to participating, but seemed skeptical of my ability to complete the interview in the space of two hours (the time available in order for me to make my flight connections). I assured him that, although it was tight, I had done a few other interviews in that space of time. "It is feasible as long as our conversation remains very focused," I explained.

I cut my arrival at the airport extremely close, having forgotten to revise my ticket to reflect the change in itinerary. After a vociferous argument with a ticket agent who insisted I didn't have enough time to catch my flight—a contention she nearly made self-fulfilling—I raced through the airport, reaching the gate with only seconds to spare. By the time I arrived in Reno, the tension from my near-missed flight had just about dissipated. The drive to Seykota's house was too far for a cab, so I rented a car. It was very early morning, and the highway winding up into the mountains offered spectacular vistas below. The classical music station I found on the radio was playing Mozart's Clarinet Concerto. The combination was glorious.

Seykota works from an office in his house, which borders Lake Tahoe. Before beginning the interview, we took a brief walk out onto the beach behind his house. It was a cold, clear morning, and the view was idyllic. The contrast between his workplace and my own—an office in the Wall Street area, with a prominent view of an ugly building—could hardly have been more striking. I plead guilty to jealousy.

In contrast to virtually all the other traders I had interviewed, Seykota's desk is not flanked by an array of quote screens, or, for that matter, even a single screen. His trading is largely confined to the few minutes it takes to run his computer program which generates signals for the next day.

In my conversation with Seykota, I was struck by the intensity of both his intelligence and sensitivity—an odd combination I thought. He has a way of looking at things from a unique vantage point. At one moment, he could be talking about analytical techniques and would appear as the consummate scientist (he holds a degree in electrical engineering from MIT), bringing up a three-dimensional diagram on the computer screen, generated by one of the many programs he had designed. Yet, in another moment, when the conversation turned to the psychology of trading, he would reveal great sensitivity and insight into human behavior.

Indeed, in recent years, Seykota has become very involved in the field of psychology. It appeared to me that psychology, and its application in helping people solve their problems, had become a more important element in his life than market analysis and trading. I suspect that Seykota would probably find this contrast somewhat artificial, in that to him, trading and psychology are one and the same thing.

Our conversation was not as focused as I had intended it to be. In fact, it went off in so many directions that we had barely scratched the surface by the time the two hours had elapsed. I continued on, assuming that I would merely catch a later flight. As it turned out, the flight that I had missed was the last direct one from Reno to New York.

Seykota later told me that he knew in our first phone conversation that I would end up spending the day. He is extremely perceptive about people. For example, at one point in our conversation, Seykota asked me, "How many minutes fast do you set your watch?" I found this question particularly striking in that in our brief time together, he had been able to pick up on one of my basic character traits. The question was also particularly timely, given my near-missed flight earlier that morning.

Seykota's success goes well beyond his trading. He impressed me as someone who had found meaning in his life, and was living exactly the life he wanted to be living.

How did you first get involved in trading?

In the late 1960s, I decided that silver had to rise when the U.S. Treasury stopped selling it. I opened a commodity margin account to take full advantage of my insight. While I was waiting, my broker convinced me to short some copper. I soon got stopped out and lost some money and my trading virginity. So I went back to waiting for the start of the big, inevitable bull market in silver. Finally, the day arrived. I bought. Much to my amazement and financial detriment, the price started falling!

At first it seemed impossible to me that silver could fall on such a bullish deal. Yet the price was falling and that was a fact. Soon my stop got hit. This was a very stunning education about the way markets discount news. I became more and more fascinated with how markets work.

About that time, I saw a letter published by Richard Donchian, which implied that a purely mechanical trend-following system could beat the markets. This too seemed impossible to me. So I wrote computer programs (on punch cards in those days) to test the theories. Amazingly, his theories tested true. To this day, I'm not sure I understand why or whether I really need to. Anyhow, studying the markets, and backing up my opinions with money, was so fascinating compared to my other career opportunities at the time, that I began trading full time for a living.

What was your first trading-related job?

I landed my first job on Wall Street in the early 1970s as an analyst with a major brokerage house. I was assigned to cover the egg and *broiler* markets. [Broilers are young chickens up to 2½ pounds dressed weight. The futures markets for both broilers and eggs have since disappeared as waning trading activity prompted their delisting by the parent exchanges.] I found it interesting that an entry level guy like me was immediately placed in charge of dispensing trading advice. I once wrote an article recommending that traders stay away from the market for a while. Management censored that comment from the market letter—likely because it didn't promise to motivate much trading.

I wanted to start applying computers to the business of analysis. Remember, in those days computers were still typically punch card devices used for accounting. The guy who was running the computer department seemed to see me as a threat to his job security, and he repeatedly chased me off his turf. After about a month at that job, I announced that I was going to quit. The head of the department called me in to find out why. It was the first time he had ever been interested in talking to me.

I went to work for another brokerage house, which was going

through a reorganization. There was a lot less management, so I took advantage of the lack of supervision by using the accounting computer to test trading systems during the weekends. They had an IBM 360 which took up a large air conditioned room. Over the course of about a half year, I was able to test about a hundred variations of four simple systems for about ten years of data on ten commodities. Today, the same job takes about one day on a PC. Anyway, I got my results. They confirmed there was a possibility of making money from trend-following systems.

I take it that computer testing of systems was not part of your job, since you did it on weekends. What were you actually hired to do?

During the week, my normal Clark Kent type job was to load new rolls of paper onto the Reuters machine when the margin turned pink. I was also responsible for tearing off the news in strips and hanging them up on the wall behind the machine. The trick was to tear between line-feeds so as to get a smooth edge. The funny thing was that hardly anyone would read the news since they'd have to lean way over the machine to see the pages. So I started reading the news and personally delivering it to the brokers. One bonus of this job was that I got to observe a lot of brokers' trading styles.

Your official position sounds like a glorified office boy. Why did you accept such a menial job?

Because I knew I wanted to be in the business, and I didn't care what I did, or what I got paid.

Why didn't you stay at your original position? At least there you were an analyst.

Because it was a stultifying environment. I disapproved of management pressures to recommend trades when I thought there were no trading opportunities. Also, I saw that being allowed access to the company computers for testing trading systems (my real desire) was a dead issue.

Did you know that you could have access to the computer at your new job?

No, but since the company had just gone through a major shake-up and most of the management had been fired, I figured there wouldn't be very much of a bureaucracy to interfere with my use of the computer.

What became of your work on computerized trading systems?

Eventually, management got interested in using my research results for managing money. I developed the first large-scale commercial computerized trading system.

What do you mean by large scale?

The program was marketed by several hundred agents of the firm, and the equity under management was several million dollars—a large amount of money in the early 1970s.

How did you get management to support you to that extent?

They were familiar with Richard Donchian, who was a pioneer in developing trend-following trading systems, although, at the time, he was doing everything by hand. Because of that exposure, they were already favorably disposed to the concept of using trading systems to manage money. Also, at the time, computers were so new that "computer system" was a great buzzword.

How did your trading program do?

The program did fine; the problem was that management couldn't keep from second-guessing the signals. For example, I remember one time the program generated a buy signal for sugar when it was trading around 5 cents. Management thought that the market was already overbought and decided not to take the signal. When the market kept on going higher, they came up with the rule that they would buy on the first 20-*point* pullback [100 points equal 1 cent]. When no such pullback developed, they modified the rule to buying on the first 30-point reaction.

As the market kept moving higher without any meaningful retracements, they changed the rule to 50 points and eventually 100 points. Finally, with sugar prices around 9 cents, they finally decided that it was a bull market, and that they had better buy before prices went much higher. They put the managed accounts long at that point. As you might guess, the sugar market peaked shortly thereafter. They compounded the error by ignoring the sell signal as well—a signal which also would have been very profitable.

The bottom line was that because of this interference, the most profitable trade of the year ended up losing money. As a result, instead of a theoretical return of 60 percent for the year, quite a few accounts actually lost money. This type of meddling was one of the main reasons why I eventually quit.

What were the other reasons?

Management wanted me to change the system so that it would trade more actively, thereby generating more commission income. I explained to them that it would be very easy to make such a change, but doing so would seriously impede performance. They didn't seem to care.

What did you do after you quit?

I just quit the research department, but I stayed on as a broker managing accounts. After about two years, I gave up brokerage to become a money manager. That shift allowed me to get away from earning my living from commissions, which I think can be a counterproductive incentive to making money for clients. I switched to a pure profit incentive fee arrangement.

Did you continue trading the system after you left?

Yes, although I substantially revised the system over the years.

What is the performance track record?

I do not publicize my track record other than my "model account," which is an actual customer account that started with $5,000 in 1972 and has made over $15 million. Theoretically, the total return would have been many multiples larger had there been no withdrawals.

With performance like that, how come you haven't been deluged with word-of-mouth requests to manage money?

I do receive requests, but I very rarely accept new accounts. If I do, it is only after considerable interviewing and screening to determine the motivations and attitudes of the client. I have found that the people I associate with have subtle, yet very important, effects on my performance. If, for example, they are able to support me and my methods over the long term, then they tend to help me. If, however, they get too concerned with the short-term ups and downs of their account, they can be a hindrance.

How many accounts did you originally start out with?

About a half dozen back in the early 1970s.

How many of those accounts are still with you?

Four. One client made about $15 million and decided to withdraw his money and manage it himself; another made over $10 million and decided to buy a house on the beach and retire.

What source did you learn from before designing your first system?

I was inspired and influenced by the book *Reminiscences of a Stock Operator* and also by Richard Donchian's five- and twenty-day moving average crossover system and his weekly rule system. I consider Donchian to be one of the guiding lights of technical trading.

What was your first trading system?

My first system was a variation of Donchian's moving average system. I used an exponential averaging method because it was easier to calculate and computational errors tended to disappear over time. It was so new at the time that it was being passed around by word of mouth as the "expedential system."

Your reference to a first system implies that you eventually changed systems. How did you know when your system needed to be changed?

Systems don't need to be changed. The trick is for a trader to develop a system with which he is compatible.

Were you incompatible with your original system?

My original system was very simple with hard-and-fast rules that didn't allow for any deviations. I found it difficult to stay with the system while disregarding my own feelings. I kept jumping on and off—often at just the wrong time. I thought I knew better than the system. At the time, I didn't really trust that trend-following systems would work. There is plenty of literature "proving" they don't. Also, it seemed a waste of my intellect and MIT education to just sit there and not try to figure out the markets. Eventually, as I became more confident of trading with the trend, and more able to ignore the news, I became more comfortable with the approach. Also, as I continued to incorporate more "expert trader rules," my system became more compatible with my trading style.

What is your trading style?

My style is basically trend following, with some special pattern recognition and money management algorithms.

Without divulging trade secrets, how have you been able to so spectacularly outperform standard trend-following systems?

The key to long-term survival and prosperity has a lot to do with the money management techniques incorporated into the technical system. There are old traders and there are bold traders, but there are very few old, bold traders.

Witty and true, but the question remains, albeit in translated form: There are many trend-following systems with money management rules; why have you done so much better?

I seem to have a gift. I think it is related to my overall philosophy, which has a lot to do with loving the markets and maintaining an optimistic attitude. Also, as I keep trading and learning, my system (that is the mechanical computer version of what I do) keeps evolving. I would add that I consider myself and how I do things as a kind of system which, by definition, I always follow. Sometimes I trade entirely off the mechanical part, sometimes I override the signals based on strong feelings, and sometimes I just quit altogether. The immediate trading result of this jumping around is probably breakeven to somewhat negative. However, if I didn't allow myself the freedom to discharge my creative side, it might build up to some kind of blowout. Striking a workable ecology seems to promote trading longevity, which is one key to success.

How would you compare the relative advantages and disadvantages of systems trading versus discretionary trading?

Systems trading is ultimately discretionary. The manager still has to decide how much risk to accept, which markets to play, and how aggressively to increase and decrease the trading base as a function of equity change. These decisions are quite important—often more important than trade timing.

What percentage of your trading is systems based? Has this percentage changed over time?

Over time, I have become more mechanical, since (1) I have become more trusting of trend trading, and (2) my mechanical programs have factored in more and more "tricks of the trade." I still go through periods of thinking I can outperform my own system, but such excursions are often self-correcting through the process of losing money.

What are the present and future prospects for trend-following systems? Do you think the growing prevalence of their use will doom them to eventual failure?

No. All trading is done on some sort of system, whether or not it is conscious. Many of the good systems are based on following trends. Life itself is based on trends. Birds start south for the winter and keep on going. Companies track trends and alter their products accordingly. Tiny protozoa move in trends along chemical and luminescence gradients.

The profitability of trading systems seems to move in cycles. Periods during which trend-following systems are highly successful will lead to their increased popularity. As the number of system users increases, and the markets shift from trending to directionless price action, these systems become unprofitable, and undercapitalized and inexperienced traders will get shaken out. Longevity is the key to success.

What are your thoughts about using fundamental analysis as an input in trading?

Fundamentals that you read about are typically useless as the market has already discounted the price, and I call them "funny-mentals." However, if you catch on early, before others believe, then you might have valuable "surprise-a-mentals."

Your answer is a bit facetious. Does it imply that you only use technical analysis?

I am primarily a trend trader with touches of hunches based on about twenty years of experience. In order of importance to me are: (1) the long-term trend, (2) the current chart pattern, and (3) picking a good spot to buy or sell. Those are the three primary components of my trading. Way down in very distant fourth place are my fundamental ideas and, quite likely, on balance, they have cost me money.

By picking the right spot to buy, do you mean determining a reaction point at which you will buy? If so, how do you avoid sometimes missing major price moves?

Oh no. If I were buying, my point would be above the market. I try to identify a point at which I expect the market momentum to be strong in the direction of the trade, so as to reduce my probable risk. I don't try to pick a bottom or top.

Does that imply that if you are bullish, you will always wait for short-term strength before entering a position, or will you sometimes buy on a reaction?

If I am bullish, I neither buy on a reaction, nor wait for strength; I am already in. I turn bullish at the instant my buy stop is hit, and stay bullish until my sell stop is hit. Being bullish and not being long is illogical.

Do you ever use contrary opinion as an aid to your trading?

Sometimes. For example, at a recent goldbug conference, virtually all the speakers were bearish. I said to myself, "Gold is probably near a bottom." [The market did indeed rally after that conference.]

Would you buy because of that type of input?

Oh no, the trend was still down. But it might get me to lighten up my short position.

What was your most dramatic or emotional trading experience?

Dramatic and emotional trading experiences tend to be negative. Pride is a great banana peel, as are hope, fear, and greed. My biggest slip-ups occurred shortly after I got emotionally involved with positions.

How about some actual "war stories"?

I prefer not to dwell on past situations. I tend to cut bad trades as soon as possible, forget them, and then move on to new opportunities. After I bury a dead trade, I don't like to dig up the details again—at least not in print. Maybe some evening, after dinner, sitting around a fire, off the record, deep in the Tahoe winter...

Can you describe specific trading mistakes that you learned from?

I had a "thing" for silver for years. One of my first losses was in silver, as were many of my worst losses. It seemed to get into my blood and hypnotize me. It inveigled me to pull my protective stops so as to avoid getting bear-raided. Naturally, it would hold momentarily and then collapse some more. I got killed so many times by silver spikes that I started thinking I was some kind of werewolf. I worked on myself with hypnosis and positive imagery. I also avoided walks in the full moon. So far it seems to be working.

How do you pick your trades?

Mostly by my trading system, although occasionally, I will get an impulsive flash and override my system. Fortunately, I don't usually take on a big enough position to do any lasting damage to my portfolio.

What are the elements of good trading?

The elements of good trading are: (1) cutting losses, (2) cutting losses, and (3) cutting losses. If you can follow these three rules, you may have a chance.

How do you handle a losing streak?

I handle losing streaks by trimming down my activity. I just wait it out. Trying to trade during a losing streak is emotionally devastating. Trying to play "catch up" is lethal.

Since you are primarily a systems trader, wouldn't following a system imply no changes of trading activity during losing periods?

I have incorporated some logic into my computer programs, such as modulating the trading activity depending on market behavior. Still, important decisions need to be made outside the mechanical system boundaries, such as how to maintain diversification for a growing account when some positions are at position limit or when markets are too thin.

Psychologically, I tend to alter my activity depending on performance. I tend to be more aggressive after I have been winning, and less so after losses. These tendencies seem OK. In contrast, a costly tendency is to get emotional over a loss and then try to get even with an overly large position.

Are you a self-taught trader, or did another trader teach you worthwhile lessons?

I am a self-taught trader who is continually studying both myself and other traders.

Do you decide where you are getting out before you get in on a trade?

I set protective stops at the same time I enter a trade. I normally move these stops in to lock in a profit as the trend continues. Sometimes, I take profits when a market gets wild. This usually doesn't get me out any better than waiting for my stops to close in, but it does cut down on the volatility of the portfolio, which helps calm my nerves. Losing a position is aggravating, whereas losing your nerve is devastating.

What is the maximum percentage of equity you will risk on any individual trade?

I intend to risk below 5 percent on a trade, allowing for poor executions. Occasionally I have taken losses above that amount when major news caused a thin market to jump through my stops.

What was your single worst "thin market" loss?

All markets are too thin when I want to get out of a bad position in a
hurry. Most markets have, on occasion, moved rapidly against me due
to surprise news. As soon as the news is digested, the market thickens
up again at a new level. During the big sugar bull market when prices
moved from 10 cents to 40 cents, I was carrying thousands of contracts
and I gave up several *cents* getting out of my position. [Each cent in sugar
is equivalent to $1,120 per contract.]

**Very few traders have enjoyed the spectacular success you have.
What makes you different?**

I feel my success comes from my love of the markets. I am not a casual
trader. It is my life. I have a passion for trading. It is not merely a hobby
or even a career choice for me. There is no question that this is what I
am supposed to do with my life.

What are the trading rules you live by?

a. Cut losses.
b. Ride winners.
c. Keep bets small.
d. Follow the rules without question.
e. Know when to break the rules.

**Your last two rules are cute because they are contradictory. Seri-
ously now, which do you believe: Follow the rules, or know when to
break the rules?**

I believe both. Mostly I follow the rules. As I keep studying the markets,
I sometimes find a new rule which breaks and then replaces a previous
rule. Sometimes I get to a personal breakpoint. When that happens, I
just get out of the markets altogether and take a vacation until I feel that
I am ready to follow the rules again. Perhaps some day, I will have a
more explicit rule for breaking rules.

I don't think traders can follow rules for very long unless they reflect their own trading style. Eventually, a breaking point is reached and the trader has to quit or change, or find a new set of rules he can follow. This seems to be part of the process of evolution and growth of a trader.

How important to trading success is varying the size of the bet?

It might be a good idea depending on the reason for doing so. Consider, though, if you had a successful modification policy, say "M" for changing system "S," then you might be better off just trading "M."

How important is gut feel?

Gut feel is important. If ignored, it may come out in subtle ways by coloring your logic. It can be dealt with through meditation and reflection to determine what's behind it. If it persists, then it might be a valuable subconscious analysis of some subtle information. Otherwise, it might be a dangerous sublimation of an inner desire for excitement and not reflect market conditions. Be sensitive to the subtle differences between "intuition" and "into wishing."

What was your worst year? What went wrong?

One of my worst years was 1980. The bull markets had ended, but I kept trying to hold on and buy back in at lower prices. The markets just kept on breaking. I had never seen a major bear market before, so I was all set up for an important educational experience.

What happened to the money management rules in your system in 1980? Did you override them?

I continued to trade even though my system was largely out of the markets due to the enormous volatility. I tried to pick tops and bottoms in what I considered grossly overbought and oversold markets. The markets just kept on going and I lost a lot. Eventually, I saw the futility of my approach and quit for a while.

What is the most important advice you can give the average trader?

That he should find a superior trader to do his trading for him, and then go find something he really loves to do.

Do you believe chart reading can be used for successful trading?

I consider trend following to be a subset of charting. Charting is a little like surfing. You don't have to know a lot about the physics of tides, resonance, and fluid dynamics in order to catch a good wave. You just have to be able to sense when it's happening and then have the drive to act at the right time.

What was your personal experience in October 1987?

I made money on the day of the October 1987 crash. I also made money for the month as a whole, and for the year, as well. I lost on the day after the crash, however, since I was short the interest rate markets. Most trend traders were likely either out or short stocks and stock indexes during the crash.

Are the markets different now than they were five to ten years ago because of the much greater current participation by professional managers?

No. The markets are the same now as they were five to ten years ago because they keep changing—just like they did then.

Does trading become more difficult as your size increases?

It becomes more difficult because it is harder to move large positions without moving the market. It becomes easier because you have more access to competent people to support you.

What type of support do you mean?

A team of experienced brokers with professional attitudes. Experienced traders can be very supportive by just being there for sharing joys and sorrows. Also, the old-timers seem to be able to smell the beginnings and endings of major moves. I also receive important support from my friends, associates, and family.

Do you use any outside advisory services?

I keep track of a lot of outside advisers, mostly by reading the business press or hearing from my brokers. The services usually break even, except when they start to gloat, then they are likely headed for trouble.

How about market letters?

Market letters tend to lag behind the market since they generally respond to demand for news about recent activity. Although there are certainly important exceptions, letter writing is often a beginning job in the industry, and as such may be handled by inexperienced traders or nontraders. Good traders trade. Good letter writers write letters.

Do you use the opinions of other traders in making trading decisions, or do you operate completely solo?

I usually ignore advice from other traders, especially the ones who believe they are on to a "sure thing." The old-timers, who talk about "maybe there is a chance of so and so," are often right and early.

At what point did you get the confidence that you could keep on winning as a trader?

I vacillate between (a) "I can keep on winning," and (b) "I have just been lucky." I sometimes get most confident of my ability just before a major losing streak.

How similar are the price patterns in different markets?

Common patterns transcend individual market behavior. For example, bond prices have a lot in common with the way cockroaches crawl up and down a wall. Unfortunately for cockroach followers, there is usually no one around to take the other side of a trade.

Does the stock market behave differently from other markets?

The stock market behaves differently from all other markets and it also behaves differently from the stock market. If this is hard to understand, it is because trying to understand the markets is a bit futile. I don't think it makes any more sense trying to understand the stock market than trying to understand music. A lot of people would rather understand the market than make money.

What do you mean, "The stock market behaves differently from the stock market"?

The stock market behaves differently from itself in that easily identifiable patterns seldom exactly repeat.

What is your long-term outlook for inflation, the dollar, and gold?

Inflation is part of the way societies sweep away the old order. All currencies eventually get debased—like it or not. Compute one penny invested at the time of Christ, compounded at 3 percent per year. Then consider why nobody has anywhere near that amount these days.

Gold tends to be dug up, refined, and then buried again. The geographical entropy of all gold on the planet seems to decrease over time. A lot has been collected in vaults. I project the trend as one toward a central world gold stash.

Do great traders have a special talent for trading?

Good traders have a special talent for trading just as good musicians and good athletes have talents for their fields. Great traders are ones who are absorbed by the talent. They don't have the talent—the talent has them.

What is the balance between talent versus work in trading success?

I don't know where one starts and the other stops.

How much of a role does luck play in trading success?

Luck plays an enormous role in trading success. Some people were lucky enough to be born smart, while others were even smarter and got born lucky.

How about a serious answer?

"Luck" or "smarts" or "gift" are words indicating an attitudinal proclivity for mastery. One tends to do well at one's calling. I think most good traders have a little extra spark about trading. Some people are natural musicians or painters or salesmen or analysts. I think it is difficult to acquire talent for trading. However, if it is already there, it can be discovered and developed.

What effect has trading had on your personal life?

My personal life is integrated with my trading life.

Is the joy of winning as intense as the pain of losing?

The joy of winning and the pain of losing are right up there with the pain of winning and the joy of losing. Also to consider are the joy and pain of not participating. The relative strengths of these feelings tend to increase with the distance of the trader from his commitment to being a trader.

When you made your first few million, did you lock some of it away to avoid the Jesse Livermore experience? [Livermore was a famous speculator of the early twentieth century who made and lost several fortunes.]

I feel the Livermore experience was a function of his psychology and had little to do with the location of his assets. In fact, I remember reading that Jesse Livermore used to lock some of his winnings away and then find a key when he needed to get at them. Therefore, locking up winnings would be necessary to emulate his experience, not to avoid it. Furthermore, you would probably also need to overtrade and have wipeouts, while you simultaneously fired up your emotions with the burning desire to "win it right back." Acting out this drama could be exciting. However, it also seems terribly expensive. One alternative is to keep bets small and then to systematically keep reducing risk during equity drawdowns. That way you approach your safe money asymptotically and have a gentle financial and emotional touchdown.

I notice there is no quote machine on your desk.

Having a quote machine is like having a slot machine on your desk—you end up feeding it all day long. I get my price data after the close each day.

Why do so many traders fail in the marketplace?

For the same reason that most baby turtles fail to reach maturity: Many are called and few are chosen. Society works by the attraction of the many. As they are culled out, the good ones are left, and the others are released to go try something else until they find their calling. The same is true for other fields of pursuit.

What can a losing trader do to transform himself into a winning trader?

A losing trader can do little to transform himself into a winning trader. A losing trader is not going to want to transform himself. That's the kind of thing winning traders do.

How would you rate the relative importance between psychology and market analysis to successful trading?

Psychology motivates the quality of analysis and puts it to use. Psychology is the driver and analysis is the road map.

You have focused a lot on the field of psychology. Can you tell by talking to a person whether that person would probably be a winning or losing trader?

Yes, the winning traders have usually been winning at whatever field they are in for years.

What traits do you look for to identify the winning trader personality?

1. He/she loves to trade; and
2. He/she loves to win.

Don't all traders want to win?

Win or lose, everybody gets what they want out of the market. Some people seem to like to lose, so they win by losing money.

I know one trader who seems to get in near the start of every substantial bull move and works his $10 thousand up to about a quarter of a million in a couple of months. Then he changes his personality and loses it all back again. This process repeats like clockwork. Once I traded with him, but got out when his personality changed. I doubled my money, while he wiped out as usual. I told him what I was doing, and even paid him a management fee. He just couldn't help himself. I don't think he can do it any differently. He wouldn't want to. He gets a lot of excitement, he gets to be a martyr, he gets sympathy from his friends, and he gets to be the center of attention. Also, possibly, he may be more comfortable relating to people if he is on their financial plane. On some level, I think he is really getting what he wants.

I think that if people look deeply enough into their trading patterns, they find that, on balance, including all their goals, they are really getting what they want, even though they may not understand it or want to admit it.

A doctor friend of mine tells a story about a cancer patient who used her condition to demand attention and, in general, to dominate others around her. As an experiment prearranged with her family, the

doctor told her a shot was available which would cure her. She constantly found excuses to avoid appearing for the shot and eventually avoided
it entirely. Perhaps her political position was more important than her
life. People's trading performance probably reflects their priorities more
than they would like to admit.

I think that some of the most flamboyant and interesting traders are
playing for more than profits alone; they are probably also playing for
excitement. One of the best ways to increase profits is to do goal setting
and visualizations in order to align the conscious and subconscious with
making profits. I have worked with a number of traders in order to examine their priorities and align their goals. I use a combination of hypnosis, breathing, pacing, visualization, gestalt, massage, and so forth.
The traders usually either (1) get much more successful, or (2) realize
they didn't really want to be traders in the first place.

**Surely, some people lose because they lack the skill, even though they
really want to win.**

It is a happy circumstance that when nature gives us true burning desires,
she also gives us the means to satisfy them. Those who want to win and
lack skill can get someone with skill to help them.

**I sometimes have dreams related to the impending direction of a
market. Although these dreams tend to be very infrequent, uncan-
nily they often prove right. Have you had any similar experiences?**

I know several people who claim to have market insights during dreams.
I think one of the functions of dreams is to reconcile information and
feelings which the conscious mind finds intractable. For instance, I once
told a lot of my friends that I expected silver to keep on going up. When
it went down instead, I ignored the signs and tried to tell myself it was
just a temporary correction. I stood to lose face and money. I couldn't
afford to be wrong. Around that time, I had dreams of being in a big,
shiny, silver aircraft that stalled out and started going down toward an
inevitable crash. I eventually dumped my silver position, even went
short, and the dreams stopped.

How do you judge success?

I don't judge success. I celebrate it. I think success has to do with finding and following one's calling regardless of financial gain.

Don't be fooled by the humor in Seykota's comments; there is a great deal of serious wisdom in his pithy replies. For me personally, the most striking comment was: "Everybody gets what they want out of the market." When Seykota first made this remark, I thought he was merely being cute. But I soon realized he was deadly serious. My reflexive response to this premise was disbelief: It implies that all losers want to lose and all winners who fall short of their goals (like myself) are fulfilling some inner need for a constrained threshold of success—a difficult proposition to swallow. Although my rigidly logical mind would normally dismiss the idea, my respect for Seykota's knowledge about markets and people forces me to consider the potential truth of the statement that everybody gets what they want out of the market—a most provocative concept.

Larry Hite

Respecting Risk

Larry Hite's interest in the financial markets was sparked by a college course, but his path to Wall Street was as circuitous as Moses' to the Land of Israel. His early adult years did not offer any clue that this was a young man headed for eventual major success. First, his academic performance was inauspicious. Then he went through a string of odd jobs, never managing to hold any for very long. Eventually, he drifted into a dual career of actor and screenwriter. While not recording any major successes, he managed to support himself, and enjoyed his work. One of his movie scripts, which never found its way into production, was optioned so often that he began to view it as a source of steady income.

One day, Hite heard H. L. Hunt on the radio describing how he made his fortune buying up lots of cheap oil right options, which gave him the opportunity for occasional windfall profits with minimal risk. That same night, Hite briefly met Brian Epstein, the manager of the Beatles, at a party. The two ideas fused in his mind, leading to another career change. He thought to himself, "Here is something [a rock promoter] that has the potential for making a lot of money with a minimal investment." Although he landed a few record contracts for some of his groups, none ever reached true stardom. Once again, although his success was limited, he managed to earn a satisfactory living in a self-employed position.

Meanwhile, Hite's real interest remained in the financial markets. "You often hear about people working on Wall Street to become screenwriters. I may be the only person who ever worked as an actor and a scriptwriter to pay for my Wall Street career," he says jokingly. In 1968, Hite finally decided to pursue his primary interest. While fascinated with the futures markets, he didn't have the slightest idea how to break into that field, so he began as a stockbroker. Several years later, he became a full-time commodities broker.

More than a decade passed before Hite, convinced that he had learned the ingredients necessary for successful long-term trading performance, took the initial steps that led to the ultimate formation of Mint Investment Management Company. He realized that his trading ideas needed to be subjected to rigorous scientific testing. With an offer of partnership, but no immediate pay, he enlisted Peter Matthews, who held a Ph.D. in statistics. One year later, he hired Michael Delman, a designer of computer systems for a defense electronics firm. Matthews and Delman brought their own ideas to the table, but perhaps even more significantly, their work provided the mathematical proof that Hite's trading concepts were indeed statistically sound. Hite is emphatic that Mint's success would not have been possible without Matthews and Delman.

Mint's objective was never to make the largest percentage return. Rather, Hite's philosophy was to aim for the best growth rate consistent with extremely rigorous risk control. It is in this perspective (return relative to risk) that Mint really shines. From the inception of trading in April 1981 through mid-1988, Mint registered an average annual compounded return of over 30 percent. But it is their consistency that is most impressive: their annual returns have ranged from a worst of plus 13 percent to a best of plus 60 percent. Their largest loss in any six-month period was only 15 percent and under 1 percent in any twelve-month period (not just calendar years).

Not surprisingly, Mint's stellar performance has resulted in a spectacular growth of equity under management. In April 1981, they began trading with $2 million; today, they manage over $800 million. Significantly, there is no evidence that the surge of money under management has had any deleterious effect on performance. Hite believes that Mint can ultimately manage $2 billion—an unprecedentedly large sum for a futures fund.

Our interview was conducted over lunch at Windows of the World atop New York's World Trade Center, on a day it was blanketed with clouds. We took the hint when we were the last ones left in the restaurant and finished the interview in Hite's office.

How did you first get interested in markets?

When I was in college, I took a business course with a professor who had a trenchant sense of humor. To give you an example, he also worked as a bank examiner. One day, before leaving the bank following an audit, he turned to the bank president and, as a joke, said, "Got you!" The man had a heart attack on the spot. After that, they did another audit and found that the bank president had embezzled $75,000. Anyway, in class one day, this professor is reviewing all the financial instruments: stocks, bonds, and so on. Then he says, "Now we come to the craziest market of all—commodities. These people trade on only 5 percent margin—and most of them borrow that." The whole class laughed, except me. For some reason, the idea of trading on 5 percent margin made perfect sense to me.

When did you first get involved in the financial markets?

Not until many years later. I was a rock promoter at the time, and on one weekend, there were three separate shootings in clubs at which the groups I managed were working. I decided it was an opportune time to change careers and pursue my true interest—the financial markets. Although I was really interested in futures, I didn't have any idea how to look for a job in that field. So I decided I would start out as a stockbroker.

My first interview was with a very old-line Wall Street firm, with offices that made you feel like you should speak in hushed tones. The man who interviewed me was the kind of guy [he adopts a pompously refined voice] who talks with his teeth together and lives in Connecticut. He tells me, "We only buy blue chips for our clients."

Not having a financial background, I was unfamiliar with the term "blue chip," but it sounded odd to me in the context of a staid investment firm. So after the interview, I looked up its derivation. I found that the origin of the term could be traced to the color of the most expensive chip in Monte Carlo. I said to myself, "Aha, now I know what this game is all about—gambling." I threw away my copy of Graham and Dodd [*Principles of Security Analysis*, considered by many to be the "bible" of stock market analysis] and bought a book called *Beat the Dealer*. I came away with the idea that successful investment was really a matter of odds, and if you could compute the odds, you could find and test methods that could beat the market.

What made you believe that you could develop methods to put the odds in your favor?

I don't know that I understood it all then, but over the years I came to realize that the markets are inefficient. I have a friend who is an economist. He would try to explain to me, as if talking to a child, why what I was trying to do was futile, because "the markets are efficient." I have noticed that everyone who has ever told me that the markets are efficient is poor. He argued that if I could develop a winning system on a computer, so could others, and we would all cancel each other out.

What is wrong with that argument?

Because people develop systems and people will make mistakes. Some will alter their system or jump from system to system as each one has a losing period. Others will be unable to resist second-guessing the trading signals. Whenever I go to a money management conference and sit down with a group to have some drinks at night, I always hear the same story. "My system worked great, but I just didn't take the gold trade, and that would have been my biggest winner."

There is a very important message here: People don't change. That is why this whole game works. In 1637, tulips in Holland traded for 5,500 florins and then crashed to 50, a 99 percent loss. Well, you might say, "Trading was relatively new then; these people were primitive; capitalism was still in its infancy. Today we are much more sophisticated." So you go to 1929 and find a stock like Air Reduction which traded at a high of $233 and after the crash fell to $31, a decline of 87 percent. OK, you might say, "The Roaring '20s were crazy times, but now things are surely different." Move ahead to 1961 and you find a stock called Texas Instruments trading at $207. It eventually dropped to $49, a decline of 77 percent. If you think we have gotten more sophisticated in the 1980s, all you have to do is look at silver prices, which in 1980 reached a peak of $50 and subsequently fell to $5, a 90 percent decline.

The point is that because people are the same, if you use sufficiently rigorous methods to avoid hindsight, you can test a system and see how it would have done in the past and get a fairly good idea of how that system will perform in the future. That is our edge.

Isn't it possible that the markets can change and the future will be very different from the past?

The markets may change, but people won't. When we were still in the testing stage, before we actually started managing any money, my partner Michael Delman came up with the concept of using holding periods as a measure of system performance. Evaluating systems solely on a calendar year basis is very arbitrary. What you really want to know are the odds for profitable performance in a holding period of any length. In our simulations, Peter determined that 90 percent of all the six-month holding periods, 97 percent of the twelve-month periods, and 100 percent of the eighteen-month periods would be profitable. After over seven years of actual trading, the numbers turned out to be 90 percent, 99 percent, and 100 percent.

I will tell you how confident I am of the future validity of our evaluation process. There is a fellow who works for us who used to be a colonel in the British army. His service specialty was dismantling bombs all over the world. I asked him, "How did you do it?" "It wasn't that difficult," he says. "There are different styles of bombs; a bomb in Malaysia is different from a bomb in the Middle East. You go there and see what kind of bomb it is and take it apart." I said, "Let me ask you a question. What happens when you come across a bomb that you don't know?" He looks me in the eye and says, "You record your first impression and hope it is not your last."

I came into the office one day and found this same steel-nerved individual virtually on the brink of tears. I asked him what was wrong. It turned out that the Fed had made a major policy change, which dramatically reversed many major market trends. Overnight, our fund, which had gone from a starting value of $10 to nearly $15, had fallen back to under $12, just after he had opened a major Swiss bank as an account. I told him, "Get them on the phone." "What?" he asked somewhat confused. I repeated [speaking more slowly and emphatically], "G-e-t t-h-e-m o-n t-h-e p-h-o-n-e."

When I was a broker, my boss taught me that if you don't call your client when he is losing money, someone else will. And, to be honest, when I was a broker, I did the same thing. When I called prospects and they complained about their broker, I would say, "Oh, how could he put you in that trade?"

So I get the account on the phone and explain that our simulations show that this type of event will occur once every few years and that I am confident that in nine months the fund will be back to a new high. "In fact," I said, "I have just borrowed some money to add to my own investment in the fund." "You really did that?" he asked in a surprised tone. I assured him that I did.

Well, the account doubled up on their investment, and the fund immediately shot straight up. Today that account is one of our biggest clients. How could I be so sure? I knew what those systems were about. What makes this business so fabulous is that, while you may not know what will happen tomorrow, you can have a very good idea what will happen over the long run.

The insurance business provides a perfect analogy. Take one sixty-year-old guy and you have absolutely no idea what the odds are that he will be alive one year later. However, if you take 100,000 sixty-year-olds, you can get an excellent estimate of how many of them will be alive one year later. We do the same thing; we let the law of large numbers work for us. In a sense, we are trading actuaries.

I have a friend who went broke trading futures. He can't understand how I can trade by following a computerized system religiously. We were playing tennis one day and he asked me, "Larry, how can you trade the way you do; isn't it boring?" I told him, "I don't trade for excitement; I trade to win." It may be very dull, but it is also very lucrative. When I get together with other traders and they start exchanging war stories about different trades, I have nothing to say. To me, all our trades are the same.

There are many money managers who use trend-following systems—and quite a few of those don't second-guess their own systems. What makes Mint different? How have you been able to achieve return/risk ratios far above the industry average?

Because we know that we don't know. No matter what information you have, no matter what you are doing, you can be wrong. I have a friend who has amassed a fortune in excess of $100 million. He taught me two basic lessons. First, if you never bet your lifestyle, from a trading standpoint, nothing bad will ever happen to you. Second, if you know what the worst possible outcome is, it gives you tremendous freedom. The truth is that, while you can't quantify reward, you can quantify risk.

I will give you an example how important this advice is. One of the world's largest coffee traders invited me to his house in London. When I walked into his library, I noticed he had just about every book ever written on power. He took me to one of the finest restaurants I have ever been at. At dinner, he asked me, "Larry, how can you know more about coffee than me? I am the largest trader in the world. I know where the boats are; I know the ministers." "You are right," I answered, "I don't know anything about coffee. In fact, I don't even drink it." "How do you trade it then?" he asked. I told him, " I just look at the risk." Well this great meal lasted for several hours. Five times he asked me what I did, and five times I told him that I managed the risk.

Three months later I heard that he had blown $100 million in the coffee market. He obviously didn't get the message. And you want to know something? He does know more about coffee than I do. But the point is, he didn't look at the risk.

So the very first rule we live by at Mint is: Never risk more than 1 percent of total equity on any trade. By only risking 1 percent, I am indifferent to any individual trade. Keeping your risk small and constant is absolutely critical. For example, one manager I know had a large account that withdrew half the money he was trading. Instead of cutting his position size in half, this manager kept trading the same number of contracts. Eventually, that half of the original money became 10 percent of the money. Risk is a no-fooling-around game; it does not allow for mistakes. If you do not manage the risk, eventually they will carry you out.

The second thing we do at Mint is that we always follow the trends and we never deviate from our methods. In fact, we have a written agreement that none of us can ever countermand our system. The trades are all the same. That is the reason why we have never had a bad trade at Mint. There are really four kinds of trades or bets: good bets, bad bets, winning bets, and losing bets. Most people think that a losing trade was a bad bet. That is absolutely wrong. You can lose money even on a good bet. If the odds on a bet are 50/50 and the payoff is $2 versus a $1 risk, that is a good bet even if you lose. The important point is that if you do enough of those trades or bets, eventually you have to come out ahead.

The third thing we do to reduce risk is diversify. We diversify in two ways. First, we probably trade more markets worldwide than any other money manager. Second, we don't just use a single best system. To provide balance, we use lots of different systems ranging from short term to long term. Some of these systems may not be that good by themselves, but we really don't care; that is not what they are there for.

The fourth thing Mint does to manage risk is track volatility. When the volatility of a market becomes so great that it adversely skews the expected return/risk ratio, we will stop trading that market.

Essentially, our approach has three lights in determining the acceptance of trading signals. When the light is green, we take all signals. When the light is yellow, we will liquidate an existing position on a signal, but we will not put on a new position. Finally, when the light is red, we liquidate existing positions automatically, and we do not take any new positions.

For example, in 1986, when coffee went from $1.30 to $2.80 and back to $1.00, we got out of our long positions on the way up at $1.70 and didn't trade the market for the rest of the price climb and subsequent collapse. Now, while we may have lost some additional profits, being out of markets like that is one of the ways we are able to achieve such rigid risk control.

So one of the key differences between you and other trend-following managers is that you have developed a way of defining when not to play?

In any situation or game, you can define a positional advantage for any player—even the weakest one. In trading, you can define three categories of players: the trade, the floor, and the speculator. The trade has the best product knowledge and the best ways of getting out of positions. For example, if they are caught in a bad position in the futures markets, they can offset their risk in the cash market. The floor has the advantage of speed. You can never be faster than the floor. While the speculator doesn't have the product knowledge or the speed, he does have the advantage of not having to play. The speculator can choose to only bet when the odds are in his favor. That is an important positional advantage.

You mentioned before that you used increased volatility as a signal to stop trading a market. How many days of past data do you use to determine your volatility filter?

Anywhere from ten to 100 days.

When you say ten to 100, are you trying to be deliberately ambiguous or do you mean you use different time frames within that range?

We look at different time windows in that range.

I fully understand the logic of your 1 percent stop-loss rule. However, my one question is: Once you are stopped out of a position without the system providing an opposite signal,* what gets you back into the trade if the market reverses to its original direction? Isn't it possible that you could get stopped out on a moderate price reaction and then miss a subsequent major move?

If the market makes a new high, we get back in.

---

*For example, if a long position is stopped out on a money management rule without a sell signal actually being generated, the system will still be in a long mode and no buy signal will be generated, no matter how high prices go. (If, however, a sell signal were generated, the system would begin monitoring for a buy signal.)

But suppose that the market goes into a wide trading range, might you not get continuously whipped between being stopped out and reentering the position at new highs?

That happens, but not enough to be a problem.

You have an incredibly strong respect for risk. Were there any personal events in your trading career that ingrained you with that attitude?

When I first became involved in commodities, I noticed that if you bought pork bellies in September and sold them before July, you almost always made a profit. So I formed a fund with a group of friends, and I put on this trade. It worked. I doubled the money. I felt like a genius.

At the time, I had a friend who followed the corn market. I didn't know anything about corn; I only knew about pork bellies. He talked me into buying the new crop corn and selling the old crop. Since this was supposed to be a relatively safe trade, in that I was offsetting my long position in one contract month with a short position in another month, I really loaded up. Shortly thereafter, the government released a surprising crop estimate. In response, the month I was long went limit-down and the month I was short went limit-up.

I was in such despair that I remember walking out to the stairway and literally getting down on my knees and saying out loud, "Dear God, I don't care how much I lose, but please don't let the account go into a debit." At the time, I was working for a sophisticated international firm, and just as I was making my providential plea, a Swiss banker came walking down the staircase. To this day, I still wonder what he must have thought.

Were there any other personal traumatic experiences caused by a failure to heed market risk?

Not for myself, but throughout my financial career, I have continually witnessed examples of other people that I have known being ruined by a failure to respect risk. If you don't take a hard look at risk, it will take you.

When I was a kid and got my first motorcycle, I had an older friend who would always get into fights. He told me, "Larry, when you are on a motorcycle, never argue with a car. You will lose." The same lesson applies to trading: If you argue with the market, you will lose.

The Hunt brothers are a perfect example. Somebody once asked me, "How could the Hunts lose? They were worth billions." Let's say you have a billion dollars, and you buy $20 billion worth of silver—I am making these numbers up for the sake of the example—you are in exactly the same risk position as the guy with $1,000 who owns $20,000 worth of silver.

I have a good friend who started from very humble beginnings; his father was a sanitation man. Anyway, he is a very bright guy and he got into option arbitrage. He was extremely good at it and made a fortune. I remember visiting him at a palatial estate he bought in England.

Well, he may have been a great arbitrageur, but he turned out to be a bad trader. He developed a trading system that made money. One day he said to me, "I am not taking the sell signal in gold; it doesn't look right to me. Besides, almost 50 percent of the signals are wrong anyway." Not only didn't he take the sell signal, he actually wound up going long. Sure enough, the market went down. I told him, "Get out!" but he insisted, "The market will come back."

Well, he didn't get out, and he lost the mansion and everything else. Now he lives in a rented box on a street with a hundred other ticky-tacky houses. To this day, I still remember the name of his estate: "Beverly." He is still one of my best friends, and his loss of that huge house had an enormous emotional impact on me. He had it and lost it all! And all because of one trade. The irony is that if he had followed his system, he would have made a fortune on that trade.

I will tell you another story. I have a cousin who turned $5,000 into $100,000 in the option market. One day I asked him, "How did you do it?" He answered, "It is very easy. I buy an option and if it goes up, I stay in, but if it goes down, I don't get out until I am at least even." I told him, "Look, I trade for a living, and I can tell you that strategy is just not going to work in the long run." He said, "Larry, don't worry, it doesn't have to work in the long run, just till I make a million. I know what I am doing. I just never take a loss." I said, "OK..."

In his next trade he buys $90,000 worth of Merrill Lynch options, only this time, it goes down, and down, and down. I talk to him about one month later, and he tells me he is in debt for $10,000. I said, "Wait a minute. You had $100,000 and you bought $90,000 in options. That should still leave you with $10,000, even after they expired worthless. How could you have a deficit of $10,000?" He said, "I originally bought the options at $4½. When the price went down to $1, I figured out that if I bought another 20,000, all it had to do was go back to $2¼ for me to break even. So I went to the bank and borrowed $10,000."

Respect for risk is not just a matter of trading; it applies to any type of business decision. I once worked for a firm where the company president, a very nice guy, hired an option trader who was brilliant, but not stable. One day the option trader disappeared, leaving the firm stuck with a losing position. The president was not a trader, and he sought my advice. "Larry, what do you think I should do?" I told him, "Just get out of the position." Instead, he decided to hold on to the trade. The loss got a little worse, but then the market came back, and he liquidated the position at a small profit.

After this incident, I told a friend who worked at the same firm, "Bob, we are going to have to find another job." "Why?" he asked. I answered, "We work for a man who has just found himself in the middle of a mine field, and what he did was close his eyes and walk through it. He now thinks that whenever you are in the middle of a mine field, the proper technique is to close your eyes and go forward. Less than one year later, this same man had to liquidate a huge *delta neutral spread position* in options [a balanced position whose value will change very little for small price moves in either direction]. Instead of just getting out, he decided to get out of the position one leg at a time. By the time he finished liquidating that position, he had gone through all of the firm's capital.

Besides errors in risk control, why do people lose money trading?

Sometimes, because their trades are based on a personal bias, instead of a statistical approach. For example, there is a regular panelist on "Wall Street Week" who is about sixty-five or seventy years old. On the show one day, he said that the lesson his father taught him was, "Bonds are the cornerstone of your portfolio." Think about that! Since this man first got into the business, he has seen interest rates go down only once out

of every eight years. [Bonds go up when interest rates decline.] Obviously, the name "bonds" means a lot more to him than the reality.

**You trade a very wide variety of markets. Do you trade them all the
same way?**

We don't trade markets, we trade money. Mickey Quenington, who is
our marketing director, once introduced me to a former chief executive
of this firm [E. F. Man, the firm to which Hite gave 50 percent ownership in his management company in exchange for financial backing].
This guy was a tough, old Irishman and he asked me, "How do you dif-
ferentiate between gold and cocoa in your trading?" I answered, "They
are both a 1 percent bet; they are the same to me." He was outraged. He
practically shouted back at me, "You mean to tell me that you don't see
any difference between gold and cocoa?" I think if it wasn't for the fact
that he liked Mickey so much, he would have thrown me out of his office.

   I married a very proper English woman who is always concerned
that her family considers me a bit crass. I was once interviewed by a
reporter from the *London Times*, who asked me what I thought about the
future direction of the London cocoa market. I told him, "Frankly, I don't
see markets; I see risks, rewards, and money." I was the last person
quoted in that article. He finished it by saying, "Mr. Hite doesn't care
about the cocoa market, all he cares about is money." My wife read the
article and said, "Great. Now I'll never be able to go home; this will just
prove to my family that they were right about you all along."

**I assume that if you trade all markets the same, you probably don't
believe in *optimization*. [Optimization refers to the process of testing
many variations of a system for the past and then selecting the best-
performing version for actual trading. The problem with this fine-
tuned approach is that the link between past and future performance
is often a very rough one.]**

Absolutely. We have a saying here: "It is incredible how rich you can
get by not being perfect." We are not looking for the optimum method;
we are looking for the hardiest method. Anyone can sit down and devise
a perfect system for the past.

188

Are there any technical indicators that you have found to be overrated?

Overbought/oversold indicators. None of them seem to prove out in testing.

Any types of indicators you consider particularly valuable?

Although I don't really trade off of them, there are two that come to mind. First, if a market doesn't respond to important news in the way that it should, it is telling you something very important. For example, when the news of the Iran/Iraq war first came out over the newswire, gold was only able to move up $1. I said to myself, "A Middle East war has just broken out and the best the gold market can do is go up $1; it has to be a great sale." The market broke sharply after that. The second item is something that Ed Seykota taught me. When a market makes a historic high, it is telling you something. No matter how many people tell you why the market shouldn't be that high, or why nothing has changed, the mere fact that the price is at a new high tells you something has changed.

Any other lessons that you learned from Ed Seykota?

Ed Seykota actually explained his philosophy one day: "You can risk 1 percent of your capital, you can risk 5 percent, or you can risk 10 percent, but you better realize that the more you risk, the more volatile the results are going to be." And he was absolutely right.

Besides your partners, who I know were integral in developing your trading systems, were there any other traders who taught you valuable lessons?

Absolutely. Jack Boyd, who hired me as a broker/analyst. Having read that Handy and Harman had said in their annual report that silver stocks totaled either three billion or seven billion ounces, I wrote a report on the silver market in which I said, "According to Handy and Harman, there is either twice as much silver as some people think or less than half." That report went over very big with Jack and helped me land the job.

Jack had been putting out trading recommendations for his firm for many years. I found that if you followed all of his recommendations, you would have made money in every year. Finally, I asked Jack how he did it. You have to picture that Jack was six foot–four. He said, "Larry, if you want to know where a market is going, all you have to do is this." He threw his charts on the floor and jumped up on his desk. He said, "Look at it, it will tell you!"

I assume by that, he meant get a perspective of the big picture.

Right, because I don't know of too many people who get rich by taking small profits. Working with Boyd was extremely important for me. From the time I met him, I knew that his approach was the right way to do it. In other words, I knew that if you traded across the board, controlled your risk, and went with the trend, it just had to work. I could see it absolutely clearly.

Any final words?

I have two basic rules about winning in trading as well as in life: (1) If you don't bet, you can't win. (2) If you lose all your chips, you can't bet.

There are two basic elements to Hite's trading philosophy. First, contrary to the opinion of many academics, Hite is firmly convinced that the markets are inefficient. This means that if you can develop a method that places the odds in your favor (and it doesn't have to be by very much), you *can* win. Second, an effective method is a necessary, but not sufficient, condition to win. In order to survive and thrive at trading, you also have to respect market risk. If you don't, sooner or later, it will get you.

Hite controls risk rigorously by applying four basic principles:

1. His system never trades counter to the market trend. There are no exceptions, and he always follows the system.
2. The maximum risk on each trade is limited to 1 percent of total equity.

3. Mint carries diversification to an extreme. First, their system is really a combination of many different systems, selected not only for their individual performance, but also for their degree of lack of correlation with other selected systems. Second, Mint trades in an extraordinarily wide spectrum of markets (nearly sixty in all), encompassing exchanges in the U.S. and five foreign countries and diverse market groups including stock indexes, interest rates, currencies, raw industrial goods, and agricultural commodities.

4. Volatility is continually tracked in each market in order to generate signals to liquidate or temporarily suspend trading in those markets where the risk/reward ratio exceeds well-defined limits.

One final observation: After merely earning a modest living at some colorful careers (such as, scriptwriter, actor, rock promoter), Larry Hite succeeded spectacularly in the single endeavor for which he had the greatest enthusiasm—fund manager. I found this to be a striking example of Ed Seykota's comment: "It is a happy circumstance that when nature gives us true burning desires, it also gives us the means to satisfy them."

Part II

Mostly Stocks

Michael Steinhardt

The Concept of Variant Perception

Michael Steinhardt's interest in the stock market dates back to his bar mitzvah, when his father gave him 200 shares of stock as a present. He recalls hanging out in the local brokerage office as a teenager, watching the ticker tape along with the old men, while his friends were out playing stickball. A very bright student, Steinhardt completed his education at an accelerated pace, graduating from the Wharton School of the University of Pennsylvania in 1960 at the age of nineteen. Steinhardt headed straight for Wall Street, landing his first job as a research assistant. In subsequent years, he held positions as a financial journalist and a research analyst. In 1967, having established a reputation as a talented analyst, Steinhardt and two other partners founded the investment firm of Steinhardt, Fine and Berkowitz—the predecessor to Steinhardt Partners. (Fine and Berkowitz left the firm in the late 1970s.)

In the twenty-one years since its inception, Steinhardt's firm has achieved a truly remarkable track record. During that time, Steinhardt Partners has realized a compounded annual growth rate of over 30 percent (just under 25 percent after subtracting a 20 percent profit incentive fee). In comparison, the S&P 500 index registered only an 8.9 percent compounded annual growth rate (dividends included) during the same period. One thousand dollars invested with the firm at its start in 1967 would have grown to over $93,000 by Spring 1988 (after deducting profit incentive fees). To put that in perspective, the same $1,000 invested in a basket of S&P stocks would only have grown to $6,400. Gain is only part of the story; Steinhardt's track record also demonstrates admirable consistency. Steinhardt Partners has only witnessed two losing years. In both cases, the net loss was under 2 percent before profit incentive fee adjustments.

Steinhardt's superior performance has been achieved by using a myriad of approaches. He is both a long-term investor and a short-term trader; he is as comfortable shorting stocks as buying them; he will shift major chunks of the firm's capital into other investment vehicles, such as treasury securities, if he feels that is the best investment choice.

To be sure, Steinhardt Partners' track record is not a solo performance. In addition to his cofounding partners, over the years, the firm has employed numerous traders and analysts. However, there was never any doubt that Steinhardt was clearly in charge. He reviews the firm's portfolio several times each day. Although he gives the firm's traders latitude to make their own judgments, Steinhardt will require a trader to rigorously justify his position if he has qualms about that position. If he feels strongly enough, Steinhardt will override the trader and liquidate the position.

Steinhardt's extreme scrutiny and control of the firm's portfolio has given him a reputation of being a very demanding man to work for—obviously, too demanding for many of the traders who have left the firm over the years. Keeping in mind that Steinhardt's wraparound desk has been constructed in the shape of a ship's bow, it is not surprising that one journalist doing a profile tagged him with the sobriquet, Captain Ahab. However, Steinhardt's tough side is very much related to his job role—much as in football coaching, toughness is probably a virtue in managing a group of traders.

I never saw Steinhardt's tough side. The man I interviewed was relaxed, soft spoken, patient, and good humored. (Of course, our interviews were always conducted outside of market hours.) Steinhardt possesses a keen sense of humor. He has been known to call friends impersonating an IRS agent, deliberately mumble fictitious orders to brokers right before the market close, and double-talk in a Dr. Irwin Corey-like manner when he wishes to pull the leg of an analyst or reporter who calls him. His conversation is also liberally sprinkled with Yiddishisms—"proprietary dreck," for example, is how he refers to newfangled fund products.

What are the major elements of your trading philosophy?

The word "trading" is not the way I think of things. I may be a trader in the sense that my frequency of transactions is relatively high, but the word "investing" would apply just as much, if not more. In my mind, trading implies an anticipation of a sale at the time of purchase. For example, if I go long stock index futures tonight because I expect tomorrow's trade number will be bullish for the market, and I plan to sell my position tomorrow—that is trading. The bulk of what I do is for a much longer duration and for more complex reasons. For example, when I went long the debt markets in 1981, I held that position for two and a half years.

Well, for purposes of this book, I would still call what you are doing trading.

How then do you define the difference between trading and investing?

I make two key distinctions. First, a trader will go short as readily as long. In contrast, the investor—for example, the portfolio manager of a typical mutual fund—will always be long. If he is uncertain about the market, he may be only 70 percent invested, but he is always long. The second distinction I make is that a trader is primarily concerned about the direction of the market. Is the market, or stock, going up or down? The investor is more concerned about picking the best stocks to invest in. There is no value judgment involved in my distinction between traders and investors, it is merely a matter of maintaining a certain thematic focus for this book. In any case, on both counts, I would certainly qualify you as a trader. To get back to my original question: How would you define your philosophy of trading?

My particular style is a bit different from that of most people. Concept number one is variant perception. I try to develop perceptions that I believe are at variance with the general market view. I will play those variant perceptions until I feel they are no longer so.

Could you give me an example of variant perception in the current marketplace?

We have been short Genentech for a year and a half. There was a period of months and months when we lost a lot of money in that position. But I stayed short because I continued to have a variant perception about the future of their drug, *TPA*. [TPA can be injected intravenously to dissolve blood clots.] It is our perception that, in a year or two, TPA will be a minor drug that will be supplanted by more effective drugs that also cost substantially less. The thrust of the entire company has been based on this one drug. If our perception is correct, this company will be earning 20 or 30 cents per share and selling for under $10. The stock is currently at $27 [June 1988], down from a high of $65. [By late November, Genentech had fallen below $15 and Steinhardt was still short.] But I think the general perception is still that Genentech is a first class biotechnology company that will produce many products that are going to revolutionize the industry. As long as my view is a variant perception, I will stay short.

That is a clear example, but it raises a question. Let's say you go short a stock because of your variant perception, and the position goes against you. If the fundamentals don't change, the more it goes against you, the more attractive the short side would appear. Yet from a money management standpoint, at some point, the position would have to be covered. It seems like there might be two basic trading principles in conflict here.

There are certain shibboleths that exist in the world of trading, which may or may not be accurate, but I have not followed them. For example, there is a general view that you shouldn't short a stock until it has already peaked and started down—that you shouldn't go short until the stock is already reflecting problems that are evident for all to see. In some sense, I can understand that. Maybe that is a superficially safer way to short stocks and you can sleep more comfortably using that approach. However, I have never done it that way. My attitude has always been that to make money in the markets, you have to be willing to get in the way of danger. I have always tended to short stocks that were favorites and backed by a great deal of institutional enthusiasm. Generally speaking, I have tended to short too early and, therefore, have usually started off with losses in my short positions. If I short a stock and it goes up a lot, it may skew my exposure a bit, but as long as my variant perception is unchanged, I'll stay short. If I'm wrong, I'm wrong.

Are you saying that as long as you think the fundamentals, as you perceive them, are unchanged, you will hang tough no matter how much the position goes against you?

Right. Of course, if it is triple horrible, I might trade around the position to take the pressure down a little bit. I would say, "OK, this looks awful; I see nothing but buyers. Why don't I join the buyers and see if I can make some money." In a matter of speaking, I dichotomize myself. I have a fundamental view, which I believe in my heart, but I try to separate that from the short-term fervor and intensity I may see in the market. So even though I am short in that type of situation, I might periodically be a buyer.

Might you actually go net long during those periods, or does your position just fluctuate between fully short and flat?

It wouldn't even remotely approach flat, because that type of buying is based on very short-lived perceptions. I might take 20, 30, or 40 percent of the position and trade with it.

If you are very negative and short in a particular stock, but are not necessarily bearish on the industry, might you sometimes hedge yourself by buying another stock in that group against your short position?

I have tried that at times, but have generally found it to be unsuccessful. What it tends to do is give me two problems instead of one. Usually, your knowledge about the second stock on the other side will tend to be relatively skimpy because you are just grasping at it to use as a hedge. If your problem is so great that you need to hedge it, why not address the

problem directly rather than taking on a totally separate position? Let's
say you are short a paper stock and the paper stocks are roaring, so you
buy another paper stock against it. Maybe your short stock will go up
more; maybe the other stock will go up more. Who knows? If you have
made a mistake, deal with the mistake; don't compound it.

**Besides the variant perception concept, what are some of the other
elements of your trading philosophy?**

Nothing that is so distinctive. I don't use stop-loss orders or such. I don't
use any rules about buying on weakness or strength. I don't look at
breakouts or breakdowns. I don't use charts.

You don't use charts at all?

Charts just leave me blank. [He adopts a Jackie Mason-like speech pattern.] I look at the stock. It has a fantastic chart. The chart has a base like
this, and then if it goes up a little bit more, boy it is a real breakout, blah,
blah, blah, blah. They all seem the same to me.

**But just from an informational standpoint, don't you use charts as
a quick and easy way to see where a stock has traded over the years?**

By watching stocks as closely as I do, I get some sense of price levels,
uptrends, ranges, and all that.

**Let's say you know that a stock has gone from $10 to $40, wouldn't
it matter to you how it went from $10 to $40?**

It makes no difference to me.

Do you have any trading rules that you could define?

Give me an example of a trading rule.

A common example might be: Before I get into a position, I know exactly where I am getting out. It doesn't necessarily have to be a risk control rule, it could be—

No, I don't have any rules about stops or objectives. I simply don't think in those terms.

At this point, there is a call on the speakerphone. The caller is giving Steinhardt some late-breaking news regarding a decision in a lawsuit against the tobacco industry. "The verdict is back. Everyone was cleared except the Liggett group who had to pay a $400,000 fine and no punitive damages." Steinhardt replies, "So it was basically a decision slightly in favor of the defendants."

I went short the tobacco stocks about a month ago. My reasoning was that if the plaintiffs won the case, the stocks would go down a lot, but if the plaintiffs lost, the stocks wouldn't go up too much, since the tobacco companies had never lost a case and winning another one wouldn't really be news. That is an example of a variant perception. It will be interesting to see how much I will lose, because my original theory was that it wouldn't be much. Here it is [reading story headline from screen], "Liggett Group Found Liable for Contributing to Smoker's Death." You know what, I won't lose anyway. A phrase like that will scare somebody.

Going back to our discussion, let's say you are short a stock because of your fundamental analysis and the stock is going against you. How would you know when your analysis is wrong because you have overlooked some unknown important element?

That situation happens fairly often. You buy or sell a stock and it doesn't act the way you think it should. I go through my portfolio six times a day. There are many stocks in the portfolio that I am not directly responsible for. For example, someone else is short Time, Inc. They are short because the magazine business is lousy, and this or that. But the stock is acting really strong and is up 10 percent from where we shorted it. I will go over to the person responsible for the Time Life position and ask several key questions: When are we going to get something that is going to surprise the world? When is something going to happen that will ease the feeling that this company is ripe for a takeover?

In a sense, I am a negative monitor of the portfolio. If there is a problem with a position I will go through it very regularly. That makes me a very difficult person here, because I only talk to people when things are lousy or when their stocks are not acting like they should.

If a stock is not acting like it should based on its fundamentals, would that be the type of market action that would change your thinking?

I try to assume that the guy on the other side of a trade knows as least as much as I do. Let's say I buy Texaco at $52 and it suddenly goes down to $50. Whoever sold Texaco at $52 had a perception that was dramatically different from mine. It is incumbent on me to find out what his perception was.

What if you can't explain it?

The explanation might be superficial or serious, but you can usually get something.

Let's take the situation of the tobacco companies. On balance, the news that came out after the close sounded bearish. If the tobacco stocks go down only modestly tomorrow and then come right back, would you cover your position?

I would cover it anyway. I would cover the position on the news.

So once the news is out, the game is over for you.

Right. That was the only reason I was short.

OK, that answers the question too simply. Assume you wanted to be short the tobacco stocks as a longer-term position and the market shrugged off today's news and closed higher tomorrow. Would you cover then?

It depends on my reasons. If I wanted to be short the tobacco companies because I felt tobacco consumption was going to decline much more than presently perceived, it wouldn't matter that much. If the market rallied tomorrow, I would have to take advantage of it and sell some more.

So you wouldn't care if the market didn't react to the news the way it should have, as long as you felt the main reason for being short was still valid.

Yes, but if the news was terrible and the stocks were up, I would try to understand why. Sometimes the market has more information and the variant action is really telling you something.

But haven't there been instances where your analysis was completely wrong?

Sure.

And you realized it somewhere down the road?

Yes, and not necessarily so quickly.

At this point, Steinhardt gets a phone call in which his side of the conversation is filled with non sequiturs and deliberate mumbling. He then explains to me his occasional habit of playing practical jokes on callers.

For example, I get a call from a broker who I haven't spoken to for a long time. I swoosh some papers around and then say, "Buy 30,000 shares of ZCU [mumbles another sentence]." Did you understand what I said?

No [I laugh].

That is exactly right, but it sounded legitimate didn't it? Anyway, he calls me back, and I have my secretary tell him I'm in the bathroom. He calls back again, frantic because it is five minutes before the close, and I am still unavailable. Then at 3:58, I call him back and say, "Haven't you done that order yet? What's the problem? Just do the damn thing!" Of course, he says, "I didn't catch the name of the stock." So I tell him [he mumbles another sentence] and hang up before he can say anything else.

Your fund is often labeled as a hedge fund because it trades very differently than a typical mutual fund. Could you elaborate on the meaning of a hedge fund.

The A.W. Jones Group has been given credit for being the first hedge fund. Originally, the term referred to a precise concept, which essentially said the following: We in the world of money management do not have the ability to forecast trends in the stock market, which are functions of a host of variables that are largely beyond the consistent ability of individuals to anticipate. But, what we as money managers can do, through careful analysis, is to make accurate judgments as to which companies are doing well versus those that are not. So, if one balanced long positions in stocks that were perceived to be relatively strong with short positions in stocks expected to act poorly, the market risk would be totally eliminated. For example, if you loved Ford and hated General Motors, and for every dollar long Ford you were short a dollar of General Motors, you might lose on your shorts, but if your judgment was good, you would come out ahead. So, the original concept of a hedge fund totally emphasized the ability to pick stocks.

Does anyone still trade that way?

No, today, the term hedge fund is somewhat of a misnomer. The term now refers to a limited partnership in which the general partner is typically paid on a performance basis, as opposed to more traditional money managers who are paid on assets managed. Typically, the manager of a hedge fund has a great deal more flexibility than a traditional money manager, and that is really the key element. That flexibility could include being able to short stocks as well as buy stocks, use options, futures, and so on. That is what a hedge fund is in general terms, but the variations on the theme cover a very wide continuum.

What happened to the original concept of a hedge fund?

The flexibility of the hedge fund structure attracted numerous young, aggressive entrepreneurs in the 1960s because it allowed them an opportunity to start their own business at an early age in a way that wasn't otherwise possible. Those were times of great stocks with wonderful stories. There were quite a number of stocks showing terrific growth.

The people that came into the hedge fund business were not theoretical practitioners of the idea of hedging, but were more interested in the idea of being their own bosses, and having the flexibility to be long a lot of stock. Although they also had the flexibility of being short, they didn't use it in any serious way. The word hedge has a very specific meaning in the English language. In most of these hedge funds, you could seriously ask, "Where is the hedge?"

So they were hedge funds in name only?

Correct. They wouldn't even call themselves hedge funds; they were embarrassed by the name. The term had a connotation of being short, and trading the short side had an anti-American ring to it. It was as if you were rooting for disaster. So they started using the term [he adopts a tone of mock pomposity] private partnership.

Ironically, today, with the disintegration of the relatively smooth secular trends of the 1950s and 1960s, the concept of a true hedge fund may make more sense than it did in its early days. Why aren't there any practitioners of the hedge fund concept in its pure form?

Because it is a very restricting approach. The premise of being a dollar long and a dollar short in some related entity requires using a lot of dollars ineffectively. How different are Ford and General Motors going to be? They are both affected by the same macroeconomic factors. If you have to put up some dollars for the long and some dollars for the short, you may be lucky to realize a 10 percent difference over a period of a year—that is, assuming you are right.

There is a group we are associated with on the West Coast that specializes exclusively in shorting stocks. The thought has been mentioned that maybe they should neutralize their market exposure by being long an equal number of dollars in the stock indexes as they are short in individual stocks, because what they bring to the party is the special ability to pick shorts. That is the closest thing to this concept I have heard recently, but they don't do it.

How does your own fund fit into the hedge fund concept?

It fits in the sense that shorting is used actively. We always have some shorts. I also spend a good deal of my time thinking about net market exposure and risk, and planning and adjusting for it. In the twenty-one years that I have been doing this, our overall exposure here has averaged about 40 percent.

You mean 40 percent net long?

Yes. In contrast, I would doubt that the most conservative of typical mutual funds has had an average exposure of less than 80 percent during the last twenty years.

On average, you have been about 40 percent net long. What range does that encompass?

I remember being 15 or 20 percent net short at one point, and, at another time, being over 100 percent net long.

So you have the flexibility of being net short as well as net long?

Yes. One of the things I would emphasize about our approach is its flexibility to shift market exposure so as to make it an exceptionally meaningful—sometimes perhaps too meaningful—tool in our investment management arsenal.

How do you determine your outlook for the general market direction, since that is obviously a very critical element of your approach?

It is really beyond definition, except to say that there are a host of variables, with some sometimes more important than others, and they change all the time. Having done it as long as I have gives me the opportunity to be 51 percent right rather than 50 percent right.

Does that imply that your main profitability comes from stock selection as opposed to net exposure adjustments for anticipated changes in the broad market direction?

No, I was being a bit facetious. It is more than a 1 percent edge, but it is not a big advantage like being right 80 percent of the time, or anything approaching that.

Relatively speaking, how important is the bias of the right market direction versus stock selection as a contributing factor to your overall superior performance?

As I look back on the past twenty-one years, there is no set pattern of successful activity. In some years, we did particularly well on the strength of a few well-chosen stocks. In other years, we did exceptionally well because we were on the right side of the market. For example, in 1973–1974, when the market went down enormously, we were up substantially, largely because we were net short. There were other periods when the bulk of our money was made in bonds. I think there is a message in the fact that there is no real pattern: Anyone who thinks he can formulate success in this racket is deluding himself, because it changes too quickly. As soon as a formula is right for any length of time, its own success carries the weight of its inevitable failure.

What made you sufficiently confident of lower stock prices to go net short in 1973–1974?

The anticipation of a recession.

Based on what?

I felt that the higher inflation rates of that period would lead to higher interest rates, which, in turn, would slow down the economy.

Were you negative on the stock market in the period preceding the major 1982 bottom as well?

Not as strongly. But in 1981 and 1982, I made an enormous amount of money by having a leveraged position in treasury notes. Although one couldn't predict the end of the rise of interest rates timing-wise, it was clear that unless interest rates came down, other areas had to be relatively unattractive. When you could get 14 percent in long-term treasury securities, in order to be competitive, stocks had to sell so much lower than they were selling at that it wasn't even worth focusing on which stocks to buy—although you might focus on the short side. What was unique in that period was the inevitability of a turn in interest rates in order for anything else to be worthwhile; it was simply a matter of timing that turn. In contrast to most other periods, this period had a clear unidirectional message: U.S. Treasury fixed income securities were by far the quintessential value of the time.

Anyone with any sense of contrarian mentality had to look at interest rates in the early 1980s as presenting a potentially great opportunity. You knew the Fed would have to ease as soon as business started to run into trouble. In addition, we had already seen an important topping in the rate of inflation.

So, some of the pieces of the puzzle were already in place?

Yes, and that is as much as you can hope for, because when they are all in place, it is too late.

You mention a contrarian mentality, but that type of thinking could have justified trying to pick a top at much lower rates.

Absolutely. People think that being a contrarian implies victory. After all, what is a contrarian but someone that goes against the crowd. It is almost a cliché that the crowd is always wrong—so the guy who stands against the crowd must always be right. Well, life doesn't work that way. There were plenty of contrarians who bought bonds when interest rates went to 8 percent for the first time, and 9 percent, and 10 percent. There was a great deal of money lost by people buying bonds at what were then all-time high yields.

There is a very important difference between being a theoretical contrarian and dealing with it in practical terms. In order to win as a contrarian, you need the right timing and you have to put on a position in the appropriate size. If you do it too small, it's not meaningful; if you do it too big, you can get wiped out if your timing is slightly off. The process requires courage, commitment, and an understanding of your own psychology.

I assume that you probably had the market run against you for quite a while in that trade.

Right, it did. It was a very painful period, because as far as most of my investors were concerned, I was an equity investor. What did I know about bonds? Who was I to contradict Henry Kaufman who was telling the world that interest rates were going to the moon? Not only was I doing something that was different than in the past, which always raises the antennas of investors—particularly those with an institutional mentality—but I was doing it in an enormous size.

Were you leveraged more than 100 percent on your position?

Yes, at one point I had three to four times the firm's capital in five-year maturities. In stocks, you have a policeman who tells you how much you can speculate: it is called margin requirements. But in treasuries, you can finance as much as 98 percent of your purchases, depending on maturity, so there is no real constraint.

How long was the period between when you started buying treasuries and the market bottom [interest rate peak]?

I started buying in the spring of 1981, and I think treasuries bottomed on September 30, 1981.

How much did rates move against you in that first half year?

I don't recall, but rates went up enough to be painful, especially given the size of my position.

Up until this time, you had primarily been a stock trader. Here on your first major foray in treasuries, you started out by incurring substantial losses. Didn't you have periods of self-doubt?

All the time. The summer of 1981 was the worst experience of my business life. A number of thoughtful, intelligent investors were really very unhappy with what I was doing—and I wasn't so sure myself.

Did you ever come close to saying, "Maybe I am wrong," and liquidating, or at least decreasing, your position?

No, never.

One of your basic principles seems to be that as long as you believe you are fundamentally right, you will stay with a position. Have there been any exceptions—that is, markets in which you didn't change your fundamental view, but the loss just got too big?

There have been some situations when I was short and simply didn't have enough courage to hang in with the full-boat of the position. That was particularly true in 1972, at the height of the "Nifty-Fifty" phenomenon. With the exception of October 1987, that was probably the worst period in my investment life. At the time, there was a theory that as long as a company continued to sustain substantially above-average secular growth, it didn't matter how much you paid for it. Many growth stocks traded at multiples that were just crazy. We went short Polaroid when it was selling at sixty times earnings, which we thought was absurd; it then went to seventy times earnings. The market seemed to lose track of reality, and we found ourselves asking, "What is the difference between forty times earnings and eighty times earnings?" By putting a different number on the secular growth rate estimate, you could justify almost any multiple That is how people were thinking in those days.

So you backed off during that period?

At times we did, because we were losing a lot of money.

Did that prove to be the right move, because stocks eventually went to much higher multiples, or would you have been better off if you had held on?

In hindsight, in almost all cases, I would have been better off sticking it out.

You mentioned that October 1987 was one of the worst market experiences in your career. Obviously, you had lots of company. But I find it surprising, you being such a contrarian. I wouldn't have expected you to be heavily long in a year with such bullish euphoria. What happened?

Actually, in the spring of 1987, I wrote a letter to my investors stating the reasons why I was cautious and substantially reducing my exposure in the market. Having done that, I kept thinking about why the market was trading at a level that was too high by historic standards. I came to the conclusion that the quintessential issue was a unique combination of phenomena occurring in the American equity markets—a substantial continuous reduction in the amount of equities outstanding, coinciding with a more liberal attitude toward debt. As long as banks were comfortable lending money, the junk bond market was good, and corporate managers saw repurchasing their shares as the right thing to do, I felt there would be an unusual upward bias to equity prices. That to me was the single most important reason in the seeming overvaluation of stocks that existed through most of 1987.

Therefore, the important question was: What was going to change this situation? The answer was a recession. And whenever that recession would come, its impact would be horrendous because the government didn't have the flexibility to fight it since they had deviated from a countercyclical fiscal policy during the expansion phase. But during the fall of 1987, not only was the economy not weakening, it was strengthening—so much so that the Fed tightened.

What I didn't anticipate was that less-than-dramatic events could have as large an impact on the market as they did. What was the real importance of the Fed tightening? Ordinarily, that might have created a 100- or 200-point decline in the stock market, but not a 500-point decline. In the light of history, what was the significance of Treasury Secretary Baker's criticism of Germany? It was merely a disagreement as to the proper valuation of currencies—hardly a unique event. In retrospect, what happened to the real world after October 19? Almost nothing. So, in some sense, you have to conclude that this problem was internal to the market; it wasn't that the market was forecasting an imminent financial debacle or great recession.

How then do you explain the extreme nature of the October 19 price break?

The problem that led to the October 19 collapse was the combination of relatively modest real world changes and an inability of the markets' mechanism to deal with the institutional changes that occurred mostly during the 1980s. The elements of stability—the individual investor and the specialist system—had been greatly reduced in importance.

Do you believe *portfolio insurance* exacerbated the decline? [Portfolio insurance is the systematic sale of stock index futures to reduce the risk exposure in a stock portfolio as prices decline. See Appendix 1 for more detail.]

That was one of the new elements. On one hand, you had a reduction in the elements of stability. On the other hand, you had the creations of the 1980s—portfolio insurance, program trading, and global asset allocation—which tended to exert a unidirectional impact. By that, I mean that participants in these strategies tend to be buyers and sellers at the same time. The stock market was not prepared to handle it.

Where were you, positionwise, coming in on October 19?

I came in very much long exposed—80 to 90 percent—and I increased my exposure during the day.

Why? Were you still bullish?

My increasing exposure was strictly a contrarian trade in the sense that when the markets have an enormous move, most of the time, it is right to take the view that there is a lot of emotionalism and extremism in that move. If you can maintain a bit of distance from the emotionalism, you tend to do well. So my buying that day is what I would have done on any 300-, 400-, or 500-point down day.

Did you stay with your long position?

No, I reduced it throughout the next two months. The magnitude of the decline and the extraordinary change in confidence that it engendered affected me as well. I thought it was better to sit back and rethink the situation with a lot of cash rather than try to hang in.

Did you think that your basic premise for being long was no longer valid?

I thought that I had underestimated the impact of the forces that had diminished market stability.

What was your percentage loss during October 1987?

I was down over 20 percent for the month.

As you look back on the October 1987 experience, are there mistakes that you believe you learned from?

There is a very good investor I speak to frequently who said, "All I bring to the party is twenty-eight years of mistakes." I really believe he is right. When you make a mistake, there is some subconscious phenomenon that makes it less likely for you to make that same mistake again. One of the advantages of trading the way I do—being a long-term investor, short-term trader, individual stock selector, market timer, sector analyst—is that I have made so many decisions and mistakes that it has made me wise beyond my years as an investor.

The typical mutual fund adheres to a buy-and-hold approach. Do you think that concept is basically a flawed strategy?

Yes, although flawed isn't quite the word I would use. I would say it is too limiting a strategy. The objective of participating in the long-term growth of American equities, willing to suffer through those periods when equities decline, is fine, but it leaves so much on the table in terms of potential professional management. It is an incomplete strategy.

Yet, the vast majority of all funds fall into that category.

I guess so, but less than before. More and more people are paying attention to market timing, not that they are necessarily qualified to do it terribly well, but because they have come to recognize what a buy-and-hold approach means. When I was a kid, it was common advice to buy a stock, put it in a vault, and forget about it. You don't hear that sort of concept anymore. We have lost confidence in the long term.

Do you think the mutual fund industry is going to change?

The mutual fund industry is certainly sensitive enough to the whims of the investing public to find products that will meet contemporary needs.

How do you handle a losing period?

As is true for so many other questions in this business, there is no pat answer or formula. There is nothing that can be articulated precisely enough to lead others in a certain direction.

In other words, one losing period may be sufficiently different from another so that, even for yourself, there may be no general wisdom that applies.

Correct.

How did you get started as a fund trader?

When I first got into this business in the late 1960s, I only had an analytical background. I was an agricultural equipment and cyclical goods analyst at Loeb Rhoades. My business was started with two other fellows who were also analysts. As our business grew, trading became more important. I became the trader for the firm, having had very little trading background.

If you had very little experience, why did you become the trader?

I probably wasn't as good an analyst as the other two.

Even in those early years, you did very well as a trader. How do you think you managed that without benefit of experience?

My father has been a gambler all his life. Although I can't remotely justify it, I feel there is an element of gambling in this business. Maybe I got that talent from my father.

You have traded the stock market for over twenty years. Have you noticed any significant changes during that time?

The amount of intellectual power on the trading desks twenty years ago was minimal compared to today. The institutional traders were typically kids from Brooklyn, who could hardly speak the language, made a minimum amount of money, and had very little discretion. So when I first started trading, it was like taking candy from a baby.

I remember once a trader needed to sell 700,000 shares of Penn Central. At the time, the stock was already in Chapter 11. The last trade was at 7, and the seller didn't bother to check the board. I bought 700,000 shares at 6⅛. The seller was relieved to sell that amount of stock at less than a dollar under the last trade. Meanwhile, I turned around and sold the 700,000 shares at 6⅞. I could have sold three times that amount at that price. I made a half million dollars on that trade, and it took me all of twelve seconds.

How long did that environment last?

Until the consolidated tape in 1975. Now there is a lot more competition; the people on the trading desks are much brighter. Another change is that retail buyers and sellers have diminished greatly in importance. The market has become institutionalized. Individuals buy stock through mutual funds. Brokerage firms don't sell customers stocks so much as they sell those horrible mutual funds and other awful things they call "financial products."

Perhaps the most important change is that the world has become much more short term oriented. All sorts of people who used to be investors are now traders. The institutions now define themselves as enterprises whose goal is to achieve the highest rate of return, when they used to define themselves as long-term investors. People's confidence in their ability to predict secular trends has greatly diminished. In 1967, it would be typical to see a report by a brokerage firm estimating McDonalds' per share earnings up to the year 2000. Those people thought they could estimate long-term earnings because companies were growing in a stable and predictable way. They believed in America and steady growth. Today, stocks don't lend themselves to the same type of secular analysis.

The implication of secular growth trend analysis not having worked in the 1970s and 1980s relates to the question of trading. In the 1950s and 1960s, the heroes were the long-term investors; today, the heroes are the wise guys. There are people like Goldsmith, who lauds the virtues of capitalism. He talks about "what I did for Goodyear." What did he do for Goodyear? He was in there for seven months, made eight zillion dollars for himself, and left the management after taking greenmail. He talks about what he did for Goodyear, because he is uncomfortable and has to somehow associate himself with the capitalist process. He and these other people have to bitch and moan about management, but they don't know their ass from their elbow about running companies. With the breakdown of certain laws, people are allowed to do things they weren't allowed to do before.

What laws are you referring to?

The Justice Department's reinterpretation of takeover laws; the definition of what is and is not monopolistic.

What would be the most important advice you could give to the layman?

One of the allures of this business is that sometimes the greatest ignoramus can do very well. That is unfortunate because it creates the impression that you don't necessarily need any professionalism to do well, and that is a great trap. So the major advice I would give anybody is: Recognize that this is a very competitive business, and that when you decide to buy or sell a stock, you are competing with people who have devoted a good portion of their lives to this same endeavor. In many instances, these professionals are on the opposite side of your trades and, on balance, they are going to beat you.

Is the implicit message that, most of the time, the novice trader would be better off having his money professionally managed?

The term professionally managed implies a credit I am not sure I would give the average professional in this business. My point is that you should have a good reason to assume that you are going to achieve a significantly superior return for investing in stocks. If you can get 9 percent or 10 percent by investing in T-bonds and 7 percent or 8 percent by investing in T-bills, what should you get in stocks to offset the incremental risk? Probably something much higher. You have to decide what that number should be, and whether you have a realistic chance of achieving it.

Don't underestimate the difficulty of the game.

Right, and forget the shibboleth that stocks are going to give you a higher rate of return because they are more risky. That is not true. They are more risky; therefore, you have to be convinced that you are going to get a higher rate of return in order to play the game. Don't assume that by investing in some mutual fund, you are going to get a higher rate of return.

Isn't that true, though? Historically, hasn't the stock market significantly beat interest rate returns?

True, but there is a lot of statistical mumbo jumbo involved. Average return calculations depend heavily on the starting date. If you start in 1968 or 1972, for example, the numbers look a lot less appealing.

What are the elements of good trading?

Good trading is a peculiar balance between the conviction to follow your ideas and the flexibility to recognize when you have made a mistake. You need to believe in something, but at the same time, you are going to be wrong a considerable number of times. The balance between confidence and humility is best learned through extensive experience and mistakes. There should be a respect for the person on the other side of the trade. Always ask yourself: Why does he want to sell? What does he know that I don't? Finally, you have to be intellectually honest with yourself and others. In my judgment, all great traders are seekers of truth.

Steinhardt's variant perception is basically a contrarian approach. But you can't be a successful contrarian by just using sentiment survey numbers or other measures of bullish consensus. The markets don't pay off that easily. Although sentiment is always very bullish at tops and very bearish at bottoms, unfortunately, extreme bullish and bearish readings are also characteristic of extended trends. The trick is not being a contrarian, but being a contrarian at the right time. Such judgments cannot be made on the basis of simple formulae. The successful contrarian needs to be able to filter out the true opportunities. Steinhardt's filters are a combination of a keen sense of fundamentals and market timing.

Flexibility is another essential key to Steinhardt's extremely favorable return/risk performance characteristics. This flexibility is demonstrated by the equal ease at which he goes short or long, as well as his willingness to trade markets other than stocks when warranted by his perception of the fundamentals. "The more things you bring to the table—shorting, hedging, participation in bond markets, futures market trading, and so on—the better off you are," he says.

One trait I have noticed among a number of the great traders is their willingness and ability to take on a particularly large position when they perceive a major trading opportunity. The nerve and skill required to step on the accelerator at the right time is certainly one of the elements that separates good traders from exceptional traders. Steinhardt's heavy position in treasury notes during 1981 and 1982 is a perfect example of this characteristic.

Conviction is probably an important quality for any trader, but it is essential to the contrarian trader. Steinhardt has repeatedly demonstrated amazing resolve in maintaining large positions during difficult times, as long as he was convinced he was still right. Witness his conviction in staying with his treasury note position during the six-month climax in interest rates in 1981, remaining immune not only to the market move against him, but also to the psychological pressures of complaining investors who questioned his sudden transition into treasuries after a career as a stock trader. Throughout it all, Steinhardt held on, and even built his position, because he remained convinced that he was right. Without his strong sense of conviction, the world probably would never have heard of Michael Steinhardt.

Steinhardt also stresses that there are no absolute formulae or fixed patterns. The markets are always changing, and the successful trader needs to adapt to these changes. In Steinhardt's view, traders who try to find fixed approaches will be doomed to failure sooner or later.

William O'Neil

The Art of Stock Selection

William O'Neil is an unreserved optimist and ebullient fan of the American economic system and its possibilities. O'Neil says, "Great opportunities occur every year in America. Get yourself prepared and go for it. You will find that little acorns can grow into giant oaks. Anything is possible with persistence and hard work. It can be done, and your own determination to succeed is the most important element."

O'Neil is living proof of his own words: a classic American success story. Born in Oklahoma during the lean Great Depression years and raised in Texas, he went on to build dual fortunes as both an immensely profitable investor and a highly successful businessman.

O'Neil began his financial career as a stockbroker for Hayden, Stone and Company in 1958. It was there that he first began the research that led to the formulation of the key elements of his investment strategy. O'Neil's trading concepts proved remarkably effective from the start. During 1962–63, by pyramiding the profits in three exceptional back-to-back trades—short Korvette, long Chrysler, and long Syntex—he managed to parlay an initial $5,000 investment into $200,000.

In 1964, O'Neil used his investment winnings to buy a seat on the New York Stock Exchange and to form William O'Neil and Co., an institutional research brokerage firm. His firm was a leader in offering comprehensive computerized stock market information and today is one of the most highly respected securities research firms in the country. William O'Neil and Co. services more than 500 major institutional accounts and 28,000 individual subscribers to their *Daily Graphs* charting service. The firm's data base contains 120 different statistics on each of 7,500 securities.

In what was certainly his boldest endeavor, in 1983, O'Neil launched *Investor's Daily* in direct competition with the *Wall Street Journal*. He financed the newspaper with his own funds, knowing that it would be many years before he could hope to break even. Skeptics abounded when the paper began with a press run under 30,000 in 1984, compared to over two million for the *Wall Street Journal*. By mid-1988, *Investor's Daily*'s subscribership had expanded to over 110,000, and the growth in circulation was accelerating. The estimated breakeven point of 200,000 subscribers no longer seems far-fetched. O'Neil believes *Investor's Daily* can eventually grow to 800,000 readers. His unflagging confidence in the paper stems from the fact that *Investor's Daily*'s financial tables contain statistical information unavailable anywhere else— earnings per share (EPS) rank, relative strength, and volume percent change. (These measures are discussed in the interview.)

In 1988, O'Neil combined his concepts in the book *How to Make Money in Stocks,* published by McGraw-Hill. The book combines clarity and brevity with excellent and very specific trading advice. It was the best-selling investment book of the year.

O'Neil's various business ventures have not impeded his performance as a virtuoso stock investor. During the past ten years, O'Neil has averaged over a 40 percent profit annually on his stock investments. Some of his biggest winners were the Canadian oils during the 1970s and Pic'n'Save and Price Co. during the late 1970s and early 1980s. Perhaps O'Neil's most famous market calls were two full-page *Wall Street Journal* ads heralding imminent major bull markets. The timing of these ads could hardly have been better: March 1978 and February 1982.

William O'Neil and Company is a no-frills operation. Rarely have I seen a more crowded office environment. O'Neil, however, does not single himself out for any special privileges. In what must surely be a rarity among chief executive officers, he shares his office with two other employees. O'Neil impressed me as being articulate, confident, opinionated, and very bullish on America.

I think it would be fair to describe your stock investment approach as individualistic and original. Where did you first develop your trading ideas?

I went through the same process that most people do. I subscribed to a few investment letters and most of them didn't do too well. I found that theories like buying low-priced stocks or stocks with low price/earnings (P/E) ratios were not very sound.

When did you first find an approach that worked?

Back in 1959, I did a study of the people that were doing very well in the market. At that time, the Dreyfus fund was a very small fund, managing only about $15 million. Jack Dreyfus, who managed the fund, was doubling the results of all of his competitors. So I got copies of their prospectus and quarterly reports and plotted on charts precisely where they had purchased each of their stocks. There were over 100 of these securities and when I laid them out on a table, I made my first real discovery: Not some, not most, but every single stock had been bought when it went to a new high price.

So the first thing I learned about how to get superior performance is not to buy stocks that are near their lows, but to buy stocks that are coming out of broad bases and beginning to make new highs relative to the preceding price base. You are trying to find the beginning of a major move so that you don't waste six or nine months sitting in a stock that is going nowhere.

I studied the stocks that were big winners in past years and tried to find the characteristics they had in common before they became major successes. I didn't just limit myself to preconceived notions like P/E ratios; I examined a lot of variables to develop a model based on how the real world worked.

Can you describe this model for picking winning stocks?

I use the easy-to-remember acronym CANSLIM. Each letter of this name represents one of the seven chief characteristics of the all-time great winning stocks during their early developing stages, just before they made huge advances.

The "C" stands for current earnings per share. The best performing stocks showed a 70 percent average increase in earnings for the current quarter over the same quarter in the prior year *before* they began their major advance. I am continually amazed by how many individual investors, and even pension fund managers, buy common stocks with unchanged or lower current quarter earnings. There is absolutely no reason for a stock to go up if the current earnings are poor. If, as our research demonstrated, the best stocks had large profit increases before they advanced rapidly in price, why should anybody settle for mediocre earnings? So, our first basic rule in stock selection is that quarterly earnings per share should be up by at least 20 to 50 percent year to year.

The "A" in our formula stands for annual earnings per share. In our studies, the prior five-year average annual compounded earnings growth rate of outstanding performing stocks at their early emerging stage was 24 percent. Ideally, each year's earnings per share should show an increase over the prior year's earnings.

It is a unique combination of both strong current earnings and high average earnings growth that creates a superb stock. The EPS rank, which is published in *Investor's Daily*, combines a stock's percent earnings increase during the past two quarters with the past five-year average percent earnings and compares that figure to every other stock we cover. An EPS rank of 95 means that a company's current and five-year historical earnings have outperformed 95 percent of all other companies.

The "N" in our formula stands for something new. The "new" can be a new product or service, a change in the industry, or new management. In our research we found that 95 percent of the greatest winners had something new that fell within these categories. The "new" also refers to a new high price for the stock. In our seminars we find that 98 percent of investors are unwilling to buy a stock at a new high. Yet, it is one of the great paradoxes of the stock market that what seems too high usually goes higher and what seems too low usually goes lower.

The "S" in the formula stands for shares outstanding. Ninety-five percent of the stocks that performed best in our studies had less than twenty-five million shares of capitalization during the period when they had their best performance. The average capitalization of all of these stocks was 11.8 million shares, while the median figure was only 4.6

million. Many institutional investors handicap themselves by restricting their purchases to only large-capitalization companies. By doing so, they automatically eliminate some of the best growth companies.

The "L" in our formula stands for leader or laggard. The 500 best-performing stocks during the 1953–1985 period had an average *relative strength* of 87 before their major price increase actually began. [The relative strength measures a stock's price performance during the past twelve months compared to all other stocks. For example, a relative strength of 80 would mean that the given stock outperformed 80 percent of all other stocks during the past year.] So, another basic rule in stock selection is to pick the leading stocks—the ones with the high relative strength values—and avoid the laggard stocks. I tend to restrict purchases to companies with relative strength ranks above 80.

The "I" in the formula stands for institutional sponsorship. The institutional buyers are by far the largest source of demand for stocks. Leading stocks usually have institutional backing. However, although some institutional sponsorship is desired, excessive sponsorship is not, because it would be a source of large selling if anything went wrong with the company or the market in general. This is why the most widely owned institutional stocks can be poor performers. By the time a company's performance is so obvious that almost all institutions own a stock, it is probably too late to buy.

The "M" in our formula stands for market. Three out of four stocks will go in the same direction as a significant move in the market averages. That is why you need to learn how to interpret price and volume on a daily basis for signs that the market has topped.

At any given time, less than 2 percent of the stocks in the entire market will fit the CANSLIM formula. The formula is deliberately restrictive because you want to pick only the very best. If you were recruiting players for a baseball team, would you pick an entire lineup of .200 hitters, or would you try to get as many .300 hitters as possible?

Since you use such a restrictive selection process, do you have a high percentage of winning trades?

I guess over the years, about two-thirds of my stock purchases were actually closed at a profit. However, I have found that only one or two stocks of every ten I have bought have turned out to be truly outstanding.

Wouldn't most of the indicators in your CANSLIM formula, such as EPS, pick up a stock before it goes to new highs? Why not just buy the stock when it is still forming a base instead of waiting for it to go to a new high?

You don't want to anticipate a breakout from a base because a stock may never break out. You can buy too soon as well as too late. The idea is to buy when there is the least probability of a loss. If you buy within the base, the stock will frequently fluctuate 10 or 15 percent in normal trading action, and it is very easy to get shaken out of the position. But if I buy at exactly the right time, the stock is usually not going to go down to my maximum 7 percent stop-loss point.

You have stated that the superior stocks have high relative strength figures—80 or higher. Although high relative strength is good, is there such a thing as it being too high? In other words, might a relative strength of 99 indicate that the stock is overextended and vulnerable to a sharp correction?

You have to look at a chart to make that determination. The key point is not how high the relative strength is, but rather how far the stock is extended beyond its most recent price base. You buy stocks that have a high relative strength if they are just beginning to emerge from a sound base-building period. However, I would generally not buy a stock with a high relative strength that is already more than 10 percent beyond its prior price base.

The "M" in the CANSLIM formula makes sense since few stocks can buck a general bear market. However, that rule sounds easier in theory than in practice. After all, how do you tell the difference between a market top and a normal bull market correction?

Top formations in the market averages occur in only one of two ways. First, the average moves up to a new high, but does so on low volume. This tells you that the demand for stocks is poor at that point and that the rally is vulnerable. Second, volume surges for several days, but there is very little, if any, upside price progress as measured by market closes. In this latter case, there may not be a pickup in volume when the market initially tops, since the distribution has taken place on the way up.

Another way to determine the direction of the general market is to focus on how the leading stocks are performing. If the stocks that have been leading the bull market start breaking down, that is a major sign the market has topped. Another important factor to watch is the Federal Reserve discount rate. Usually, after the Fed raises the rate two or three times, the market runs into trouble.

The daily *advance/decline line* is sometimes a useful indicator to watch for signs of a market top. [The advance/decline line illustrates the difference between the total number of New York Stock Exchange stocks advancing each day versus the number declining.] Frequently, the advance/decline line will lag behind the market averages and fail to penetrate prior peaks after the averages reach new highs. This indicates that fewer stocks are participating in the market advance.

When you believe that the general market has entered a bearish phase, would you advise going short rather than merely liquidating longs?

I don't normally advise people to sell short unless they are professional traders. Selling short is quite tricky. I myself have only made significant profits on the short side of two of the last nine bear markets.

A stock should never be sold short because its price looks too high. The idea is not to sell short at the top, but at the right time. Short selling of individual stocks should only be considered after the general market shows signs of a top. The best chart pattern to short is one in which a stock breaks out on the upside of its third or fourth base and then fails. The stock should be breaking down toward the low end of its previous base pattern on increased volume. After the first serious price break below the base, there will usually be several pullback attempts. The prior base will now provide an area of overhead supply, as all investors who bought in that zone will be losing money, and a number of them will be eager to get out near breakeven. Therefore, pullbacks to failed price bases also provide good timing for short sales.

Does the element of unlimited risk present any special problem in short selling?

No, because I never take unlimited risk. If a short position goes against me, I will be out after the first 6 or 7 percent loss. Before you sell any stock short, you should decide the price at which you will cover that short position if a loss occurs.

Besides the CANSLIM formula, which is critical to your stock selection process, risk control obviously plays an important role in your overall strategy. Can you talk a little bit more about that element of trading?

My philosophy is that all stocks are bad. There are no good stocks unless they go up in price. If they go down instead, you have to cut your losses fast. The secret for winning in the stock market does not include being right all the time. In fact, you should be able to win even if you are right only half the time. The key is to lose the least amount of money possible when you are wrong. I make it a rule never to lose more than a maximum of 7 percent on any stock I buy. If a stock drops 7 percent below my purchase price, I will automatically sell it at the market—no second-guessing, no hesitation.

Some people say, "I can't sell that stock because I'd be taking a loss." If the stock is below the price you paid for it, selling doesn't give you the loss; you already have it. Letting losses run is the most serious mistake made by most investors. The public doesn't really understand the philosophy of cutting losses quickly. If you don't have a rule like cutting a loss at 7 percent, then in bear markets like 1973–74, you can lose 70 or 80 percent on your holdings. I have seen people go bankrupt in that type of situation. If you aren't willing to cut your losses short, then you probably should not buy stocks. Would you drive your car without brakes?

In my book, I repeat a story told by Fred C. Kelly, the author of *Why You Win or Lose,* that provides the best example I know of how the typical investor procrastinates when it comes to making a selling decision. A man has rigged up a turkey trap with a trail of corn leading into a big box with a hinged door. The man holds a long piece of twine, connected to the door, that he can use to pull the door shut once enough turkeys have wandered into the box. However, once he shuts the door, he can't open it again without going back to the box, which would scare away any turkeys lurking on the outside.

One day, he had a dozen turkeys in his box. Then one walked out, leaving eleven. "I should have pulled the string when there were twelve inside," he thought, "but maybe if I wait, he will walk back in." While he was waiting for his twelfth turkey to return, two more turkeys walked out. "I should have been satisfied with the eleven," he thought. "If just one of them walks back, I will pull the string." While he was waiting, three more turkeys walked out. Eventually, he was left empty-handed. His problem was that he couldn't give up the idea that some of the original turkeys would return. This is the attitude of the typical investor who can't bring himself to sell at a loss. He keeps expecting the stock to recover. The moral is: To reduce your stock market risk, stop counting turkeys.

OK, you use your CANSLIM methodology for selecting stocks, and your 7 percent rule for getting out if you are wrong. How do you decide when to liquidate a winning stock position?

First, you should hold a stock as long as it is performing properly. Jesse Livermore said, "It is never your thinking that makes big money, it's the sitting." Second, you have to realize that you will never sell the exact top. Therefore, it is ridiculous to kick yourself when a stock goes higher after you sell. The goal is to make substantial profits on your stocks and not be upset if the price continues to advance after you get out.

Your writings express disdain for a number of factors that many people consider important, including P/E ratios, dividends, diversification, and overbought/oversold indicators. Could you explain what you think is wrong with the conventional wisdom regarding these subjects. Let's start with P/E ratios.

To say that a stock is undervalued because it is selling at a low P/E ratio is nonsense. In our research, we found there was a very low correlation between the P/E ratio and the best-performing stocks. Some of these stocks had P/E ratios of 10 when they started their major advance; others had P/E ratios of 50. During the thirty-three years in our survey period

[1953–1985], the average P/E ratio for the best-performing stocks at their early emerging stage was 20, compared to an average P/E ratio of 15 for the Dow Jones Average during the same time. At the end of their expansion phase, these stocks had an average P/E ratio of approximately 45. This means that if, in the past, you were not willing to buy stocks with above-average P/Es, you automatically eliminated most of the best-performing securities.

A common mistake a lot of investors make is to buy a stock solely because the P/E ratio looks cheap. There is usually a very good reason why a P/E ratio is low. Many years ago, when I was first beginning to study the market, I bought Northrop at four times earnings and watched in disbelief as the stock eventually declined to two times earnings.

Another common mistake is selling stocks with high P/E ratios. I still remember in 1962 when an investor barged into my friend's brokerage office, declaring in a loud voice that Xerox was drastically overpriced because it was selling at fifty times earnings. He went short at $88. Xerox eventually went to $1,300, adjusting for stock splits.

Your thoughts on dividends?

There is no correlation between dividends and a stock's performance. In fact, the more a company pays in dividends, the weaker their posture because they may have to pay high interest rates to replace funds paid out in dividends. It is naive to hold stocks that are going down because they pay dividends. If you are getting a 4 percent dividend and the stock goes down 25 percent, your net yield is a 21 percent loss.

How about overbought/oversold indicators?

I rarely pay any attention to overbought/oversold indicators. I once hired a well-known professional who specialized in such technical indicators. At the very point during the 1969 market break when I was trying to convince portfolio managers to liquidate stocks and move to cash, he was telling them it was too late to sell because his indicators said the market was very oversold. Once his indicators were oversold, the market break really accelerated.

The final item on my list of your most prominent conventional wisdom targets is diversification.

Diversification is a hedge for ignorance. I think you are much better off owning a few stocks and knowing a great deal about them. By being very selective, you increase your chances of picking superior performers. You can also watch those stocks much more carefully, which is important in controlling risk.

How many issues would you advise a typical investor to hold at any one time?

For an investor with $5,000, one or two; $10,000, three or four; $25,000, four or five; $50,000, five or six; and $100,000 or more, six or seven.

Aside from the subjects we have just discussed, is there anything else you consider a major public misconception?

Most investors think that charts are hocus-pocus. Only about 5 to 10 percent of investors understand charts. Even a lot of professionals are totally ignorant about charts. Just as a doctor would be foolish not to use X-rays and EKGs, investors would be foolish not to use charts. Charts provide valuable information about what is going on that cannot be obtained easily any other way. They allow you to follow a huge number of different stocks in an organized manner.

Earlier, you talked about using volume as a clue that the market averages were topping. Do you also use volume as an indicator in trading individual stocks?

The volume in a stock is a measure of supply and demand. When a stock is beginning to move into new high ground, volume should increase by at least 50 percent over the average daily volume in recent months. High volume at a key point is an extraordinarily valuable tip-off that a stock is ready to move.

Volume can also be used in a reverse manner. When prices enter a consolidation after an advance, volume should dry up very substantially. In other words, there should be very little selling coming into the market. During a consolidation, declining volume is generally constructive.

How do you handle a losing streak?

If you hit a losing streak, and it is not because what you are doing is wrong, that tells you the whole market may be going bad. If you have five or six straight losses, you want to pull back to see if it is time to start moving into cash.

The "M" in your CANSLIM formula emphasizes the importance of being out of the market—at least on the long side—during major bear phases. Since most mutual funds, by their very structure, remain heavily invested in stocks throughout both bull and bear markets, does this imply that you believe mutual funds are a poor investment?

This is going to surprise you. I think mutual funds are an absolutely outstanding way to invest. I believe that every person should own their own home, own real estate, and have an individual stock account or own mutual funds. Those are the only ways you can make any substantial income above your salary. Although I think mutual funds are an excellent investment, the problem is that most people don't know how to handle them. The key to success in mutual funds is to sit and not to think. When you buy a fund, you want to be in it for 15 years or more. That is how you will make the really big money. But in order to do that, you need the courage to sit through three, four, or five bear markets. The typical diversified growth stock fund will go up 75 to 100 percent in a bull market, but it will decline by only 20 to 30 percent in a bear market.

So you treat a fund very differently from an individual stock account?

Very, very differently. With an individual stock, you absolutely have to have a stop-loss point, because you never know how far down the stock is going. I remember selling a $100 stock one time and it eventually went to $1. I didn't have any idea it was going down that far, but what would have happened if I had held on to it? One mistake like that and you can't come back.

In contrast, in a mutual fund, you should sit through the bear markets. Since most funds will be diversified in 100 or more stocks across the American economy, when stocks recover after a bear market, these funds will recover as well—they almost have to. Unfortunately, in a bear market, most people get scared and decide to switch, ruining their long-term holding plan. Actually, when a good, diversified growth fund is down sharply, you should buy more.

Would it be fair to say that the general public tends to treat funds like they should individual stocks and stocks like they should funds? By that I mean, they tend to hold on to their losers in individual stocks, but liquidate their mutual funds when they are down sharply.

Yes, that is exactly right. Because of the emotional element, most of what people do in the market is wrong.

Along that line, what are the biggest mistakes investors generally make?

In my book I have a chapter on eighteen common mistakes.

The following list of common mistakes is excerpted from O'Neil's book *How to Make Money in Stocks*, published by McGraw-Hill in 1988.

1. Most investors never get past the starting gate because they do not use good selection criteria. They do not know what to look for to find a successful stock. Therefore, they buy fourth-rate "nothing-to-write-home-about" stocks that are not acting particularly well in the marketplace and are not real market leaders.

2. A good way to ensure miserable results is to buy on the way down in price; a declining stock seems a real bargain because it's cheaper than it was a few months earlier. For example, an acquaintance of mine bought Interna-

tional Harvester at $19 in March 1981 because it was down in price sharply and seemed a great bargain. This was his first investment, and he made the classic tyro's mistake. He bought a stock near its low for the year. As it turned out, the company was in serious trouble and was headed, at the time, for possible bankruptcy.

3. An even worse habit is to average down in your buying, rather than up. If you buy a stock at $40 and then buy more at $30 and average out your cost at $35, you are following up your losers and mistakes by putting good money after bad. This amateur strategy can produce serious losses and weigh you down with a few big losers.

4. The public loves to buy cheap stocks selling at low prices per share. They incorrectly feel it's wiser to buy more shares of stock in round lots of 100 or 1,000 shares, and this makes them feel better, perhaps more important. You would be better off buying 30 or 50 shares of higher-priced, sounder companies. You must think in terms of the number of dollars you are investing, not the number of shares you can buy. Buy the best merchandise available, not the poorest. The appeal of a $2, $5, or $10 stock seems irresistible. But most stocks selling for $10 or lower are there because the companies have either been inferior in the past or have had something wrong with them recently. Stocks are like anything else. You can't buy the best quality at the cheapest price!

It usually costs more in commissions and markups to buy low-priced stocks, and your risk is greater, since cheap stocks can drop 15 to 20 percent faster than most higher-priced stocks. Professionals and institutions will not normally buy the $5 and $10 stocks, so you have a much poorer grade following and support for these low-quality securities. As discussed earlier, institutional sponsorship is one of the ingredients needed to help propel a stock higher in price.

5. First-time speculators want to make a killing in the market. They want too much, too fast, without doing the necessary study and preparation or acquiring the essential methods and skills. They are looking for an easy way to make a quick buck without spending any time or effort really learning what they are doing.

6. Mainstream America delights in buying on tips, rumors, stories, and advisory service recommendations. In other words, they are willing to risk their hard-earned money on what someone else says, rather than on knowing for sure what they are doing themselves. Most rumors are false, and even if a tip is correct, the stock ironically will, in many cases, go down in price.

7. Investors buy second-rate stocks because of dividends or low price/earnings ratios. Dividends are not as important as earnings per share; in fact, the more a company pays in dividends, the weaker the company may be because it may have to pay high interest rates to replenish internally needed funds that were paid out in the form of dividends. An investor can lose the amount of a dividend in one or two days' fluctuation in the price of the stock. A low P/E, of course, is probably low because the company's past record is inferior.

8. People buy company names they are familiar with, names they know. Just because you used to work for General Motors doesn't make General Motors necessarily a good stock to buy. Many of the best investments will be names you won't know very well but could and should know if you would do a little studying and research.

9. Most investors are not able to find good information and advice. Many, if they had sound advice, would not recognize or follow it. The average friend, stockbroker, or advisory service could be a source of losing advice. It is always the exceedingly small minority of your friends, brokers, or advisory services that are successful enough in the market themselves that merit your consideration. Outstanding stockbrokers or advisory services are no more frequent than are outstanding doctors, lawyers, or baseball players. Only one out of nine baseball players that sign professional contracts ever make it to the big leagues. And, of course, the majority of ballplayers that graduate from college are not even good enough to sign a professional contract.

10. Over 98 percent of the masses are afraid to buy a stock that is beginning to go into new high ground, pricewise. It just seems too high to them. Personal feelings and opinions are far less accurate than markets.

11. The majority of unskilled investors stubbornly hold onto their losses when the losses are small and reasonable. They could get out cheaply, but being emotionally involved and human, they keep waiting and hoping until their loss gets much bigger and costs them dearly.

12. In a similar vein, investors cash in small, easy-to-take profits and hold their losers. This tactic is exactly the opposite of correct investment procedure. Investors will sell a stock with a profit before they will sell one with a loss.

13. Individual investors worry too much about taxes and commissions. Your key objective should be to first make a net profit. Excessive worrying

about taxes usually leads to unsound investments in the hope of achieving a tax shelter. At other times in the past, investors lost a good profit by holding on too long, trying to get a long-term capital gain. Some investors, even erroneously, convince themselves they can't sell because of taxes—strong ego, weak judgment.

Commission costs of buying or selling stocks, especially through a discount broker, are a relatively minor factor, compared to more important aspects such as making the right decisions in the first place and taking action when needed. One of the great advantages of owning stock over real estate is the substantially lower commission and instant marketability and liquidity. This enables you to protect yourself quickly at a low cost or to take advantage of highly profitable new trends as they continually evolve.

14. The multitude speculates in options too much because they think it is a way to get rich quick. When they buy options, they incorrectly concentrate entirely in shorter-term, lower-priced options that involve greater volatility and risk rather than in longer-term options. The limited time period works against short-term option holders. Many options speculators also write what are referred to as "naked options," which are nothing but taking a great risk for a potentially small reward and, therefore, a relatively unsound investment procedure.

15. Novice investors like to put price limits on their buy-and-sell orders. They rarely place market orders. This procedure is poor because the investor is quibbling for eighths and quarters of a point, rather than emphasizing the more important and larger overall movement. Limit orders eventually result in your completely missing the market and not getting out of stocks that should be sold to avoid substantial losses.

16. Some investors have trouble making decisions to buy or sell. In other words, they vacillate and can't make up their minds. They are unsure because they really don't know what they are doing. They do not have a plan, a set of principles, or rules to guide them and, therefore, are uncertain of what they should be doing.

17. Most investors cannot look at stocks objectively. They are always hoping and having favorites, and they rely on their hopes and personal opinions rather than paying attention to the opinion of the marketplace, which is more frequently right.

18. Investors are usually influenced by things that are not really crucial, such as stock splits, increased dividends, news announcements, and brokerage firm or advisory recommendations.

As someone who has spent a lifetime researching stocks and the American economy, do you have any opinions about the quality of research provided by Wall Street firms?

An article in *Financial World* found that top-rated analysts generally underperformed the S&P average. One major problem is that 80 percent of brokerage firm research is written on the wrong companies. Each industry analyst has to turn out his or her quota of reports, even though only a few industry groups are leaders in each cycle. There is insufficient screening to determine which reports should actually be written. Another major problem with Wall Street research is that it seldom provides sell recommendations.

I would assume, given the consistency of your success as a stock investor for over twenty-five years, that you don't think very much of the random walk theory.

The stock market is neither efficient nor random. It is not efficient because there are too many poorly conceived opinions; it is not random because strong investor emotions can create trends.

In the most general sense, trading success requires three basic components: an effective trade selection process, risk control, and discipline to adhere to the first two items. William O'Neil provides a perfect illustration of the successful trader. He has devised a specific strategy for selecting stocks (CANSLIM), he has a rigorous risk control rule, and he has the discipline not to deviate from his selection and risk control strategies. In addition to the specific stock selection methodology detailed in this chapter, traders and investors should find the advice regarding common mistakes, listed near the end of the interview, particularly useful.

David Ryan

Stock Investment as a Treasure Hunt

David Ryan does not believe in buying low-priced stocks. But that was not always the case. He remembers flipping through the *Wall Street Journal* when he was thirteen years old and finding a $1 stock. He ran with the paper in hand to his father and asked, "If I go up to my room and get a dollar, can I buy this stock?" His father told him that it didn't quite work that way. "You have to do some research about a company before you invest in the stock," he explained.

A few days later, leafing through the *Wall Street Journal* again, Ryan found an article on Ward Foods, which made Bit-O-Honey and Chunky candy bars. It seemed like a perfect investment, since he ate a lot of candy. His father set up an account for him, and he bought ten shares of the stock. He recalls getting all his friends to buy the candy bars so the company would make more money and his stock would go up. That was the official start of Ryan's career as a stock investor.

Ryan's interest in the stock market increased as he grew older. By the time he was sixteen years old, he was subscribing to a weekly chart service and attending investment seminars by William O'Neil and other market analysts. In college, he read every book on the stock market he could find.

William O'Neil was Ryan's idol. After graduating college in 1982, he decided to try to get a job at O'Neil's company. He told the receptionist of his interest in O'Neil's work and his willingness to accept any job, no matter how menial, just to get his foot in the door. He was even willing to work for free. Ryan was hired, and within four years, his investment success led to his appointment as the youngest vice-president of the company, with responsibilities as a portfolio manager and as O'Neil's direct assistant in stock selection for institutional clients.

Ryan achieved a degree of fame in his own regard when he won the 1985 stock division of the U.S. Investing Championship, a contest run by former Stanford University Professor Norm Zadeh. His return that year was a phenomenal 161 percent. As if to demonstrate that his performance was no one-year fluke, Ryan reentered the contest in 1986, virtually duplicating his previous year's performance with a 160 percent return second-place finish. In 1987, he won the contest once again with another triple-digit return year. For the three years as a whole, his compounded return was a remarkable 1,379 percent.

Although most of the traders I interviewed have a love for trading, none have the unbridled enthusiasm demonstrated by Ryan. To Ryan, the whole process of stock selection is like a terrific game—a treasure hunt as he describes it—and he still can't believe he is getting paid to do it.

The offices of the traders I interviewed ranged from the unadorned to the elaborate, but Ryan clearly had the low end of the spectrum staked out. Instead of an office, plain or otherwise, I was surprised to find Ryan's workplace to be a cubicle within a noisy, floor-sized room. Ryan didn't seem to care about the lack of amenities. I suspect that as long as he was supplied with his charts and computer runs, he would probably be content to work in a hall closet.

Did your original job at William O'Neil & Co. involve any market analysis?

No, but once I was in, I just started studying and studying.

On your own time, I take it.

Yes. I would take stuff home every night and on weekends.

What kind of things were you studying?

I would go over our charts. I studied the company's past recommendations. I studied historical models of great winning stocks to ingrain in my mind what a stock looked like before it made a major move. I tried to get to the point where I was looking at the exact same things O'Neil did. He was my role model.

Were you trading at this time?

Yes, I opened a $20,000 account shortly after I started working for the company [1982].

How did you do?

Initially, I ran the account up to about $52,000 by June 1983. Then I gave it all back, including some of my starting capital. By mid-1984, my account was down to $16,000.

Do you know what you did wrong?

Yes. I sat down and studied every mistake that I had made from June 1983 through the middle of 1984. Probably my biggest mistake was that even though we were in a moderate bear market—the Dow came down from 1,296 to 1,078—I continued to play as aggressively as I had during the bull market from August 1982 through June 1983. I also made the mistake of buying stocks that were overextended. By that I mean I was buying stocks that had already moved 15 to 20 percent above their price bases. You should only buy stocks that are within a few percent of their base; otherwise, the risk is too great.

I turned it around by learning from all the mistakes that I had made. In late 1984, I sold a piece of real estate I owned and put all the money in a stock account.

Were you confident, despite your poor performance during mid-1983 to mid-1984, because you felt that you had figured out what you were doing wrong?

Yes, because I had studied very hard and was determined to be disciplined, I thought I was going to do very well. So in 1985 I entered the U.S. Investing Championship. I won the stock division that year with a 161 percent return. I reentered the contest in subsequent years and substantially exceeded 100 percent returns in 1986 and 1987 as well. I was doing the exact same thing over and over again. I was buying stocks when they had all the characteristics I liked.

How are you doing this year [May 1988]?

So far this year, I am down. We are in a different type of market: Stocks aren't moving as quickly as they have in the last three years. I am playing with a much smaller amount this year, because I think the potential for making a lot of money is much more limited.

You mentioned earlier that for a while you read virtually every book on the markets you could find. What reading list would you give to someone starting out who is serious about becoming a successful stock trader?

Essential reading on top of the list is O'Neil's book, *How to Make Money in Stocks* (McGraw-Hill, New York, NY 1988). Another book that is must reading is *How I Made Two Million Dollars in the Stock Market* by Nicholas Darvas (Lyle Stuart, Inc., Secaucus, NJ, 1986). A lot of people laugh at that title, but it is fun reading and you learn a ton. Another book I would recommend is *Reminiscences of a Stock Operator* by Edwin Lefevre [reputedly about Jesse Livermore]. Livermore himself wrote a very good thin volume, *How to Trade in Stocks* (Institute for Economic & Financial Research, Albuquerque, NM, 1986).

Any others?

A good one on what to look for in individual stocks is *Super Performance Stocks* by Richard Love (Prentice Hall, Englewood Cliffs, NJ, 1977). The book has a great study on some of the greatest winners of all time. Another good one on picking stocks is *Profile of a Growth Stock* by Kermit Zieg and Susannah H. Zieg (Investor's Intelligence, Larchmont, NY, 1972). I would also recommend Marty Zweig's book, *Winning on Wall Street* (Warner Books, Inc., New York, NY, 1986) and Stan Weinstein's *Secrets for Profiting in Bull and Bear Markets* (Dow, Jones-Irwin, New York, NY, 1988), which has some good sections on short selling. Finally, on Elliott Wave analysis, which I think has some validity, there is *Elliott Wave Principle* by Frost and Prechter (New Classic Library, Inc., Gainesville, GA, 1978) and a book called *Super Timing* by an English fellow named Beckman (Milestone Publishers, London).

All those books are good, but you learn the most from the market itself. Every time I buy a stock, I write down the reasons why I bought it [he pulls out a binder containing annotated charts]. Doing this helps cement in my mind the characteristics of a winning stock. Maybe even more important, it helps me learn from my mistakes.

What kind of things did you learn by keeping your trader's diary?

Not buying overextended stocks, using O'Neil's criteria for stock selection, and being as disciplined as possible. The more disciplined you can get, the better you are going to do in the market. The more you listen to tips and rumors, the more money you're likely to lose.

Has keeping this diary been an important part of your success?

Absolutely.

Can you describe your procedure for selecting stocks?

I start out by going through the stock charts and writing down the stocks with strong technical action. In other words, I write down all the stocks

I want to take a closer look at.

Your company follows 7,000 stocks; you can't possibly look at 7,000 charts on a regular basis.

I don't look through 7,000, but in a week I probably go through about 4,000 charts. So, I see a majority of the data base. Keep in mind there are probably about 1,500 to 2,000 stocks that trade under $10, and I don't like to look at those anyway.

Is that a good rule: Avoid stocks under $10?

Yes, because they are usually down there for a reason.

Doesn't that knock out a lot of the OTC stocks?

Yes, a lot of the smaller OTC stocks.

But aren't those sometimes the best buys—the stocks that no one is paying any attention to?

Sometimes. But many of those stocks stay down there for years and years. I would rather wait until they prove themselves by moving up to the $15 to $20 range.

After you have reviewed the charts and written down the stocks that interest you, what do you look at next to screen your selection?

I look at the five-year earnings growth record and the last two quarters of earnings relative to the previous year's levels. The quarterly comparisons show you if there is any deceleration in the earnings growth rate. For example, a 30 percent growth rate over the last five years may look very impressive, but if in the last two quarters earnings were only up 10 percent and 15 percent, it warns you that the strong growth period may be over. Of course, those two factors—the five-year earnings growth record and the earnings during the past two quarters—are combined in our *earnings per share* (EPS) rank. [See the O'Neil chapter for a detailed explanation of the EPS.]

What are you looking for in an EPS figure?

As high as possible—at least above 80, and preferably above 90. Actually, a lot of stocks I buy have an EPS rank of 99.

In my experience, markets usually anticipate. One thing that surprises me about the EPS is that I would think that the price of the stock would run up well before the earnings growth starts to be extremely positive.

That is what a lot of people think. They say, "It's too late to buy the stock; the earnings are already on the table." However, in analyzing hundreds of the biggest winners, we found that, in many cases, the earnings had been on the table for a while.

What would cause a stock to just sit despite very good earnings?

The broad stock market may be weak and holding back the stock, but once the weight of the market comes off, these stocks just go right through the roof.

How about if the stock market is OK? What would keep the stock from taking off in that type of situation?

Perceptions—people might not believe that the earnings are going to continue as strongly as they had in the past.

What else are you using besides the EPS and the earnings breakdown to screen your stock selections?

The *relative strength* is very important. [The relative strength ranks a stock's price change relative to all other stocks surveyed. See the O'Neil chapter for a detailed definition.]

What are you looking for in relative strength?

At least above 80, and preferably above 90.

Intuitively, I would almost think that—

"It has already gone too far. It can't get any stronger."

Well, not necessarily that it can't get any stronger, but it seems to me that, by definition, every stock has to have a high relative strength when it tops. How do you avoid sometimes buying the highs, if you are restricting yourself to high relative strength stocks?

I am usually able to avoid that because in my first step of screening the charts, I generally rule out stocks that are overextended from their base. Very often the stocks with the highest relative strength continue to out-perform the market for months and months. For example, Microsoft had a relative strength of 97 when it was at $50 a share. It eventually moved to $161.

Are you implying that the higher the relative strength the better?

Yes, I would rather go with a relative strength of 99 than 95. However, once the relative strength starts falling off, I usually get out of the stock.

So you are not only paying attention to the relative strength value itself, but also the trend of the relative strength.

Right. If the relative strength starts breaking an uptrend, then I would be very cautious, even if it is still well above 80.

Am I going in the right order, EPS to relative strength, in terms of how you filter down your initial stock list?

I would probably place relative strength first, then EPS. Many times the relative strength takes off before that big earnings report comes out.

Do you also use the relative strength of the industry as a filter in your stock selection?

Yes. *Investor's Daily* ranks industry groups between 0 and 200. I usually want the industry group to be in the top 50.

To continue the screening process, after checking the stock's relative strength, the EPS, and the industry relative strength, what is your next step?

I check the number of shares outstanding. I am looking for stocks with less than thirty million shares and preferably only five to ten million shares. Stocks with more than thirty million shares are more mature; they have already split a few times. It is a case of supply and demand: Because you have more supply, it takes a lot more money to move those stocks.

What else do you look at?

You want some institutional ownership, because they really power a stock higher, but you don't want too much sponsorship. I would say 1 percent to 20 percent mutual fund sponsorship is the ideal range.

Are there any other important elements that go into the stock selection process?

Yes. There should be something new that attracts people to that stock. For example, Reebok had shoes that were hot. Compaq had a fantastic portable computer. Microsoft was a leader in the software field.

Doesn't that rule out most companies that have been around for a while?

Yes. You don't want to be playing General Electric because there is usually nothing really hot or brand new going on. Occasionally, there are exceptions. For example, General Motors has gone virtually sideways for the last five years, and it looks like they are trying to turn their situation around.

With General Motors, might the "new" be the recent shift to high styling?

Yes, but in most cases, you are going to find the new in emerging entrepreneurial growth companies.

I would imagine if you go through 7,000 stocks, there must be quite a large number that meet your criteria.

On average, there are probably only about seventy stocks that meet the criteria, because it is tough to meet all the conditions. Then I cut those seventy down to about seven.

How do you cut down from seventy to seven?

I pick those stocks that have all the characteristics plus a great-looking base pattern. I also look at how the stock has done in the past. For example, has the stock doubled before? A lot of the stocks I buy have already doubled and tripled before I buy them.

You actually prefer to buy a stock that has already doubled as opposed to a stock that is in a long base?

Yes, because that shows me there is something very unusual going on, and if the situation is that good, a doubling may just be the beginning. It is probably going to double again. To sum it up, I am looking for the strongest stocks in the market, in terms of both earnings and the technical picture.

Since you use an extremely rigorous selection process, do you have a high percentage of winners in your stock picks?

No, only about 50/50, because I cut the losers very quickly. The maximum loss I allow is 7 percent, and usually I am out of a losing stock a lot quicker. I make my money on the few stocks a year that double and triple in price. The profits in those trades easily make up for all the small losers.

How long do you typically hold a stock?

I usually hold my big winners for about six to twelve months, stocks that aren't that strong about three months, and my losers less than two weeks.

Do you pick an objective on the stocks you buy?

No. I usually wait until the stock runs up, builds another base, and then breaks down. That is when I liquidate.

Do you think people should only use market orders?

In a dull market that is just trading back and forth, you could put in a limit order. But if you really think the stock is going to make a big move—and that should be the only reason you are buying the stock to begin with—then there is no reason to haggle over an eighth of a point. Just buy the stock. The same thing applies to the downside; if you think the stock is going to drop, just sell it.

I learned the lesson about market orders in 1982 when I was trying to buy Textone, which was trading at $15, for $14¾. The next day it jumped 1½ points, and I couldn't bring myself to buy the stock at $16½ when I could have bought it at $15 a day earlier. That stock eventually went to $45.

One element of your trading style is buying a stock when it makes a new high. Wouldn't the fundamental screening conditions you use have been in place well before that point?

In some cases, they might have been. But I am trying to buy a stock when you have the most chance of making money. When a stock is coming off the low end of a base back to the high end, there will be a lot of people who bought it near the highs and sat with a loss for months. Some of those people are going to be happy to get out at even, and that creates a lot of overhead resistance.

So, a stock which is at new highs has much more of an open running field?

Right, because no one ahead of you is at a loss and wants to get out at the first opportunity. Everybody has a profit; everybody is happy.

But the downside of that is if you wait for a breakout to new highs, a lot of times the market will pull back into the trading range. How do you avoid getting whipsawed in those situations?

You can tell a lot by the volume. If the volume doubles one day and the stock moves to a new high, it is telling you a lot of people are interested in the stock and buying it.

So volume becomes very important as a filtering process to avoid getting whipsawed.

Yes. If the stock moves to new high ground, but the volume is only up 10 percent, I would be wary.

Do you buy it the first day the stock breaks out to new highs, or do you wait for it to consolidate for a few days?

I want to buy it as soon as it goes to new highs.

If you buy a stock at new highs and it then pulls back into the range, at what point do you decide it was a false breakout? For example, assume a stock that has been trading between $16 and $20 goes to $21 and you buy it. What do you do if two days later the stock is back to $19?

If it reenters its base, I have a rule to cut at least 50 percent of the position.

If it reenters its base at all? Do you mean even if it is just below the top end of the base, or do you require some minimum penetration?

No, if it just reenters the base. In some cases, it will break out and come back to the top of the base, but not reenter. That's fine, and I will stay with the stock. But if the top of the base was $20 and it breaks back to $19¾, I want to sell at least half of the position because the stock didn't keep on moving. Frequently, when a stock drops back into its base, it goes all the way back down to the lower end of the base. In the example, if it goes from $21 down to $19¾, it will often go all the way back down to $16. Therefore, you want to cut your losses quickly.

From a technical perspective, is the price going back into the base a bearish indicator?

Yes. Stocks should be at a profit the first day you buy them. In fact, having a profit on the first day is one of the best indicators that you are going to make money on the trade.

Do you use the table in *Investor's Daily* that lists the stocks with the greatest percentage increase in volume relative to the past fifty-day average volume levels?

Yes, I use it to help spot stocks that are just about ready to take off.

Are you using it to verify stocks you have already picked out?

Yes. After I have done my weekly screen to select the stocks I am interested in buying, I sometimes wait for the stock to hit that column as a timing signal.

Can you elaborate on using volume as a trading tool?

When a stock that has been moving up starts consolidating, you want to see volume dry up. You should see a downtrend in volume. Then when volume starts picking up again, it usually means the stock is ready to blast off.

So, in the consolidation phase, decreasing volume is good. If you continue to see very high volume, do you start thinking potential top?

Yes, because that shows that a lot of people are getting out of the stock. You want an increase in volume when the stock breaks out, but you want a decrease in volume as the stock consolidates.

Any other volume signals you look for?

When the market, or a stock, is bottoming, you want to see increased volume combined with an absence of further price progress on the downside. For example, if the Dow declines from 2,200 to 2,100, trades down to 2,085 the next day, and then closes higher on increased volume, it demonstrates support. It suggests that there are a lot of buyers coming in.

The screens you have described in selecting stocks are essentially O'Neil's *CANSLIM* methodology. [See the O'Neil chapter for definition.] Did you add any of your own elements to his approach?

Yes, I learned that most of our greatest winning recommendations started off with prices under thirty times earnings. O'Neil says the P/E [price/earnings] ratio is not important. I think it is, in that your success ratio is a lot higher on lower P/E ratio stocks.

But I guess not *too* low P/E ratios?

When I'm talking about lower P/E ratio stocks, I mean stocks that have a P/E ratio that is between even and up to two times the S&P 500 P/E ratio. So if the S&P 500 is at fifteen times earnings, you should try to buy stocks with P/E ratios between 15 and 30. Once you start going much beyond double the S&P 500 P/E ratio level, your timing has to be more exact. You are bound to make a few more mistakes on higher P/E ratio stocks.

Do you therefore avoid high P/E ratio stocks?

Yes, in many cases I do. The most profitable situation is when you find a stock with a strong earnings trend that is trading at a P/E ratio in line with the broad market ratio.

If you avoid high P/E ratio stocks, wouldn't that have prevented you from catching the whole biomedical group move?

That was a little different because of the fact that the whole group was trading at high P/E ratios.

Does that imply that there should be an exception made for a new industry?

Yes, you don't want to be absolutely rigid with these rules.

Has the basic market behavior stayed the same in the 1980s versus the 1970s and the 1960s?

Yes, the same types of stocks work time after time. It hasn't changed at all. We can take one of the greatest winning stocks from 1960 and line it up with one of the best stocks in 1980 and they are going to have exactly the same characteristics.

Do you have any thoughts on the subject of short selling?

I need more time to study it and more experience. However, to pick a short, I think you need to flip all these characteristics we were talking about. Instead of a good growth record, you should look for a poor five-year growth record and quarterly earnings that are decelerating. The stock should be losing relative strength, breaking uptrends, and starting to hit new lows.

Do you think that short selling may be a critical element for superior performance if we go into a long bear market?

Yes, I think it would help. But, Bill O'Neil will tell you that shorting is about three times as hard as buying stocks. Bill says he has made substantial money in only two of the past nine bear markets. He thinks the best thing you can do in a bear market is just sit it out.

How do you recognize a bear market before it's too late?

By how well my individual stocks are doing. If, during the bull phase, the leaders start losing, it indicates that a bear market is developing. If I have five or six stocks in a row that get stopped out, a caution flag goes up.

What else do you look for to signal a bear market?

Divergence between the Dow and the daily *advance/decline line* [a graph of the cumulative net difference between the number of New York Stock Exchange stocks advancing each day versus the number declining]. The advance/decline tends to top out a few months before the Dow does.

Did that happen in 1987?

The advance/decline topped out during the first quarter of 1987, well before the stock market peak in August.

Were you looking for a top because of that?

Not at that point, because a lot of the individual stocks were still doing very well. The big clue that the market was really topping was after the Dow came off its high at 2,746, there was a very feeble, low-volume rally, and then the market got hit for another 90-point loss. At that juncture, I decided it was time to move out of the market.

Because the rally was on low volume?

Yes, and the fact that there were very few stocks that participated in the rally; the advance/decline line did not move as high as it did on the previous rally. Also, in late August, the discount rate was raised for the first time in three years. I think that really stabbed the market.

You haven't been in the business that long. Do you have the confidence that you will be able to trade successfully almost every year for a long time?

Yes, because I have established a very defined set of principles that will provide the foundation for successful trading for years to come. Also, I plan to never stop learning.

Do you feel you are getting better as a trader?

Yes. If you try to learn from every single trade that you make, you are only going to get better and better as time goes on.

Why are you so much more successful than the typical stock investor?

Because I am doing something that I love to do and find fascinating. After eight or nine hours at work, I go home and spend more time on the markets. I have the charts delivered to me on Saturdays, and I go through them for three or four hours on Sunday. I think if you love what you are doing, you are going to be a lot more successful.

A lot of people who invest use their spare time to study the market and still have only mediocre, or even losing, results.

That is probably because they have not found a disciplined system for picking stocks. They read an article and say, "That sounds like a good stock, I'll buy it." Or they buy a stock because their broker recommends it.

What advice would you give the novice trader?

The single most important advice I can give anybody is: Learn from your mistakes. That is the only way to become a successful trader.

Any final comments?

The greatest thing about the market is that it is always fun to be looking for that next big winner—trying to find the stock with all the characteristics that are going to make it have a big move. The feeling isn't any different now than when I was only trading 500 shares. There is still the same satisfaction of knowing you found a stock before it made its big move.

You make it sound like a game.

It is. To me it is like a giant treasure hunt. Somewhere in here [he pats the weekly chart book] there is going to be a big winner, and I am trying to find it.

The conventional wisdom about how to make money in stocks is summarized by the semi-facetious advice: Buy low and sell high. David Ryan would disagree. His philosophy can be summarized as: Buy high and sell higher. In fact, Ryan usually will not consider buying any stock selling for less than $10.

Ryan's success is basically due to using a precise methodology and applying great discipline to follow it. As Ryan has clearly demonstrated, a trading methodology doesn't have to be original to be extremely successful. Ryan readily acknowledges that most of his approach has been learned directly from the writings and teachings of William O'Neil. With the help of hard work and in-depth study, he has been able to apply O'Neil's trading philosophy with great effectiveness.

When traders deviate from their own rules, they invariably tend to lose. Ryan is no exception. During mid-1983 to mid-1984, he witnessed a period of extremely poor performance. He let his previous trading success go to his head by repeatedly breaking one of his own cardinal rules: Never buy an *overextended stock* [a stock that is trading far above its most recent price base]. The 1983–1984 experience made a lasting impression on Ryan, and he has not repeated that mistake.

Maintaining a trader's diary is an essential element of Ryan's approach. Every time he buys a stock, Ryan annotates the chart with his reasons for buying the stock. Whenever he liquidates or adds to an existing position, a new chart is included with updated comments. This approach has helped Ryan reinforce in his mind the key characteristics of winning stocks. Perhaps, more important, reviewing his past entries has helped him avoid repeating similar trading mistakes.

Ryan's basic approach, like William O'Neil's approach, is to buy value and strength. He also believes in focusing on the very best stocks as opposed to diversifying his portfolio. One important observation Ryan made, which many other traders may find helpful, is that his best trades are usually winners right from the start. Thus, he has little reservation about getting out of a losing trade quickly. The maximum he will risk on any trade is a 7 percent price decline. A rigid stop-loss rule is an essential ingredient to the trading approach of many successful traders.

Marty Schwartz

Champion Trader

I interviewed Marty Schwartz at his office after trading hours. I found him to be very opinionated and intense about the subject of trading. This intensity occasionally spills over into anger when a raw nerve is hit (such as program trading). In fact, Schwartz readily admits that he finds anger a useful trait in trading. None of this "going with the market flow" philosophy for Schwartz. In his view, the marketplace is an arena and other traders are the adversaries.

I was also struck by Schwartz's dedication to his daily work routine. He was doing his market analysis when I arrived and continued to run through his calculations during our interview. When I left that evening, his analysis was still unfinished. Although he appeared very tired, I had no doubt that he would finish his work that evening. Schwartz has followed his daily work routine religiously during the past nine years.

Schwartz spent a decade losing money on his trading before he found his stride as a remarkably successful professional trader. During his earlier years, he was a well-paid securities analyst, who, as he describes it, was always broke because of market losses. Eventually, he changed his trading methodology, in the process of transforming himself from a repeated loser to an amazingly consistent winner. Not only has Schwartz scored enormous percentage gains in every year since he turned full-time trader in 1979, but he has done so without ever losing more than 3 percent of his equity on a month-end to month-end basis.

Schwartz trades independently from an office at home. He is proud of the fact that he has no employees. Solitary traders of this type, no matter how successful, are usually unknown to the public. Schwartz, however, has attained a degree of fame through repeated entries in the U.S. Trading Championships, run by Norm Zadeh, a Stanford University professor. His performance in these contests has been nothing short of astounding. In nine of the ten four-month trading championships he entered (typically with a starting stake of $400,000), he made more money than all the other contestants combined. His average return in these nine contests was 210 percent—nonannualized! (In the one remaining four-month contest he witnessed a near breakeven result.) In his single entry in a one-year contest, he scored a 781 percent return. Schwartz's entry into these contests is his way of telling the world that he is the best trader around. In terms of risk/reward ratios, he may well be.

Please start by telling me about your early days.

How far back do you want me to go?

From whenever you think is appropriate.

Well it is very relevant to go back to my childhood, quite frankly. Should I lay down on the couch? I grew up in New Haven in a family of modest means. I was very hard working. When I was seven or eight I would go out with a snow shovel and come back with $10 after a snowstorm.

Even now, I still put in about twelve hours a day. I feel uncomfortable not doing the work; that's why I am doing it now as you are sitting here. I calculate a lot of mathematical ratios and oscillators, and I post my own charts. My attitude is that I always want to be better prepared than someone I'm competing against. The way I prepare myself is by doing my work each night.

As I grew up, I realized that education was my ticket, probably because it was strongly emphasized in my family. I studied hard and was an honor student in high school.

I was accepted to Amherst College, which was one of the great experiences of my life. When I went to freshman orientation they said, "Look to your left and right and realize that half of you are going to be in the top half of the class and half of you are going to be in the bottom half." Most of those who matriculated there, including myself, were in the top 5 percent of their high school class. Perceiving that I wasn't going to be at the top of everything was a difficult first realization.

It was the first time in my life I had to struggle. I even had to get a tutor for calculus because I just wasn't getting the concept. But when I finally got it, when the light bulb clicked on, it was like looking at a magnificent painting. I really experienced the joy of learning and working hard there. Before, studying was only a means to an end; now, I found that learning itself was a real joy. Amherst had a profound influence on me.

After graduating in 1967, I was accepted to the Columbia Business School. At the time, the government had just ended graduate school military deferments. Since I was unhappy at Columbia and combat in Vietnam didn't appeal to me, I joined a U.S. Marine Corps reserve unit that was recruiting officers.

You have to be somewhat crazy to be in the Marines; it is a very unusual organization. They push you to the edge and then rebuild you in their own mold. However, I have developed a great respect for that bureaucracy, because throughout the Marine Corps history, they've been consistent in their training procedure. As a second lieutenant you have forty-six lives under your control, so you must be well skilled. They put you under a lot of pressure. If you couldn't cut the mustard, you didn't get the bars. We had an attrition rate that I believe approached 50 percent.

I was the only reservist in Officers Candidate School in Quantico at that time. There were 199 regulars who went to Vietnam, but I came home; that was the deal I made when I was recruited. I was also the only Jewish person there, and they weren't too favorably disposed toward Jews. One time, the platoon sergeant drew the Star of David on my forehead with a magic marker. I wanted to knock the crap out of him, but I figured he didn't really know the historic significance of what it meant. I knew he was just trying to find any kind of pressure point that would make me break. The hardest thing I had to do was scrub the magic marker off my forehead. That's a bitch [he laughs]. Anyway, I persevered and made it through successfully. I consider that a really fine achievement. The feeling improves as time passes, and you forget the real pain of the experience.

The rigorous Marine training gave me the confidence to believe that I could perform at levels beyond my previous expectations. Just as Amherst had strengthened my mind, the Marines strengthened my body. The two experiences convinced me that I could do almost anything if I worked hard enough and provided the groundwork for my successful trading. That's not to say it worked right away, because it didn't.

After getting out of the Marines, I returned to Columbia and held some boring part-time jobs while I completed my M.B.A. My first full-time job was as a securities analyst at Kuhn Loeb. I specialized in the health and retail field, and I stayed there for two years. I found that, on Wall Street, the best way to receive a pay increase was to change jobs. The company you work for never wants to pay you as much as a company trying to recruit you.

I left for XYZ in 1972. I want to leave out the firm's name and other particulars for reasons that will soon become obvious. This proved to be one of the most difficult periods in my life and career. XYZ had thirty analysts, divided into three subgroups of ten. Because the research director didn't want to work, he had one of the senior analysts of each group review the work of the analysts. The policy was that our research reports would be circulated and critiqued by the other analysts within the subgroups prior to being sent out.

I had written a bearish report on hospital management stocks, saying that the industry would eventually go to a utility rate of return. As part of the normal routine, the draft was circulated among the other analysts, one of whom got drunk one night on a flight home from California and told a client about my report. He even sent him a copy of the report in progress. What right did he have to send out my work? The stocks began plummeting prior to the report's release, because the client started spreading rumors that a negative report was about to be issued.

It was a bitter experience. I had to testify for six hours before the New York Stock Exchange. My company's counsel told me, "We will represent you, but should our interests diverge at any point, we will inform you."

At the time, did you know what had happened?

No, I didn't, but I assumed that everything would be all right if I told the truth, which I did. I was totally exonerated; the exchange realized I had been set up. The drug analyst eventually confessed because an exchange official found out what happened by piecing it all together. It was a rotten, bitter experience for me, and I was very sour. I shut the door of my office and stopped working. I lost the spark, the drive, the desire to succeed.

What were you doing at that time?

I was still doing reports, but I didn't have my heart in it. Besides that whole negative experience, it was early 1973, and I felt the market was topping out. I had become very interested in technical analysis. At the time, the advance/decline line had formed a major top many months earlier. I felt that the market and the stocks I was covering were going to go down. Still, people wanted to know how many widgets a company was selling and at what price. I lost the spirit to write bullish reports, because if stock prices are going down, who cares how many widgets are being sold. I was covering growth stocks, which in those days sold at forty or fifty times earnings. It was all so ridiculous!

Were you discouraged from writing bearish reports? Also, what ever happened to the bearish report that was leaked?

Nobody wrote bearish reports on Wall Street at that time. I was allowed to complete the bearish report on the hospital management industry, but I don't believe they ever intended to publish it. Of course, after it was leaked, they were forced to rush it to the printer to save their scalps.

What eventually happened?

I lost my job in the bear market and was out of work for four months. That was a very interesting period, because I believe you learn the most through adversity. I had about $20,000, which in those days was a lot of money, and I was going to trade. I found a real lunatic who had developed computer programs for trading commodities. At the time, he had to rent time on a monster machine to run programs that today you could do on any PC. He was using different moving averages, that sort of thing. I put some of my money in with him, and I lost most of it—along with my dreams of glory.

Having dissipated my capital, I decided I had to go back to work. I was in for a shock. Although I had been totally honest and forthright, I was tainted. "Oh, aren't you the guy who wrote that report?" It didn't matter that I had been totally ethical and exonerated. People don't want to get involved with any controversy, even if it wasn't of your own making.

A friend of mine helped me get a job at Edwards & Hanly, which, although it was a retail-oriented firm, had a group of analysts who became real stars. It was there that I met Bob Zoellner, the managing partner of the firm. He was a great, great trader. He almost single-handedly kept the firm afloat in 1974 by shorting stocks and making money in the firm's capital account, while they were losing money on the operating side. He started his own hedge fund in 1976 and went on to become an extraordinary success.

I always had a good nose as a securities analyst, and it has stood me in good stead. When I noticed that the head of research, who never went out to lunch, began going out to lunch regularly, I started interviewing for another job. So, when the firm went bankrupt in fall 1975, I had another job lined up at Loeb Rhoades.

In 1976, I met my wife-to-be and she had a profound effect on me. She made me realize that my life was not a dress rehearsal; it was the real thing and I had been screwing it up. Although I had steadily earned good salaries, I was still almost broke because I consistently lost money in the market.

We got married in March 1978. By that time, I was working at E. F. Hutton. Being married made going on business trips harder and harder. When you are twenty-five, seeing friends from college in different cities around the country is very exciting, but when you get in your thirties, it gets real stale. My wife literally had to push me out the door when I had to go on these trips.

I resented what I called the "tap dances," which made you feel like a piece of meat. You meet with portfolio managers to give them your views on the stocks you follow, so that they will give commission business to your firm. On a typical trip, you might have five appointments in Houston, fly to San Antonio for dinner, and then fly to Dallas later that night to be ready for breakfast the next morning. I got sick of it.

I wanted to have a family, but I felt that I wasn't able to handle it financially. I had resisted getting married because I was afraid of being tapped out. But, at that point, I wondered whether it had been a self-fulfilling prophecy. People seem to know how to handle failure because they can produce it themselves. It almost becomes a negative cause and effect cycle, whereby they produce it, they know how to handle it, and they wallow in it.

By mid-1978, I had been a security analyst for eight years and it had become intolerable. I knew I had to do something different. I always knew I wanted to work for myself, have no clients, and answer to no one. That, to me, was the ultimate goal. I had been brooding for years, "Why wasn't I doing well when I was groomed to be successful?" I decided it was now time to be successful.

When a brokerage firm wants to hire you, they'll give you anything. Once you are there, they are far less responsive. So, when I was being romanced by Hutton, I asked for a quote machine in my office. I was the only securities analyst that had a quote machine. During my last year at Hutton, I started closing the door to my office so that I could watch the market. I talked to my friend Bob Zoellner several times a day, and he taught me how to analyze market action. For example, when the market gets good news and goes down, it means the market is very weak; when it gets bad news and goes up, it means the market is healthy.

During that year, I started taking trial subscriptions to a lot of different newsletters. I consider myself a synthesizer; I didn't necessarily create a new methodology, but I took a number of different methodologies and molded them into my own approach.

I found a guy, Terry Laundry, who lived in Nantucket and had an unorthodox approach called the Magic T Forecast. He was an MIT engineering graduate with a math background, and that appealed to me. His basic theory was that the market spent the same amount of time going up as going down. Only the amplitude was different.

In my experience, markets come down a lot quicker than they go up. Doesn't that contradict the theory?

The market movement before it goes down may be a distributive process. I call them M-tops. The point you use to measure the time element is not the price high, but an oscillator high, which precedes the price high. That, in fact, is a major cornerstone of his work. The theory had different properties that I learned, and it has been extremely helpful to me.

For the record, what is the name of Laundry's book?

There is no book. He just extolled his theory through his various newsletters. He also had some pamphlets. Actually, it was kind of funny. After I mentioned him in a *Barron's* article, he got a lot of inquiries for his pamphlets. He is a little eccentric. His response was, "I don't have any copies available." He should have printed them and made some money.

I developed and synthesized a number of indicators that I used to determine when the market was at a lower-risk entry point. I focused on determining mathematical probabilities. Although occasionally there are situations where the market goes three standard deviations instead of two, based on the likelihood that 98 percent of the moves will stop at two standard deviations, I'll take that bet any day of the week. And, if I am wrong, I am going to use risk control and stop myself out X dollars away. That is the most critical element.

Anyway, I subscribed to all these letters, developed a methodology, and traded like crazy. By mid-1979, I had run $5,000 up to $140,000 in just two years.

When did you turn from a loser to a winner?

When I was able to separate my ego needs from making money. When I was able to accept being wrong. Before, admitting I was wrong was more upsetting than losing the money. I used to try to will things to happen. I figured it out, therefore it can't be wrong. When I became a winner, I said, "I figured it out, but if I'm wrong, I'm getting the hell out, because I want to save my money and go on to the next trade." By living the philosophy that my winners are always in front of me, it is not so painful to take a loss. If I make a mistake, so what!

Did you make a complete transition from fundamental to technical analysis?

Absolutely. I always laugh at people who say, "I've never met a rich technician." I love that! It is such an arrogant, nonsensical response. I used fundamentals for nine years and got rich as a technician.

But you were still doing fundamental analysis as an analyst?

Yes, to earn a salary. But my wife said to me, "Go out on your own. You're thirty-four and you've always wanted to work for yourself. The worst that can happen is that you'll go back to doing what you were doing before."

I always pictured myself as being brave, courageous, and strong, but when it came time to take the chance, I was scared out of my mind. I had $140,000, of which about $30,000 was tied up in tax deals and $92,500 was used to pay for a seat on the American Stock Exchange. That left me with about $20,000 when I went on the floor as a market maker. I borrowed $50,000 from my in-laws, which gave me $70,000 of working capital.

I started off losing in my first two days in the business. I got involved in Mesa Petroleum options because Zoellner, whom I profoundly respected, thought they were significantly undervalued. I called him the second day from the floor, "Are you sure you are right?" I must have had a grand total of ten options. I was down $1,800 and dying. I was petrified because, in my mind, I was down almost 10 percent, since I didn't consider my in-laws' money part of my own working capital. The third day, Mesa options started going up and I never looked back.

After the first four months, I was ahead by $100,000. The next year I earned $600,000. After 1981, I never earned less than seven figures. I remember talking to a good friend of mine in 1979 and saying, "I don't think anybody can make $40,000 a month trading options." Now I can do that in a day without a problem.

You were doing very well on the floor. Why did you leave?

It was very slow during lunchtime in those years. I used to go to an upstairs office to eat my lunch. While I was at my desk eating a sandwich,

I would do my charts and look for different ideas. I came to realize that I could see much more sitting at the desk, looking at a machine, than being at a post, trading an option. On the floor, the specialists chose the symbols they wanted to keep on the quote machines, because they paid the rent on them. So you always had to run around to find what you wanted to see. I felt much more comfortable upstairs.

About a year and a half later, after I started earning a lot of money, the floor wasn't big enough. There was a much bigger arena to play in. Another reason for my move was the fact that, in 1981, a change in the tax laws made it more lucrative to trade futures than stocks and options.

In my futures trading, I didn't try to make two one year, four the next, eight the next, etc. I didn't earn significantly more in my futures trading in 1987 than I did in 1982, because I used my profits to invest in real estate and other things to enhance the quality of my life.

I was broke in the 1970s, and I never wanted to be broke again. My philosophy was that if you make money every month, nothing bad is going to happen to you. So, you won't be the richest person. You'll never be the richest person anyway. What difference does it make? I'm proud of my futures trading, because I took $40,000 and ran it up to about $20 million with never more than a 3 percent drawdown.

Did you continue trading stocks during this period?

Yes, but with a different mentality. I traded stocks from a little longer time horizon. I don't feel the same pressure when I own 100,000 shares of stock as when I own 100 S&Ps.

Will you trade stocks as readily from the short side as the long side?

No, I find it harder to trade stocks from the short side.

Because of the uptick rule?

No, it is just easier to short the S&P, because you get so much more bang for the buck. Also, I hate the specialist system; they are always trying to con you to death. I'll give you my view on specialists: Never in my life have I met a less talented group of people who make a disproportionately large amount of money relative to their skills. Having the specialist book is the most extraordinary advantage one could ever ask for. In normal markets, the specialists can always define their risk. If they have a bid for 20,000 down ⅛, they can buy the stock, knowing they can always get out ⅛ lower. So, they are protected. I always tell my friends to have their daughters marry the son of a specialist.

I can't stand most established institutions. I have a me-against-them mentality, which I believe helps me be a better, more aggressive trader. It helps as long as I maintain an intellectual bias in my work and discipline in money management.

What was your experience during the week of the October 19 stock crash?

I came in long. I have thought about it, and I would do the same thing again. Why? Because on October 16, the market fell 108 points, which, at the time, was the biggest one-day point decline in the history of the stock exchange. It looked climactic to me, and I thought that was a buying opportunity. The only problem was that it was a Friday. Usually a down Friday is followed by a down Monday.

I don't think Monday would have been nearly as bad as it was, if Treasury Secretary James Baker had not started verbally bludgeoning the Germans about interest rates over the weekend. He was so belligerent. Once I heard Baker, I knew I was dead.

So, you knew that you were in trouble over the weekend?

Yes. Also, Marty Zweig, who is a friend of mine, was on "Wall Street Week" on Friday evening, talking about a possible depression. I called Marty the next day, and he said he thought there was another 500 points risk in the market. Of course, he didn't know it was going to happen in one day.

What made him so bearish at the time?

I think his monetary indicators were terribly negative. Remember, the bonds were sinking rapidly at the time.

What happened that Monday? When did you get out?

The high in the S&P on Monday was 269. I liquidated my long position at 267½. I was real proud of that because it is very hard to pull the trigger on a loser. I just dumped everything. I think I was long 40 contracts coming into that day, and I lost $315,000.

One of the most suicidal things you can do in trading is to keep adding to a losing position. Had I done that, I could have lost $5 million that day. It was painful, and I was bleeding, but I honored my risk points and bit the bullet.

That's another example where my Marine training came into play. They teach you never to freeze when you are under attack. One of the tactics in the Marine Corps officer's manual is either go forward or backward. Don't just sit there if you are getting the hell beat out of you. Even retreating is offensive, because you are still doing something. It is the same thing in the market. The most important thing is to keep enough powder to make your comeback. I did real well after October 19. In fact, 1987 was my most profitable year.

You liquidated your long position very well on October 19. Did you think about actually going short?

I thought about it, but I said to myself, "Now is not the time to worry about making money; it is the time to worry about keeping what you have made." Whenever there is a really rough period, I try to play defense, defense, defense. I believe in protecting what you have.

The day of the crash, I got out of most of my positions and protected my family. Then at 1:30 P.M., with the Dow down 275 points, I went to my safe deposit box and took my gold out. Half an hour later, I went to another bank and started writing checks to get my cash out. I started buying Treasury bills and preparing for the worst. I had never seen anything like what was going on.

You were seriously worried about the banks going under?

Why not? The stories I heard, subsequently, from people on the operations side of the business would have stopped the hearts of the public if they had known what was going on. The banks weren't meeting any of the calls at the brokerage firms. On Tuesday morning, we were within hours of the whole thing totally collapsing. So my caution was well advised.

I think my fear of a depression is related to my father graduating college in 1929. If you talk to people who got out of college at that time, it is as though a ten-year period is missing from their lives. There was just nothing substantial going on in this country. That always stuck with me, because I feared it so much. I think that is one of the reasons why I don't try to increase my earnings geometrically. On the day of the crash, when I looked at my son in his crib, I thought, I don't want him ever to ask me, "Dad, why didn't you do everything you could have done?"

When did you start trading again?

Wednesday of that week. It was funny because I started out trading only one or two S&P contracts at a time. The S&P was trading in *full point increments* [equivalent to $500 per contract, compared to $25 for a minimum tick], and I didn't know how to handicap what was going on. From past experiences, I knew we were in some sort of opportunity period, but they were rewriting the rule book. My attitude is: Never risk your family's security. I didn't need to make any more money at that point. On Wednesday, the market got up to an area where I thought it should be shorted. I ended Wednesday short twelve S&P contracts, which for me was a miniscule position.

That night, Bob Prechter [editor of the *Elliott Wave Theorist,* a widely followed advisory letter] put out a negative hotline message. The next morning, the market was under tremendous pressure, partially because of that recommendation, but mainly because one of the biggest fund managers in the country was trying to liquidate a monster long position. It has been stated that he lost $800 million during that period.

I called the S&P pit just before the opening that morning, and my clerk said, "Decembers are offered at 230, offered at 220, offered at 210, trading at 200 even." I yelled, "Cover!" I made a quarter of a million dollars on twelve contracts! It was one of the most memorable trades of my life.

What are your thoughts about program trading? [See Appendix 1 for definition.]

I hate it. There used to be a natural ebb and flow in the market, but program trading killed it. Those firms doing program trading wield extraordinary power to move the market, and the locals have simply become accomplices. I'm not just paranoid, because I've adjusted to it and been successful. But I hate it.

Some people say that all this criticism of program trading is a bunch of nonsense.

Well, they are idiots.

No, some of them are very intelligent people.

No, they are idiots. I can prove to any one of them that they are idiots.

How do you prove it?

There is something I would like the regulators to investigate. The market closes near the high or low of the day much more frequently than it used to. During the last two years, the market has closed within 2 percent of the high or low of the day about 20 percent of the time. Mathematically, that type of distribution is impossible by chance.

You talk about program trading as if it is immoral. What is unethical about trading stocks against futures?

Because the program traders also have the other side of the equation to do. You have the so-called Chinese wall in investment banking, where they don't want the arbitrageurs and investment bankers on the same floor for fear they might talk to each other. Well, I would like the SEC to explain to me how they can allow agency program traders sitting alongside principal traders for the firm's own account.

Your example introduces an element of frontrunning, which obscures the basic question. What I am trying to get at is: What is immoral about buying stock and selling futures (or the reverse trade) because prices in the two markets are out of line?

Because I've seen situations in which a firm has information about a debt/equity swap a day ahead of time. For example, when the state of New Jersey sold $2 billion worth of stock and moved it into the bonds, this firm knew about it the day before. Since they knew they were going to be selling $2 billion worth of stock the next day, from 4:00 to 4:15, they sold thousands of futures contracts to set up the trade. That stinks.

The example you just gave is (a) a case of trading on inside information, (b) frontrunning, and (c) an outright trade. It is not a program trade. Let me give you an example. Let's say a trading firm has a computer program that signals when stocks are overpriced or underpriced relative to futures, and they are not doing any customer business—

Let me give you an example first. If these brokerage firms need an 80-cent discount to take off a customer program, they will take off their own position at a 50-cent discount. They have the edge and can run in front of their clients because their transaction costs are lower—they're not paying commissions to themselves.

I keep trying to separate these things out. Let's take an example where there is no frontrunning or customer business—just somebody trading their own money, trying to take out an arbitrage profit. If that is their methodology, why is it any worse than your methodology?

Because it is a dumb game. Anybody who puts on a basket of stocks to earn 80 basis points above the T-bill yield is an idiot! They are the same idiots I tried to get away from when I left security analysis. Who the hell needs to earn 80 basis points over Treasury bills? The brokerage firms sell them this bill of goods because it is a way of creating more order flow, which on Wall Street today has become the ultimate power.

Are you saying program trading is wrong, even for some entity that is not trading customer money?

I grew up being a security analyst, analyzing things and buying something for value. Trading stocks against stock index futures, in and out, serves no useful purpose.

They are buying and selling, and you are buying and selling. What's the difference?

I am trying to earn infinity when I trade.

What makes that style any more right than the style which is trying to arbitrage the market?

I guess it is their constitutional right and they are able to do it, but there are some incredible abuses as a consequence. I scream at the kids who work for these brokerage firms: "You SOBs have no integrity, no ethics! You know what will happen? You are going to kill the game." Now they are swearing at me. When they stopped doing proprietary program trading they said, "Are you happy? You got your wish!" I said, "No, it is not quite finished yet." I didn't tell them the conclusion, which comes when they are no longer earning $300,000 or more a year, and they find out what they are really worth; when they are hitting the bricks and can't get a job for $50,000. Then it will have come full circle.

Speaking of circles, we seem to be moving in one on this subject. Let's go on. What stands out as your most dramatic trading experience?

The most gut-wrenching time was in November 1982. I had a much smaller net worth then, and I took a $600,000 loss in one day.

What happened?

It was Election Day, and the Republicans did much better than expected in the congressional races. The market ran up 43 points, which at that time was one of the largest point advances in history. I was short, and like an imbecile, I sold more with the S&P locked at the 500-point limit against me and less than an hour left in the trading session.

My wife, who was working with me at the time, was out that day. The next day she came into work, and every ten minutes she would say, "Get smaller, get smaller." I kept taking losses, just getting out of the position.

Whenever you get hit, you are very upset emotionally. Most traders try to make it back immediately; they try to play bigger. Whenever you try to get all your losses back at once, you are most often doomed to fail. That is true in everything—investments, trading, gambling. I learned from the crap table at Las Vegas to keep only X dollars in my pocket and never to have any credit, because the worst thing you can do is to send good money after bad. If you can physically remove yourself from the premises, which is the same thing in futures trading as getting flat, you can see things in a whole different perspective.

After a devastating loss, I always play very small and try to get black ink, black ink. It's not how much money I make, but just getting my rhythm and confidence back. I shrink my size totally—to a fifth or a tenth of the position that I trade normally. And it works. I think I ended up losing only $57,000 in November 1982, after taking a $600,000 hit on November 4.

Is there any trading mistake that you could isolate as responsible for that Election Day, 1982, loss?

Adding to shorts when the futures market is already locked-limit against you and the cash market looks like it is 200 points higher is pretty stupid.

When you look back, do you say, "Why did I do it?"

I think because I had huge gains the month before. I've always had my biggest setbacks after my biggest victories. I was careless.

Do you still make trading mistakes? By that, I mean deviations from trading principles you consider valid—not losing trades.

You always make trading mistakes. I made one just recently—a terrible mistake. I was short the S&P and short the bonds, and I got nervous because the bonds moved above their moving average. However, T-bills had not followed suit. One of my rules is not to have a position when my moving averages in T-bills and bonds diverge—that is, when one moving average is above the price and the other below—because interest rates can't move very far until one confirms the movement of the other. According to my rules, I should have moved my bond position from short to flat; instead, I reversed from short to long. I paid dearly for that mistake. Whereas, I had lost only about $20,000 on my original short position, the next day I had a six-figure loss—my largest loss of the year.

The great thing about being a trader is that you can always do a much better job. No matter how successful you are, you know how many times you screw up. Most people, in most careers, are busy trying to cover up their mistakes. As a trader, you are forced to confront your mistakes because the numbers don't lie.

From time to time, you have alluded to your trading rules. Can you list them?

[Reading from a list and extemporizing] I always check my charts and the moving averages prior to taking a position. Is the price above or below the moving average? That works better than any tool I have. I try not to go against the moving averages; it is self-destructive.

Has a stock held above its most recent low, when the market has penetrated its most recent low? If so, that stock is much healthier than the market. Those are the types of divergences I always look for.

Before putting on a position always ask, "Do I really want to have this position?"

After a successful period, take a day off as a reward. I've found it difficult to sustain excellent trading for more than two weeks at a time. I've had periods where I can be profitable for twelve days in a row, but eventually you just get battle fatigue. So, after a strong run of profits, I try to play smaller rather than larger. My biggest losses have always followed my largest profits.

This next rule is a major problem for me; I'm always trying not to break it. The rule: Bottom fishing is one of the most expensive forms of gambling. It's OK to break this rule on occasion if you have sufficient justification. For example, today, I bought the S&Ps when they were down sharply. Two weeks ago, I had written down the number 248.45

as the best entry for the S&P. The low today was 248.50. Consequently, I was able to buy into weakness today and make a good deal of money. I had a plan, I carried it out, and it worked. It doesn't always work. It was risky, but I wasn't pyramiding wildly into it, and I knew how much I was risking.

That brings me to my next rule: Before taking a position, always know the amount you are willing to lose. Know your "uncle point" and honor it. I have a pain threshold, and if I reach that point, I must get out.

When T-bonds and T-bills differ in respect to their individual relationship between price and the moving average—one above the moving average, the other below—have no position until one confirms the direction of the other. [Generally speaking, a price above its moving average implies a price uptrend, while the reverse case implies a price downtrend.]

Then, the last words I have at the bottom of the page are: Work, work, and more work.

Is there anything to add to that list?

The most important thing is money management, money management, money management. Anybody who is successful will tell you the same thing.

The one area that I am constantly trying to improve on is to let my gains run. I'm not able to do that well. I'm always working on it. To my dying day, I'll probably still be working on it.

Is that because you do something wrong?

I just love to take profits. I hear music when the cash register rings. The irony is: How can I be willing to risk 400 points on the downside and only take 200 points of a 1,000-point move on the upside?

On the risk side, you have a method, a plan. Have you experimented with trying to use similar discipline on the profit side?

Yes, but I haven't been able to perfect it. I have had varying degrees of success, but it is my greatest criticism of myself.

Why the difficulty in this area?

I think it all relates to my fears of some cataclysmic event. I'm like W. C. Fields: I have several bank accounts and a few safe deposit boxes with gold and cash. I'm extremely well diversified. My thought process is that if I screw up in one place, I'll always have a life preserver someplace else.

Any other rules you can think of?

Yes. If you're ever very nervous about a position overnight, and especially over a weekend, and you're able to get out at a much better price than you thought possible when the market trades, you're usually better off staying with the position. For example, the other day I was short the S&P and got nervous because the bond market was very strong on the night session. The next morning, the stock market was virtually unchanged. I was so relieved that I could get out without a loss, I covered my position. That was a mistake. A little later that day, the S&P collapsed. When your worst fears aren't realized, you probably should increase your position.

What has been your worst drawdown percentagewise?

My records were just evaluated for a money management deal. Over my entire career as a full-time trader, based on month-end data, my biggest drawdown was 3 percent. I had my worst two months around the birth of my two children, because I was worried about whether I was going to get the tennis ball in the right place in Lamaze class.

My philosophy has always been to try to be profitable every single month. I even try to be profitable every single day. And I've had some extraordinary runs—over 90 percent of my months have been profitable. I'm particularly proud of the fact that, in virtually every year, I didn't have a losing month before April. I probably don't make as much money as I could because of that, but I'm more concerned about controlling the downside.

You start off every year with a clean slate?

That's my philosophy: January 1, I'm poor.

Do you trade smaller in January?

Not necessarily. It is just that my attention is greater.

Do you take your losses more quickly in January?

No, I always take my losses quickly. That is probably the key to my success. You can always put the trade back on, but if you go flat, you see things differently.

Greater clarity?

Much greater clarity because the pressure you feel when you are in a position that is not working puts you in a catatonic state.

Getting back to managed money, I wonder, after years of making plenty of money trading on your own, what possible motive could you have for bothering with managing other people's money?

I felt that I was getting a little stale, and this presents a whole new challenge. Also, after October 1987, I realized that downside risk can't be adequately measured. The way to get more personal leverage is with an outside pool of money.

How much money are you going to be managing?

I don't want to be specific about the amount, but I'm only taking on one or two large pools of money. I don't want to deal with multiple investors, even though I'm certain I could raise a great deal more money if I went with a public underwriting.

The more people you have involved, the more potential headaches. For example, when I met a large fund manager, he asked me how many employees I had. I told him, "None." He told me he had seventy. When he wants to quit, it will be more difficult because he'll have their lives in his hands. I don't want that kind of pressure.

You seem rather isolated here. Do you like working alone?

It took me several years to be able to accept working alone. I used to go to a downtown office because a lot of my friends were there. But, as time passed and fewer of those people were still there, the attraction diminished significantly. Now, I have half a dozen people I talk to on the phone daily. I've taught my methodologies to a number of them, and they have methodologies of their own.

Have you ever tried training people to be traders working for you?

I hired four people, but nobody lasted. They all became intimidated. I tried to clone myself and it didn't work. I taught them all my methodologies, but learning the intellectual side is only part of it. You can't teach them your stomach.

Why do most traders lose money?

Because they would rather lose money than admit they're wrong. What is the ultimate rationalization of a trader in a losing position? "I'll get out when I'm even." Why is getting out even so important? Because it protects the ego. I became a winning trader when I was able to say, "To hell with my ego, making money is more important."

What do you tell people who seek your advice?

I always try to encourage people that are thinking of going into this business for themselves. I tell them, "Think that you might become more successful than you ever dreamt, because that's what happened to me." I have the freedom I always wanted, both financially and structurally. I can go on vacation at any moment. I live in Westhampton Beach half of the year and in New York the other half. I have a wonderful lifestyle. My kids think all fathers work at home.

What is the best advice you can give to the ordinary guy trying to become a better trader?

Learn to take losses. The most important thing in making money is not letting your losses get out of hand. Also, don't increase your position size until you have doubled or tripled your capital. Most people make the mistake of increasing their bets as soon as they start making money. That is a quick way to get wiped out.

Marty Schwartz's story should encourage those whose initial attempts at trading have met with failure. Here is a trader who was unsuccessful over a ten-year period, managing to lose enough money to keep himself near broke, despite consistently earning good salaries. Yet, Schwartz was eventually able to turn things around and become one of the world's best traders.

How did he do it? There were two essential elements. First, he found a methodology that worked for him. Throughout his losing years, Schwartz used fundamental analysis to determine his trades. It was not until he immersed himself in technical analysis that he became successful. The point here is not that technical analysis is better than fundamental analysis, but rather that technical analysis was the methodology that was right for him. Some of the other traders interviewed in this book, such as James Rogers, have been very successful using fundamental analysis to the complete exclusion of technical analysis. The key lesson is that each trader must find his or her own best approach.

The second element behind Schwartz's transition to success was a change in attitude. As he describes it, he became successful when his desire to win took precedence over his desire to be right.

Risk control is an essential element of Schwartz's trading style, as attested to by his incredibly low drawdowns. He achieves this risk control by always knowing his "uncle point" on any trade. No doubt, his approach of sharply reducing position size after large losses, as well as extended winning streaks, contributes heavily to his success. The rationale for reducing position size after a destabilizing loss is apparent.

However, the reason for taking the same action after a winning streak deserves further elaboration. As Schwartz explains it, he has always experienced his biggest losses after his biggest gains. I suspect this is true for the majority of traders. Winning streaks lead to complacency, and complacency leads to sloppy trading.

Most traders cite similar rules (such as discipline and hard work) as the reasons for their success. Therefore, it is always a treat when a top trader provides a rule that is unique and rings true. I was fascinated with Schwartz's observation about maintaining a position that you are worried about, when the market action doesn't justify your fears. The implicit concept is that if the market is letting you off the hook easily on a position for which there was a basis for fear (such as a fundamental development adverse to the position or a technical breakout in the opposite direction), there must be strong underlying forces in favor of the direction of the original position.

Part III

A Little Bit of Everything

James B. Rogers, Jr.

Buying Value and Selling Hysteria

Jim Rogers began trading the stock market with a paltry $600 in 1968. In 1973, he formed the Quantum Fund with partner George Soros. The Quantum Fund proved to be one of the best-performing hedge funds, and in 1980, having amassed a small fortune, Rogers retired. "Retired" is the word Rogers uses to describe the management of his personal portfolio, an endeavor that requires considerable ongoing research. His retirement also includes teaching investment courses at the Columbia University Graduate School of Business.

I was eager to interview Rogers because of his stellar reputation as one of the shrewdest investors of our time and because his comments on television financial interview shows and in the print media always seemed to strike a note of common sense with rare clarity. Since I did not know Rogers, I sent him a letter requesting an interview, explaining that I was working on a book on great traders. I included a copy of my previous book on the futures markets, which I inscribed with a quotation from Voltaire that I deemed particularly appropriate: "Common sense is not so common."

Rogers called a few days later to thank me for the book and to indicate his willingness to participate. "However," he cautioned, "I am probably not the person you want to interview. I often hold positions for many years. Furthermore, I'm probably one of the world's worst traders. I never get in at the right time." He was referring to the distinction I had made in my letter, indicating that I was interested in great traders rather than great investors.

As I use the term, a "trader" would be primarily concerned with which direction the stock market was heading, while an "investor" would concentrate on selecting stocks with the best chance of outperforming the market overall. In other words, the investor was always long, while the trader might be long or short. I explained my use of these terms to Rogers and stressed that he was indeed the type of person I wished to interview.

I arrived at Rogers' home, a baronial, eclectically furnished townhouse, on a fall-like spring afternoon. The atmosphere seemed more reminiscent of a comfortable English manor than a home in New York City. In fact, if my only exposure to New York City was that afternoon's conversation with Rogers in his antique-filled sitting room, with its pleasant views of the Hudson, I would conclude that New York City was an eminently peaceful place to live. After greeting me, Rogers immediately stated, "I still think you have the wrong man." Once again, he was referring to the fact that he did not consider himself to be a trader. This is the note on which the following interview begins.

As I told you in our phone conversation, I don't consider myself a trader. I remember when I went to buy German stocks in 1982, I said to the broker, "I want you to buy me X, Y, and Z stocks." The broker, who didn't know me, asked, "What do I do next?" I said, "You buy the stocks and send me the confirmations." He asked, "Do you want me to send you some research?" I said, "Please don't do that." He asked, "Do you want me to send you opinions?" I said, "No, no, don't." He asked, "Do you want me to call you with prices?" I said, "No, don't even give me prices, because if you do, once I see that these stocks have doubled and tripled, I might be tempted to sell them. I plan to own German stocks for at least three years, because I think you are about to have the biggest bull market you've had in two or three generations." Needless to say, the broker was dumbfounded; he thought I was a madman.

Now I don't consider that trading; it was determining that there was about to be a major change in a market and taking a position. By the way, I got that one right. I bought the German stocks at the end of 1982 and sold them out in late 1985 and early 1986.

What made you so bullish on Germany at that time?

The bull market had started here in August 1982. More important, Germany had not had any kind of bull market since the previous all-time high in 1961, twenty-one years earlier. The German market had crumbled in 1962 and had essentially gone sideways since then. In the meantime, the German economy had boomed. So there was basic value there.

Whenever I buy or sell something, I always try to make sure I'm not going to lose any money first. If there is very good value, then I'm probably not going to lose much money even if I'm wrong.

But you could have bought that market ten years earlier on the same theory.

That's absolutely right. You could have bought it in 1971 for exactly those reasons and watched German stocks sit for ten years, while we had a major bull market in the U.S. But this time there was a catalyst. You always need a catalyst to make big things happen. At the time, the catalyst was the upcoming German elections. I figured the Socialists were going to be thrown out, and I knew that the opposition party, the Christian Democrats, had a platform designed to encourage investment.

My basic assessment was that if the conservative Christian Democrats won the election after having been out of power for so many years, they were going to make major changes. I also knew that many German companies were holding back from investing in capital equipment and expansion in 1982 in anticipation of a conservative victory. Therefore, if the conservatives did win, there would be a real explosion of pent-up capital investment.

Was the election a toss-up at the time?

Not in my mind.

I mean in terms of the polls.

I guess so, because when the conservatives did win, the market exploded that same day.

What if they had lost?

I still didn't think I would have lost any meaningful money for the reasons I mentioned before. I had every anticipation that there was going to be a major change, and that the bull market would last for two, three, or four years.

It sounds like you have a great deal of conviction when you put on a trade.

Yes, I usually do; otherwise, I don't bother doing it. One of the best rules anybody can learn about investing is to do nothing, absolutely nothing, unless there is something to do. Most people—not that I'm better than most people—always have to be playing; they always have to be doing something. They make a big play and say, "Boy, am I smart, I just tripled my money." Then they rush out and have to do something else with that money. They can't just sit there and wait for something new to develop.

Do you always wait for a situation to line up in your favor? Don't you ever say, "I think this market is probably going to go up, so I'll give it a shot"?

What you just described is a very fast way to the poorhouse. I just wait until there is money lying in the corner, and all I have to do is go over there and pick it up. I do nothing in the meantime. Even people who lose money in the market say, "I just lost my money, now I have to do something to make it back." No, you don't. You should sit there until you find something.

Trade as little as possible.

That is why I don't think of myself as a trader. I think of myself as someone who waits for something to come along. I wait for a situation that is like the proverbial "shooting fish in a barrel."

Are all your trades fundamentally oriented?

Yes. Occasionally, however, the Commodity Research Bureau charts
will provide a catalyst. Sometimes the chart for a market will show an
incredible spike either up or down. You will see hysteria in the charts.
When I see hysteria, I usually like to take a look to see if I shouldn't be
going the other way.

Can you think of any examples?

Yes. Two years ago, I went short soybeans after they had gone straight
up to $9.60. The reason I remember it so vividly is because that same
evening, I went to dinner with a group of traders, one of whom was talking about all the reasons why he had bought soybeans. I said, "I really
can't tell you why all the bullish arguments are wrong; all I know is that
I'm shorting hysteria."

How do you pick the time to go against the hysteria?

I wait until the market starts moving in gaps.

**In the midst of it all, or do you wait for some sign of an end to the
move, for example, a reversal day?**

No, I don't know about reversal days.

**That brings to mind a classic example of hysteria. In late 1979–early
1980, the gold market witnessed an incredible accelerated advance.
Did you go short that market?**

Yes, I sold gold at $675.

That was almost $200 too early!

I told you I'm not a good trader. I'm nearly always too early, but it was
only about four days before the top.

I didn't say you were way off timewise, but pricewise it must have been a pretty scary ride. When you do a trade like that, isn't there a point where you have second thoughts?

Yes, when it goes to $676 [he laughs].

But you stayed with the trade?

Yes, in that case, because it was chaos. It was something that couldn't last. It was the gold market's dying gasp.

Was that a matter of recognizing the fingerprint of a market in its final blowoff, or was it a matter of gold being overpriced?

Both. Gold was overpriced, but basically it was—I like your terminology—the "fingerprint" of hysteria. Just about every time you go against panic, you will be right if you can stick it out.

So when you see panic, do you automatically go against it?

The panic, the hysteria, in and of itself is only a catalyst to make me look to see what is going on. It doesn't mean I'm going to do anything. In the case of the early 1980 gold market, I had a view of the world that was bearish for gold. Volcker had just become the Federal Reserve Chairman a few months earlier and said that we were going to beat inflation. I believed he meant it. I also happened to be bearish on oil at the time, and I knew that if oil went down, gold would go down as well.

Was that because you thought gold and oil should move together, or because you thought the rest of the world believed that?

At that time, everybody in the world believed that.

But, did you believe that the relationship was true?

I knew that it was *not* true.

The reason I asked is that I have always felt that the relationship between gold and oil was a coincidental correlation.

Yes, that was all it was. For one very short period of time, gold and oil moved together.

Does that mean you will sometimes do a trade based on a relationship you know doesn't really make any sense, simply because you think that the rest of the world believes it?

Rarely. I usually like to look at what I think is the fact, the truth. The main item then was that I thought Volcker meant it when he said he was going to break the back of inflation. The fact that oil was ready to go down anyway was just the kicker.

Actually, the decisive step came in October 1979, when the Fed changed its policy from controlling interest rates to controlling money supply growth. Yet the gold market apparently didn't believe it, because it went up for several months after that point. In situations like that, are the markets too wound up in their hysteria to pay attention to changing fundamentals?

Absolutely. It is amazing how sometimes something important will happen, and the market will keep going despite that. Now, I am experienced enough to know that just because I see something doesn't mean that everyone sees it. A lot of people are going to keep buying or selling just because that has been the thing to do.

So, just because the market doesn't respond to some important news, such as the October 1979 change in Fed policy, doesn't mean that it isn't important.

All the better. If the market keeps going the way it shouldn't go, especially if it is a hysterical blowoff, then you know an opportunity will present itself.

Can you think of a more recent example?

Yes, October 1987. October 19 is my birthday, by the way. At the end
of 1986 and the beginning of 1987, I had predicted that we would have
one more big move up in the stock market and then witness the worst
bear market since 1937. But I didn't know it was going to happen on my
birthday. It was the best birthday present I ever had.

Did you have any idea that the break could be as large as it was?

When John Train interviewed me in January 1987, I told him, "Somewhere along the way, the market is going to go down 300 points in one
day." He looked at me as though I were a madman. I envisioned that the
Dow would be around 3,000, and 300 points would only be 10 percent.
In 1929, the market went down 12 percent in one day. Ten percent in
one day was not such a big move, given the kind of markets we were
having then. The market had already seen a number of 3, 4, and 5 percent days. So I said, "Why can't the market go down 300 points in a
day?" Little did I know it would be 508 points.

**Why did you pick 1937 as a comparison in your prediction for a
stock market collapse?**

Because in 1937, the Dow went down 49 percent in six months. What I
was trying to say was that we were going to have a major, fast, deep,
horrible collapse, as opposed to say 1973–1974, when the market went
down 50 percent, but it took two years.

Why did you use 1937 as an analogy as opposed to 1929–1930?

Because 1929–1930 went on to be a major depression. I knew we were
going to have a bear market caused by a major financial collapse. I was
not convinced we were going to have a depression. I was differentiating
between a financial and economic collapse.

Why were you expecting a financial collapse?

It was the atmosphere. Money was flooding the world. Every stock market in the world was at an all-time high. You had all these stories of young guys, three years out of school, making half a million dollars a year. That is not reality. Whenever you see that in a market, you are near a top. So, I went into the summer positioned for a collapse.

Were you short stocks or long puts?

I was short stocks and short calls. I don't buy options. Buying options is another fast way to the poorhouse. Someone did a study for the SEC and discovered that 90 percent of all options expire as losses. Well, I figured out that if 90 percent of all long option positions lose money, that meant that 90 percent of all short option positions make money. If I want to use options to be bearish, I sell calls.

When did you cover your positions?

During the week of October 19. If you remember, by that time, everybody thought that the financial structure of America was over.

Did you cover then because we had hysteria going the other way?

That is exactly right. That week was a textbook case of hysteria. Under those kind of conditions, if you are still solvent, you have to step in there and go against it. Maybe that was going to be the one time it was the end of the world, and I would have been wiped out too. But 95 percent of the time when you go against that kind of hysteria, you are going to make money.

Between October 1987 and January 1988, I didn't have any shorts. That was one of the few times in my whole life that I didn't have any shorts. Whether I am bullish or bearish, I always try to have both long and short positions—just in case I'm wrong. Even in the best of times, there is always somebody fouling up, and even in the worst of times, there is somebody doing well.

Are you implying that after the collapse, you couldn't find any stocks you wanted to be short?

I thought that if I were right and the world wasn't coming to an end right away, everything was going to go up—including those stocks that I knew, fundamentally, were coming apart at the seams. In January [1988], I started putting a couple of shorts back on, and even though I am losing money on one of those shorts, I am happy to do it because I feel more comfortable having the protection of some short positions.

A lot of people blame the October 1987 break on program trading. Do you consider that scapegoatism?

Absolutely. The people who blame it on that do not understand the market. Politicians and people who lose money always look for scapegoats. In 1929, they blamed the crash on short sellers and margin requirements. There were lots of good reasons why the stock market went down. What they should focus on is why there were sellers on October 19, but no buyers.

I remember why I became even more bearish on the weekend before October 19. The week before, [Federal Reserve Chairman] Alan Greenspan announced that the balance of trade was getting much better and things were under control. Two days later, the balance of trade figures came out, and they were the worst in the history of the world. Right away I said, "This guy is either a fool or a liar. He doesn't have any idea what is going on." Then on the weekend before October 19, you had [Treasury Secretary] Baker telling the world we were going to stick it to the Germans by letting the dollar go, because the Germans weren't loosening monetary and fiscal policy as Baker had demanded. It looked like the trade wars of the 1930s all over again.

I was in a panic—and I was already short! I called Singapore that Sunday night to add to my shorts. [Singapore opens earlier than we do.] So all those guys who came in on Monday to sell had very, very good reasons to sell, and there were no buyers around. There were no buyers, because there was no reason for people to buy. Even the buyers were scared and bearish that Monday.

Are you saying the crash was caused by Greenspan and Baker?

There were a lot of causes: Greenspan, Baker, the fact that money was tight, the steady worsening of the balance of trade, and you had a market that had spiked up to 2,700 six weeks earlier. If you check, you will see that, during 1987, while the S&P and the Dow were going up, the rest of the market was quietly eroding away. In December 1986, I shorted the financial stocks, and throughout 1987, I didn't lose any money, even though the Dow and the S&P were going through the roof.

Were there any times you faded hysteria and lost?

Yes, one of my greatest lessons happened in my early days and taught me about bear markets. In January 1970, a time when I still bought options, I took all the money I had—which wasn't very much—and bought puts. In May 1970, the market caved in, and the day the market hit bottom, I sold my puts. I had tripled my money. I was a genius! "I'm going to be the next Bernard Baruch," I said to myself.

My plan then was to wait for the market to rally and this time to sell short instead of buying puts so that I would make money faster. Sure enough the market rallied, and I took everything I had and went short. Needless to say, two months later, I was completely wiped out because I didn't know what I was doing.

One of the stocks I had shorted was Memorex. I sold Memorex at 48. In those days, I didn't have the staying power—psychologically, emotionally, and, most important, financially. I ended up covering my shorts at 72. Memorex eventually went to about 96 and then went straight down to 2.

I was dead right, absolutely, flat-out, perfectly right to short that stock at 48. I just ended up getting completely wiped out. The market didn't care that I was dead right. That is one of the reasons that I now know about hysteria.

What did you learn from that particular experience?

That the market is going to go higher than I think it can and lower than I think it will. I had a tendency to think that if I knew something, everybody knew it. I would just read things in the paper; I didn't have any inside information. What I now know is that they don't know what I know. Most people don't have the foresight to look six months, one year, or two years out. The Memorex experience taught me that anything can happen in the stock market, because there are a lot of people in the market who don't understand what is going on.

Are you looking for a very pronounced bear market beyond what we have already seen?

Yes, eventually I expect the market to break the October 1987 low.

Do you expect a very deep recession as well?

Right now [April 1988], I'm still looking mainly for a financial collapse. However, the politicians may foul it up and turn it into an economic collapse.

Can we get a financial collapse without actually having a very serious recession?

Sure. It has happened lots of times. That is why I used 1937 as an example before. I don't expect the economy to collapse because as the dollar keeps getting weaker—which is what I expect—many parts of the American economy will do well—steel, agriculture, textiles, mining.

So even if the stock market falls below the October low, you can still see the economy doing well?

Absolutely. Unless the politicians foul it up.

By doing what?

Raising taxes, tariffs, protectionism. There are lots of things the politicians can do to foul it up, and I'm sure they will—they always have. I know we will have a financial crisis. And, if the politicians get it wrong, we may get an economic collapse as well.

What is going to trigger the financial collapse?

The trade figures will start getting worse again, and this will eventually precipitate another dollar crisis.

What do you see as the main cause of the trade deficit?

The budget deficit, by and large, causes the trade deficit. You are not going to get rid of the trade deficit until you get rid of the budget deficit.

Given the magnitude of the deficit problem, is there anything that can be done at this point?

The basic problem in the world today is that America is consuming more than it is saving. You need to do everything you can to encourage saving and investment: Eliminate taxation of savings, the capital gains tax, and dual taxation of dividends; bring back the more attractive incentives for IRAs, Keoghs, and 401Ks. At the same time, you need to do everything you can to discourage consumption. Change our tax structure to utilize a value added tax, which taxes consumption rather than saving and investing. Cut government spending dramatically—and there are lots of ways of doing it without hurting the economy too badly. We would have problems, but the problems would not be nearly as bad as when they are forced on us. If we don't bite the bullet, then we are going to have a 1930s-type collapse.

Your answer implies that there are relatively painless ways to cut government spending "dramatically." Could you provide some specific examples?

I'll give you two examples; I could give you a dozen. The U.S. government spends $5 billion a year to support the domestic price of sugar so that Americans can pay 22 cents a pound wholesale, when it is selling for 8 cents a pound in the world market. Five billion dollars! We would be better off if the government told every sugar grower, "We'll give you $100,000 a year for the rest of your life, a condominium, and a Porsche if you just get out of the sugar business." We would save billions of dollars a year, and the whole country would be better off because we would all be paying less for sugar.

If you really want to save a big number, do you know what our annual balance of trade deficit is? One hundred and fifty billion dollars. Do you know what it costs us each year to keep American troops stationed in Europe? One hundred and fifty billion dollars. American troops were sent there as an army of occupation forty-three years ago! Most people in this country weren't even born when the decision was made to send our troops to Europe. They are doing nothing there but sitting around, drinking beer, getting fat, and chasing girls. The GAO has said that we don't have enough bullets to fight even a thirty-day war in Europe. Yet it costs us $150 billion a year to keep those guys there. I would submit to you that if we stop spending that $150 billion a year and bring those troops home, the Europeans would defend themselves. And the kicker is: Do you know who they would buy their guns from? They would buy their guns from us, because they don't have a very good defense industry establishment.

But those are very unlikely actions. No politicians are even talking about those solutions.

I understand that. With the present cast of jerks in Washington, it is not going to happen. The politicians are going to foul things up. They are not going to do what has to be done. They are going to be more concerned about keeping their votes and winning the next election. That is going to continue until we are forced into solving our problems. Then it is going to be a disaster.

If the politicians don't act, do we eventually face a choice between very high inflation or a deep recession?

It is going to be an extreme. What I suspect will happen—and I am just speculating, I don't have to make this decision yet—is that somewhere along the line a recession will develop. Initially, the politicians will say, "We've got to bite the bullet and suffer through this. This is good for us; it will help clean out our system." People are going to buy that for a while. Then it is going to start to hurt. Then it is really going to start to hurt. At that point, the politicians are going to give up, and they are going to start to inflate their way out of it. But the only way to inflate your way out at that point is to really print money!

In that scenario, we start off with a recession and end up with very high inflation.

Right, but we could have wild inflation first and then deflation. Another very real possibility is that we will eventually have exchange controls. Fortunately, I don't have to make my investment decisions for two or three years forward right now.

What kind of exchange controls?

By exchange controls I mean limitations on capital flows. If you want to go to Europe, you can't take more than $1,000. You can't ship money out of the country without the government's approval.

What happens to the relative values of currencies in a situation like that?

The dollar disappears. What would bring on exchange controls is the dollar getting weaker and weaker. The politicians would then try to bring in Draconian exchange controls, which would just make the situation worse.

When you say disappear, are you talking about the dollar becoming like the Argentine peso?

Why not? Why couldn't it happen? Remember the Civil War expression, "I don't give a damn about a greenback dollar."

You talk about the collapse of the dollar as if it's an inevitability.

In 1983, we were the largest creditor nation in the world. In 1985, we became a debtor nation for the first time since 1914. By the end of 1987, our foreign debts were greater than all of the foreign debts of every nation south of the Rio Grande put together: Brazil, Mexico, Peru, Argentina, and all the rest.

Can I paraphrase the chain of events you imply as follows: Nothing meaningful will be done to change the budget deficit situation. The continued budget deficit will guarantee that the trade deficit situation stays bad or even gets worse. That, in turn, guarantees that sooner or later, the dollar will come under extreme pressure.

Absolutely. That's why I'm not long the dollar.

How does the bond market fit into this scenario?

At some point, foreigners are going to stop putting money into this country because of the weakening dollar. That means the American public will have to finance the debt. We have only a 3 to 4 percent savings rate. To get the American public to finance that debt, interest rates would have to be very high. If the Federal Reserve tries to avoid high rates by printing more money, then the dollar just disappears and the Fed loses control completely. That is the case where you get hyperinflation and 25 to 30 percent interest rates. Either way, we are going to have high rates. You might start out with lower rates first if the politicians decide to bite the bullet by having a recession. But then, they will eventually give up and start printing money.

But, sooner or later, the bond market collapses.

Absolutely. Sooner or later, we repeat the English experience of not having a long-term bond market. But I don't know when sooner or later is. It could be three years; it could be ten.

How far did British bonds fall in the situation you are referring to?

About 70 percent.

What kind of things do you look at in deciding which scenario will happen first: deflation or inflation?

Money supply, government deficits, trade deficits, inflation figures, the financial markets, and government policy. I look at all those things for the U.S. and key foreign countries as well. It is one big, three-dimensional puzzle. However, if you had a three-dimensional puzzle, you could eventually put it together. But this puzzle is not one in which you can spread out the pieces on a great big table and put them all together. The picture is always changing. Every day some pieces get taken away and others get thrown in.

While we are on the topic of scenarios, do you have a long-term outlook for gold?

In 1934, they set the price of gold at $35 an ounce and gold production declined every year between 1935 and 1980. Production kept going down because there was no incentive to look for gold. During that whole forty-five-year period, the consumption of gold kept going up, especially during the 1960s and 1970s, when we had the electronic revolution. Demand got bigger and bigger, while at the same time, the supply was going down. You would have had a great bull market in gold in the 1970s, no matter what. Even if inflation was at zero percent, you still would have had a big bull market in gold during the 1970s, because of supply and demand.

The situation has changed entirely in the 1980s. There is nothing like taking the price of gold from $35 to $875 to make people go into the gold business. Gold production has gone up every year since 1980. Just based on known projections for mine openings and expansions, gold production is scheduled to go up every year until at least 1995. At the same time, there have been major technological advances in the recovery processes for gold. In short, there is much more gold available than there used to be, and that trend will continue at least into the mid-1990s.

I own some gold as an insurance policy, but I don't think gold is going to be the great inflation hedge of the 1990s that it was in the 1970s, because supply and demand is so different. I don't know what the inflation hedge of the 1990s will be yet, but fortunately, I don't have to decide today.

The supply/demand picture you are painting for gold is obviously negative. But if you put that together with a situation in which, using your own words, "the dollar disappears," wouldn't such an event swamp the internal supply/demand balance of gold?

Certainly, gold may keep its purchasing power. It may do better, it may do worse, but it's not going to be the best market.

In other words, gold was yesterday's inflation hedge.

Generals always fight the last war. Portfolio managers always invest in the last bull market. The idea that gold has always been the great store of value is absurd. There have been many times in history when gold has lost purchasing power—sometimes for decades.

I should add something else about gold. Remember that three-dimensional puzzle I was talking about, where there are always pieces being removed and added. Don't forget South Africa in that puzzle. Gold is more complicated because of the South African situation. I fully expect South Africa to eventually blow up, because I think that the government has painted itself too far into a corner. If there were a revolution tomorrow and the blacks took over, the South African whites would dump all their gold. So the price would actually go down a lot.

In a situation like that, I would think the price of gold would go up sharply, because of the panic related to disruptions in mine production.

While the revolution is going on, the price will go up, but after that, it will go down. The move down will completely confuse everybody. They will ask, "Why is the price of gold moving down?" But you will want to buy after that move down, because the euphoria of the revolution will also bring chaos.

We have talked about your long-term views for the stock market, bonds, currencies, and gold. Any thoughts about oil?

Yes, when the recession hits—and I guarantee it will some day—the price of oil is going to go way down. You can put that in writing; I don't mind saying that. It certainly is going to go under $12. Whether that is $11 or $7 or $3, I don't know. [The price of oil was approximately $16 at the time of this interview.]

Given the general scenario you are talking about—the stock market going down, the dollar going down, etc.—is there anything that the average guy can do to protect himself?

Buy European and Far Eastern currencies; buy Treasury bills; buy farm land.

How did you first get interested in trading?

Investing. I stumbled onto Wall Street. In 1964, I had just finished college and was going on to graduate school. I got a summer job through a guy I met, who happened to work for a Wall Street firm. I didn't know anything about Wall Street at the time. I didn't know the difference between stocks and bonds. I didn't even know that there *was* a difference between stocks and bonds. All I knew about Wall Street was that it was somewhere in New York and something unpleasant had happened there in 1929.

After that summer, I went to Oxford during 1964–1966. Whereas all the Americans I knew at Oxford were interested in politics, I was more interested in reading the *Financial Times*.

Were you trading while you were at Oxford?

Very lightly. I was an odd lotter. The money I was investing in the market was my scholarship money at Oxford. I would get my scholarship money at the beginning of the year and invest as long as I could.

Not exactly deep pockets.

[He laughs] If I had lost much money in either of those two years—

So you actually started making money right off the bat?

Yes, I was making money. That was the bull market of 1964–1965. By the time I left Oxford in the summer of 1966, the bear market had started, but I had already paid off my bills. I was lucky. If I had gone to Oxford during 1965–1967, I probably would have gotten wiped out.

What happened after Oxford?

I was in the army for a couple of years, and since I didn't have any money, I couldn't follow the market. In 1968, the day I got out of the army, I went to work on Wall Street. I invested everything I could. My first wife used to say, "We need a TV." I said, "What do we need a TV for? Let's put the money in the market, and we could have ten TVs." She said, "We need a sofa." I said, "We could have ten sofas if we just put the money in the market for a little while."

What kind of job did you get on Wall Street?

Junior analyst.

Covering what stocks?

Machine tools and then advertising agencies.

Were you investing in the stocks you were covering?

I invested in anything.

Successfully?

I came into the market on August 1, 1968, right at the top. But I still had some money left, and in January 1970, I figured out it was going to be a bear market. I don't know how I figured it out. As I mentioned earlier, I took all the money I had and bought puts. By May, I had tripled my money. In July, I started shorting stocks, and by September, I was wiped out. Those first two years were great: I went from being a genius to a fool.

So you were back to ground zero in September 1970. What happened then?

I saved everything I had and put it back into the market. I didn't care about a TV or a sofa. The wife got rid of me. I was the entrepreneurial spirit personified. Just like those guys who build up great retail chains, and plow everything back into their stores, I was plowing everything back into the market.

Were you trading just stocks at this time?

Bonds, stocks, currencies, commodities.

When did you get involved in these different markets?

I traded all of them almost from the very beginning. Bonds and stocks from day one. Currencies fairly early too. When I was at Oxford, I kept as much money in dollars as I could, because I knew they were going to devalue sterling any day. I knew it was coming, and it did—a year after I left. Once again, I was a little early. Even then, I had a strong awareness of currencies.

In the late 1960s, I also got involved in commodities by buying gold. In my early years in the business, I remember interviewing for a job. The fellow asked me, "What do you read in the *Wall Street Jour-*

nal?" I said, "One of the first things I read is the commodity page." The guy was stunned, because he did too. This was back before commodities were *commodities*. He offered me a job, and when I turned him down, he almost strangled me. This job interview was in 1970, and I was already trading commodities.

Going from ground zero in September 1970, where did you start picking up tradingwise to build up to your ultimate trading success?

My early losses taught me a lot. Since then—I don't like to say this kind of thing—I have made very few mistakes. I learned quickly not to do anything unless you know what you are doing. I learned that it is better to do nothing and wait until you get a concept so right, and a price so right, that even if you are wrong, it is not going to hurt you.

Did you have a losing year after that point?

No.

How did the Quantum Fund get started?

George Soros was the senior partner, and I was the junior partner. We started off with one senior partner, one junior partner, and one secretary.

How did you know George Soros?

In 1970, I went to work for him at Arnhold and S. Bleichroeder. We left in 1973 because new brokerage firm regulations did not allow you to get a percentage of the trading profits. We could have stayed, but we couldn't have managed money. So we had to leave—fortunately. We left and started our own firm.

What kind of trading did you do for the Quantum Fund? As I understand it, that fund was managed differently from the typical fund.

We invested in stocks, bonds, currencies, commodities, everything— long and short—all over the world.

Did you and George make independent trading decisions?

No. If you broke down the division of labor, he was the trader and I was the analyst.

Did you come up with the idea, for example, shorting the dollar, and did he decide the timing of when to do it?

Yes, sort of.

What if you disagreed on a market?

Usually if we disagreed, we just did nothing.

So, you both had to agree on a trade to do it?

There were no rules. Sometimes we would disagree and do the trade anyway, because one of us felt more strongly. But that type of scenario rarely came up, since we were usually in agreement, and once we worked things through, it was pretty clear that the trade was either right or wrong. When we thought something through, a consensus was formed. I hate to use that word, because consensus investing is a disaster, but we almost always seemed to come together.

When you were trading leveraged products such as commodities and currencies, how did you determine what your allocation was?

Until we ran out of money, we were always leveraged to the hilt. When we bought something and ran out of money, we would look at the portfolio and push out whatever appeared to be the least attractive item at that point. For example, if you wanted to buy corn and ran out of money, you either had to stop buying corn or sell something else. It was an amoebic process. You know how amoebas grow—they grow out this way, then they run into pressure so they grow out the other way. It was a very amoebic portfolio.

You never evaluated the risk of your positions on an individual basis? So, if you lost money in one market and had to reduce your portfolio, you might just as easily cut back in another market?

Right. We would always cut back on what we thought were the least attractive positions in the portfolio.

Even today, that sounds like a very unconventional fund. Back then, I imagine it was probably unique in terms of its investment strategy.

It certainly was unique. I still don't know anybody who trades all the markets. By all the markets, I mean all the currencies, commodities, bonds, and stocks—long and short—all over the world. I am retired now, and I still do all these markets. People say to me, "You're retired? We have a full staff and can't even keep up with all these markets. What do you mean you are retired? You are short stocks all over the world!"

I must admit, I find it amusing when you say you are retired.

Now in my retirement, I'm more active than anybody, and people say, "How do you follow all these things?"

I have the same question.

I don't see how you can invest in American steel without understanding what is going on in Malaysian palm oil. As I explained before, it is all part of a big, three-dimensional puzzle that is always changing.

How do you find enough time to spend on all those markets? Just the reading itself seems to be a monumental chore.

I do not do it nearly as actively as I used to. Over the years, I have spent a great deal of time pouring a lot of stuff into my head. I have developed a great deal of perspective on many markets. When I teach, students are always astonished by the range of historical markets that I am familiar with. I know about these markets because I have pored over many commodity, bond, and stock books so many times, for so many years. As an example, I knew about the great bull market in cotton in 1861, when cotton went from ½ cent to $1.05.

How do you find out about a market like that?

I start by finding the anomalous years in a long-term historical chart. When I see a picture like the 1861 cotton market, I ask myself, "What caused that? Why did that happen?" Then I try to figure it out. From that, you learn an enormous amount.

In fact, one of the courses I teach at Columbia, which the kids call "Bulls and Bears," requires each student to find a major historical market move. It doesn't matter which market, or whether the move was up or down. My instructions are for them to tell me what one could have known at the time to see the big move coming. When rubber was at 2 cents everyone said, "How can rubber ever go up?" Yet it went up twelvefold. Somebody saw it. I always ask them, "What could you have seen at the time?" I always nail them. They will say, "I knew the market would go up because there was going to be a war." But I will make them tell me how they could have known at the time that there was a war coming. The course gives them historical perspective across a broad spectrum of markets and teaches them how to analyze.

I have lived through or studied hundreds, possibly even thousands, of bull and bear markets. In every bull market, whether it is IBM or oats, the bulls always seem to come up with reasons why it must go on, and on, and on. I remember hearing hundreds of times, "We are going to run out of supply." "This time is going to be different." "Oil has to sell at $100 a barrel." "Oil is not a commodity [he laughs]." "Gold is different from every other commodity." Well, damn, for 5,000 years it has not been different from every other commodity. There have been some periods when gold has been very bullish, and other periods when it has gone down for many years. There is nothing mystical about it. Sure, it has been a store of value, but so has wheat, corn, copper—everything. All these things have been around for thousands of years. Some are more valuable than others, but they are all commodities. They always have been, and they always will be.

I guess the 1987 stock market is a prime recent example of the "this time is going to be different" complacency.

Right. There was going to be a shortage of stocks again. In 1968, one of the major Wall Street houses published a great learned thesis on why there was a shortage of stocks developing, and why the bull market had to keep going up for years—right at the top. In 1987, you started hearing it all over again: "There is a shortage of stocks, because everybody is buying in all this stock." At the bottom of the bear market [he begins a laugh that builds steadily] there is going to be a shortage of money— I assure you—with a gigantic surplus of stocks.

While editing this chapter, I came across the following item in a *Time* magazine story about the incredible bull market on the Tokyo Stock Exchange (August 8, 1988, p. 29). One could hardly ask for a better current example of "this time is going to be different." The subject of the Japanese stock market actually comes up slightly later in this interview.

The explosive growth worries some Western financial experts, who fear that the boom could go bust. If that happened, investors with heavy losses in Tokyo could be forced to pull money out of other markets, triggering another crash. Japanese stocks are already trading at astronomical prices in comparison with the profits of the companies that issued the shares, at least by American standards. On the New York Stock Exchange, such price-earnings ratios run about 15 to 1, while in Tokyo the multiples are often four times as high. Nippon Telegraph & Telephone trades at 158 times its earnings. "Japanese authorities have allowed a speculative bubble to grow," warns George Soros, manager of the New York City–based Quantum Fund, "At no time in the past has a bubble of this magnitude been deflated in an orderly manner."

Such worries are groundless, argue analysts in Tokyo. The Japanese attribute the high price-earnings ratios in part to accounting rules that allow companies to understate earnings to keep their taxes lower. Another factor propping up prices is so-called cross-holding of stock. Because many Japanese companies hold large blocks of other companies' stock, which out of tradition are seldom traded, fewer shares are available for purchase so their prices rise.

Is there a lot of similarity between different cases of market hysteria?

It's always the same cycle. When a market is very low, there comes a time when some people buy it because it has become undervalued. The market starts to go up, and more people buy because it is a fundamentally sound thing to do, or because the charts look good. In the next stage, people buy because it has been the thing to do. My mother calls me up and says, "Buy me XYZ stock." I ask her, "Why?" "Because the stock has tripled," she answers. Finally, there comes the magical stage: People are hysterical to buy, because they know that the market is going to go up forever, and prices exceed any kind of rational, logical economic value.

The whole process then repeats itself on the downside. The market gets tremendously overpriced and it starts to go down. More people sell because the fundamentals are turning poor. As the economics deteriorate, more and more people sell. Next, people sell just because it has been the thing to do. Everybody knows it is going to go to nothing, so they sell. Then the market reaches the hysteria stage and gets very underpriced. That's when you can buy it for a pop. But for a long-term investment, you usually have to wait a few years and let the market base.

Talking about extreme bull markets, I recently read that Australia sold a 1½ acre plot in Tokyo for $450 million that they bought for $250,000 twenty-five years ago. Is Japan the *tulipmania* of our day? [During 1634–1636, a speculative frenzy in tulips swept Holland, causing such an enormous rise and collapse in tulip bulb prices that the event is still famous today.]

I guarantee that the Japanese stock market is going to have a major collapse—possibly within the next year or two. Many of our stocks are going to go down 80 to 90 percent in the bear market. A lot more of theirs are going to go down 80 to 90 percent.

Is there any way the average U.S. trader can take advantage of that?

Short Japanese stocks, short Japanese indexes, short Japanese calls, buy Japanese puts. A lot of Japanese stocks trade here and you can just short them. You can short the Japanese index, which trades in Singapore and Osaka. Most American brokers can do it for you. There are at least five major Japanese corporations which have options traded on the Chicago Board Options Exchange. Although I think a collapse is coming, you have to be very careful about going short Japan, because they might change the rules on you at any time.

I don't know if you remember the Kuwaiti stock market of 1980–1981. In that market, you could buy stocks with a postdated check. You could buy $10 million worth of stocks with a postdated check; you could buy $100 million worth of stock that way. It didn't matter. Everybody was doing it. In the end, there was a passport clerk who owned $10 billion worth of stocks! All of it on postdated checks.

Although that market was a very clear example of hysteria, I didn't short it. I thought about it that long [he snaps fingers]. The reason I didn't go short was because I knew when the market caved in, they would create rules so that I would never get my money out. Of course, the market eventually collapsed. If I had gone short they would have blamed it on me and said I caused the damn thing by shorting. People were even blaming me for the October crash last year, because I said it was going to happen. Some people claim I caused oil prices to collapse, because I said the price of oil was going to go down. I wish I were that influential or powerful.

To get back to Japan, I have a few Japanese shorts, and I'm going to have more. But whatever I do in Japan, I know when the crisis comes, I don't want to be around near the bottom, because the Japanese are going to protect themselves. And whatever they do to protect themselves, it ain't going to be good for Jim Rogers. I guarantee that.

You may not be able to get your money out?

Yes, they could freeze the currency. They could have three different tiers of currency. God knows what they will do.

Wouldn't you be protected if you were short a Japanese market that traded on an American exchange like the CBOE?

Suppose they create two levels of currencies and the guy on the other side of the trade can't meet his obligation.

The clearinghouse is responsible.

OK, fine, I'm happy to hear it. That's the best news I've had in a long time. Still, whatever I do, I'm going to be careful. If the Japanese stock market goes from 30,000 to 24,000 or 20,000 that's fine. But you better think about getting out of it before the last bit if it goes to 12,000. If you wait that long, you may get your profits out, but it is going to be very painful.

Why did you leave the Quantum Fund?

I didn't want to do the same thing for the rest of my life. I always wanted to have more than one career. When I came to New York in 1968, I was a poor boy from Alabama. By 1979, I had made more money than I knew existed in the world. Also, we were getting very big. We had started with three people, and by 1979, we had fifteen people. They wanted to know when they could go on vacation, get raises, etc. I wasn't interested in any of that; I was interested in investing. I didn't want to get bigger.

In September 1979, I decided it would be my last year. But then, in October, there was a big collapse in the stock market, which we sailed right through. It was so much fun that I decided to stay on one more year. I left in 1980.

Was 1980 the start of your "retirement"?

Yes, in 1980, I just cashed in my chips and retired.

Is that the point you became an independent trader?

The term I really prefer is "unemployed."

Well, you teach at Columbia.

That's unemployed. I did it as a part-time thing starting in 1983 so that I could play squash.

I thought it was the love of teaching.

It has developed into much more. But when I started out, I didn't even want to teach. I just wanted to learn how to play squash.

You're not being facetious? You actually started teaching so you could play squash?

I'm dead serious. Columbia is right here and the Dean kept pestering me to teach a course. I told him, "I don't think people should go to business school." I thought that, for many people, business school was a waste of time. I still think so. But one thing I wanted to learn in my retirement was how to play squash. So I made a deal with the Dean to teach one course per semester for free, in return for lifetime access to the Columbia gym. He agreed. I thought I got a great deal, but he was smarter than I was—I'm still teaching.

I take it, at this point, you really enjoy it.

Oh, it's good fun, yes. And Columbia is terrific.

What courses are you teaching?

Security analysis, investment analysis, and the "Bulls and Bears" course we talked about before.

Of the multitude of your trading experiences, do any stand out as particularly dramatic?

Lots. My October 19 birthday present that I talked about earlier was probably the best. August 1982 is another. I put a gigantic part of my net worth into bonds throughout 1981 and 1982, and in August 1982, they skyrocketed.

Any negative dramatic experiences?

August 1971 was a very exciting time. We were long Japan and short America, and one Sunday night, Nixon announced that he was taking America off the gold standard. I didn't even know it had happened. I had been off somewhere on my motorcycle, and I came in Monday morning without having read the papers. That week the Japanese stock market went down 20 percent, and the U.S. stock market went up. We were losing heavily on both sides.

Did you have to liquidate your positions right off the bat?

You can't liquidate at a time like that. Who can you sell to in Japan? Who could you buy from in the U.S.? If you covered your shorts, you made things worse. In a situation like that, you have to figure out whether you are right or wrong. If there was going to be a major fundamental change forever, the first loss is the best loss. But if fundamentally you are basically correct, then you do nothing but sit there and let the market hysteria wash around you.

Did you stay with your positions?

Yes.

So, you really had to ride out a rather treacherous paper loss.

There is no such thing as a paper loss. A paper loss is a very real loss.

What was the analysis that gave you the confidence to stay with your positions?

Our analysis was that this was not the end of the world. America had simply taken a short-term step, and it was not going to solve our country's long-term problems.

Did that position actually turn out to be OK?

It turned out fine. The Nixon announcement was just another step in the
dissolution of the *Bretton Woods Agreement* [a 1944 international pact
that, among other things, established guidelines for foreign exchange rate
stabilization] and the decline of America. America was rallying in its
own bear market.

**So, you saw it as a cosmetic move that wasn't going to change the
trend, and you stayed with your position.**

Right.

**Is that a general principle: When government measures are imple-
mented to counteract a trend, you should sell the rally after the
government action?**

Absolutely. It should be written down as an axiom that you always invest against the central banks. When the central banks try to prop up a
currency, go the other way.

What is the biggest public fallacy regarding market behavior?

That the market is always right. The market is nearly always wrong. I
can assure you of that.

What else?

Never, ever, follow conventional wisdom in the market. You have to
learn to go counter to the markets. You have to learn how to think for
yourself; to be able to see that the emperor has no clothes. Most people
can't do it. Most people want to follow a trend. "The trend is your friend."
Maybe that is valid for a few minutes in Chicago, but for the most part,
following what everyone else is doing is rarely a way to get rich. You
may make money that way for a while, but keeping it is very hard.

But actually, your whole style of trading involves staying with a trend for years. So isn't what you are saying contradictory?

That kind of trend—a trend that is economically justified—is different. You have to see the supply/demand balance change early, buy early, and only buy markets that are going to go on for years. By "trend following," I meant buying a market just because it goes up and selling it just because it goes down.

What trading rules do you live by?

Look for hysteria to see if you shouldn't go the opposite way, but don't go the opposite way until you have fully examined the situation. Also, remember that the world is always changing. Be aware of change. Buy change. You should be willing to buy or sell anything. So many people say, "I could never buy that kind of stock," "I could never buy utilities," "I could never play commodities." You should be flexible and alert to investing in anything.

If you were counseling the average investor, what would you tell him?

Don't do anything until you know what you are doing. If you make 50 percent two years in a row and then lose 50 percent in the third year, you would actually be worse off than if you just put your money in a money market fund. Wait for something to come along that you know is right. Then take your profit, put it back in the money market fund, and just wait again. You will come out way ahead of everybody else.

Are you ever wrong on a major position play? That is, are one of your almost sure shots ever wrong, or are they so well selected that they just invariably go?

I don't want to make it sound like I don't know how to lose money—because I know how to lose money better than most people—but there has not been a major mistake in a long time. But you have to remember that I don't trade that often. It is not as though I'm making three decisions a month. I may make three decisions a year, or five decisions a year, and I'll stay with them.

How often do you make a trade?

Well, there is a difference between making a trade and deciding to buy bonds in 1981. I've owned bonds since 1981, but I sell around the position. I make trades, but basically I own them. I went short the dollar at the end of 1984. Now, I have made a fair amount of trades in currencies since the end of 1984, but it is basically one trade with a lot of trades around it.

Very few investors or traders are as successful as you have been over time. What makes you different?

I don't play. I just don't play.

I can understand that. But still, very few people can analyze the same fundamentals you are looking at and so consistently be correct in assessing all the variables.

Just don't do anything until you know you've got it right. As an example, until you see American agriculture hit a low, then no matter what happens in the world—unless the world is going to stop eating—you can't go wrong. American agriculture is now so competitive, and so many marginal farmers have been washed out, that it has to go up. You just watch American agriculture deteriorate, deteriorate, deteriorate, and then you buy. You may buy early or late. In my case, usually a little bit early. But, so what? The worst that happens is you bought it too early. Who cares?

Is there anything else besides the fact that you are very selective that sets you apart?

I have no boundaries. I am totally flexible. I am open to everything, and I pursue everything. I have no more compunction about speculating in Singapore dollars or shorting Malaysian palm oil than I do about buying General Motors.

What happens when you have one scenario for currencies, one for the stock market, one for the bond market, and not everything meshes?

Then I won't do anything. It happens all the time. I don't do anything until all the pieces fit.

What is your opinion about chart reading?

I haven't met a rich technician. Excluding, of course, technicians who sell their technical services and make a lot of money.

Do you use charts yourself?

Yes, I look at them every week. I use them for knowledge, to see what is going on. I learn a lot about what is going on in the world by looking at charts.

But you don't ever look at charts and say, "I've seen this type of pattern before and it usually means the market is topping."

I look at charts to see what has happened.

Not what will happen?

What has happened. If you don't know what has happened, you'll never know what is going to happen. The charts say to me that there is a runaway bull market. They give me facts, but that's it. I don't say—what is that term you used earlier, reversal?—there is a reversal here. I don't even know what a reversal is.

A reversal simply is—

Don't tell me. It might mess up my mind. I don't know about those things, and I don't want to know.

Do the markets behave any differently now because so much money is being managed by trend-oriented systems?

No. They may not always have been on a computer, but there always have been systems. I guarantee that you can go back 100 years in the market and not find a single decade where there hasn't been some kind of system, some kind of new formula developed to play the markets.

So the markets today are basically the same as the markets in the 1970s, 1960s, and 1950s.

The same as the markets in the nineteenth century. The same things make markets go up and down. They have not changed the rules of supply and demand.

Do you have any goals at this point?

I'm looking for adventure. I'd like to be able to wean myself more and more from the markets. There are two problems. First, investing is such a wonderful pastime that it is hard to give up. I haven't changed from when I was twenty-two years old. I always wanted to read and know everything that was going on and figure out the future. The second problem is what do I do with my funds if I just stop? If I turn it over to my friendly broker at XYZ, I would be broke in five years, and then I would have to go back to work.

Any last words?

Good investing is really just common sense. But it is astonishing how few people have common sense—how many people can look at the exact same scenario, the exact same facts and not see what is going to happen. Ninety percent of them will focus on the same thing, but the good investor—or trader, to use your term—will see something else. The ability to get away from conventional wisdom is not very common.

Jim Rogers' unique approach may be difficult to emulate in its entirety, but many of his trading principles are of great relevance to all traders. His basic concepts are:

1. *Buy value.* If you buy value, you will not lose much even if your timing is wrong.

2. *Wait for a catalyst.* Bottoming markets can go nowhere for very long periods of time. To avoid tying up your money in a dead market, wait until there is a catalyst to change the market direction.

3. *Sell hysteria.* This principle is sound, but its application is far from easy. Rogers' methodology can be paraphrased as follows: Wait for hysteria, examine to see whether the market is wrong, go against the hysteria if fundamentally validated, be sure you are right, and then hold on tight. The tricky parts are the last two steps. Very few traders have Rogers' analytical skills and intuitive insights to wade through the maze of facts and statistics in the "three-dimensional puzzle" of world markets and arrive at the correct long-term projections with uncanny high accuracy. Without this type of accuracy, the ability to sit tight could be a lethal virtue. And, even if you can predict long-term economic trends with a sufficient degree of accuracy, there still remains the problem of being able to sit tight, particularly when the financial steamroller of market hysteria is running counter to your position.

For example, I doubt many traders would have been able to sell gold at $675, stay short while it surged to $875 in only four days, and then hold the position through the subsequent long-term collapse, eventually liquidating at a large profit. Even if you have the steel nerves necessary to duplicate this feat, you probably lack the financial resources to outstay this type of market or the same high degree of accuracy in picking your shots. Perhaps this particular concept should come with a caution label attached: Warning! Any attempts by the unskilled practitioner to apply the method described herein can lead to financial ruin.

4. *Be very selective.* Wait for the right trade to come along. Never trade for trading's sake. Have the patience to sit on your money until the high probability trade sets up exactly right.

5. *Be flexible.* Biases against certain markets or types of trades limit your field of opportunity. A trader who says, "I will never go short," has a distinct disadvantage compared to the trader who is willing to go short as well as long. The trader who is open to examining a broad range of markets has a distinct advantage over someone who is willing to participate in only one market.

6. *Never follow conventional wisdom.* Keep this principle in mind and you will be less likely to buy stocks after the Dow has already moved from 1,000 to 2,600 and everyone is convinced that there is a shortage of stocks.

7. *Know when to hold and when to liquidate a losing position.* If you believe the market is going against you because your original analysis was flawed (such as when you realize you overlooked an important fundamental factor), then as Rogers states: "The first loss is the best loss." However, if the market is going against you, but you are convinced your original analysis was right, then sit out the hysteria. As a cautionary word, this latter condition should be applied *only* by traders who fully understand the risks involved.

Mark Weinstein

High-Percentage Trader

After a brief period as a real estate broker, Mark Weinstein became a full-time trader. His start in trading was so naive that he virtually threw his money away. After that early failure, Weinstein withdrew to seriously study the markets and earn another trading stake. With the exception of one disastrous trading experience, Weinstein was a successful trader from that point on. He has intensively traded a wide variety of markets, including stocks, stock options, stock index futures, currencies, and commodities. Although he is reluctant to divulge specific details, it is clear that he has profited handsomely in all these trading arenas.

I met Mark Weinstein through a mutual friend. Although he was very intrigued by the project, his desire for anonymity made him reluctant to tell his story. He would call me and say, "OK, I will do it, let's schedule the interview." Then the next day he would call and say, "I changed my mind. I don't want the publicity." This pattern was repeated several times, with each decision accompanied by lengthy phone conversations regarding the merits and drawbacks of doing the interview. Finally, in exasperation, I said, "Mark, we could have done three interviews in the time we have spent talking about it." That was our last conversation regarding the matter until about two months later when, impressed by the caliber of traders who had agreed to participate in this book, Weinstein decided to do the interview.

Weinstein met me at my office one summer evening. Because the building turns off the air-conditioning after 5:00 P.M., we were forced out into a corner lobby, which, although warm, was at least less stifling. The interview was conducted over a dinner of deli sandwiches and soda.

Through our phone conversations, I knew Weinstein had a strong tendency to go off in many directions in any conversation—that's how his mind works, one topic leads him to think of five others and their various interrelations. Dreading a mammoth editing task, I stressed to Weinstein the need for remaining focused on the specific questions. I could tell that Weinstein was making an extra effort to heed this advice. This fact notwithstanding, the interview lasted five hours and yielded a 200-page transcript.

How did you first get involved in trading?

Back in 1972, when I was a real estate broker, I had a friend who was a commodity broker. He and I had gone to school together.

Did your friend get you interested in the markets?

It didn't take much to get me interested because my father's hobby was gambling. He was very good at percentages, and I used to watch him at the crap tables. In a sense, I think being a trader is in my genes. Also, trading fascinated me because of my mathematics and science background in college and because I had a commodity broker friend who was into computer strategies.

Do you remember your first trade?

I remember it exactly. I opened up a commodity account with $8,400, and I went long corn based on a recommendation made by the firm's grain analyst. Three days later, I was out $7,800.

Did your broker friend advise you to follow the analyst's recommendation?

Yes, and he also followed it. What I didn't realize then was that the market had been rising for some time and was already overbought when I went long. It wasn't even a bad reaction. I just got in on the move too late. I didn't have enough margin to keep the position going. Also, my guts turned on me, and I didn't want to put up any more money.

It sounds to me like your friend let you put on a position that was clearly out of line with any money management principles.

It was one of those get-rich-quick schemes.

Did you know anything about the markets at the time?

Absolutely nothing. If I flipped through a chart book, it looked like a collection of TV test patterns to me.

Did you have any idea of the risk involved?

I knew that the chances of my winning were very slim because I didn't know what I was doing.

Didn't it occur to you that you should learn something before you started?

No, because I was desperate for a change; I didn't like being a real estate broker.

Was the money that you invested a substantial part of your savings at the time?

It was all the money I had.

When did you get enough money to come back into the markets?

It took me approximately six or seven months. I worked seven days a week and rented as many apartments as I could get my hands on. I also sold a few co-ops. By that time, I had saved up about $24,000. I took out $4,000 to live on, and used the remaining $20,000 to open an account.

Did you make any effort to learn anything about the markets in the interim?

Yes. I studied the gold market, learned how to chart, and became familiar with the concept of overbought and oversold markets. I figured that if I bought a severely oversold market and left myself enough money for two margin calls, I couldn't lose unless something drastic happened in the economy. That was my method.

But if you use that approach in a trending market, you are going to get killed.

It worked in that market. I guess ignorance was bliss.

What were your trading results the second time around?

I did well for several years after that and managed to build a small fortune. But a lot of that was due to luck.

It couldn't have all been luck. What were you doing right when you were making money?

In relation to what I know now, there was very little that I was doing right. I think I just had good markets. In those days, commodities seemed to follow chart patterns a lot better than they do now. Very few people knew anything about technical analysis then, so the markets were much more orderly. I got a break by learning as much as I could about technical analysis at a time when it was working pretty well.

Did you have a method for controlling risk?

No, and I still don't. I depended on my nervous system and gut reaction. I covered positions when I did not feel right about them. Sometimes it would be after two days; sometimes after two hours.

Were you spending all day trading?

All day and all night. I was losing friends left and right. I sat in a studio apartment with charts plastered on every wall. I probably looked like a madman to the friends I had left.

So this was really a full-time endeavor.

Not only an endeavor—it was an obsession! I slept with it; I dreamt about it. Sometimes I would stay up all night thinking about what I would do the next day. If I didn't need sleep, I would have done it twenty-four hours a day. At that point, it wasn't the money that was motivating me. I was hooked on the game: on the challenge of trying to figure out the market.

Did you sometimes wake up with a feeling that you knew the gold market was going higher or anything like that?

No, it had nothing to do with the direction of the market. It was just an extension of what I was doing during the day. I would take so much of it to sleep that I ended up exploring unconsciously what I had been doing consciously that day.

Did you have any goals when you set out?

Well, the great American dream is to make a million dollars, and that was particularly true in those days. I never really had a materialistic dream until I started vacationing and traveling in Europe.

When was this? How many years after you started trading?

It was in the mid-1970s. I had been trading for about three or four years.

Had you passed the million dollar mark by that point?

Yes, and I had made enough money to be able to relax, start vacationing, and think about things I wanted to buy. At that point, I was feeling
confident enough to know that I could replace the money I spent with
my trading profits. I figured the next logical step was to start appreciat-
ing the money I was making. I saw a castle in the south of France that I
wanted. I was particularly impressed that the castle had a moat around
it, and the idea of living there appealed to me. It was on the market for
only $350,000, and I figured it would take about $50,000 a year to keep
it up.

That doesn't sound like a lot of money for a castle.

Today it is probably worth $5 million. When I came back to the U.S., I
wanted to make the money to pay for the castle almost immediately. That
was a tremendous mistake.

**I don't understand. You already had the money to buy the castle;
you didn't have to make it.**

Even though I had the money, I still looked at it in terms of how much
it cost. I know people in this business who have $17 million in their trad-
ing account and won't buy a new car.

So you didn't take your money out of the account to buy the castle.

No, I came back and decided that making the money was going to be my
goal.

**In other words, your next $350,000 in profits was going to go for the
castle.**

Exactly.

What happened?

On my next trade, I put on a large long position in soybeans. The market closed up the first day, and I had about a 25 percent profit on my money. I was planning to get out of the position at the end of the week. The biggest mistake I made was having a specific target of what I wanted out of the trade.

The target being determined not by market analysis, but rather by the $350,000 you wanted to make on the trade. Did you trade differently because you were trying to make money for a specific purpose?

Yes, I didn't consider the risk and took on too large a position. I was not using any type of rational judgment. I was being guided by my material desires. The market went up again the next day, but collapsed suddenly late in the session, locking limit-down.

Did you get stuck with your position at limit-down?

Yes, I couldn't get out. The next day I showed up at the brokerage office and the market opened offered limit-down. I waited all day to see if it would come off of locked limit-down, but it didn't.

I take it that you would have liquidated your position if you could have.

If the market had traded, I would have sold out at any price.

Do you remember your emotions at the time?

I was in a state of shock and had no decision-making capability left whatsoever. I couldn't fall asleep, and found myself almost praying the market would somehow trade the next day. On the third day, I called the office about a half an hour before the opening, and they told me it didn't look like there was any hope. I didn't even bother going in because I couldn't face the people in the office. I was certain that they were getting a big thrill out of my situation.

Why is that?

There were a few other professional traders in the office who were never able to make the kind of money I had been making. When this situation developed, they were almost relieved. It seemed to justify all those years of their not taking positions like I did. They were really heartless. The only person who was really upset was my broker, and, frankly, that was probably because he was afraid of losing the account.

Did the other traders kid you about it?

They overconsoled me and then laughed about it behind my back. They wanted to see me come in and fall apart. That is why I stopped coming to the office.

Do you think they relished your predicament because it made them seem less deficient as traders?

It went beyond that. I think there are a lot of people in this business who just enjoy watching others lose money.

Once you stopped going into the office, what did you do during the day?

I checked with other brokerage houses, trying to get price quotes.

Why didn't you just call your own broker?

I was too embarrassed, and I didn't want to take the derision.

Your own broker was kidding you?

I didn't know what to think of him. I was starting to get paranoid and hostile because nothing could be done. I went to a competing firm and spoke to their grains analyst. I was looking for someone to hold my hand. He told me I would be OK, because the fundamentals were still strong and there would be a tremendous demand for soybeans if the market went down another day. Of course, on the fourth day, the market locked limit-down again.

How much were you losing each day?

About $125 thousand a day. This was at a time when the average annual salary was $15,000. I was not born rich, and I couldn't stop thinking of my loss in those terms.

Could you put that loss in perspective relative to your account size?

Before that trade, I had nearly $1.5 million in my trading account. So I was losing nearly 10 percent of my equity level prior to the trade each day.

     I was devastated. I felt like I was wounded in a trench and watching myself bleed to death. The market went limit-down five days in a row, and I lost over $600,000. On the fifth day, I remember sitting in a park holding hands with a girl I had picked up, literally crying on her lap. I was practically in a psychotic state. I thought about getting out of the business altogether. I started to think that what everybody was telling me was true—maybe it was just luck that I had made money all those years. I worried that if I continued trading, I could wind up losing it all, and being forced to go back to some job I didn't like.

Which was more devastating, the large monetary loss, or your feelings about going from success to failure?

It was the money and the limit situation, and the fact that I couldn't act. My exact thoughts were: Here I am, a person who thought it was un-American to go short, and what I found out was really un-American was not being able to get out of a position.

So you felt cheated by not being able to get out?

I definitely felt cheated. To this day, I think there is something wrong with limit price moves.

Are you implying that price limits that were supposedly created to protect the public actually work against them by preventing people from getting out of their losing positions?

Yes. I think the market should be totally free of restraints.

There is talk about putting limits on stock markets as a way of reducing volatility. Would that actually be jumping from the frying pan into the fire?

Absolutely. Now, the average investor knows that if he wants to get out, he can at least get out at some price. Imagine if this guy calls his broker and finds out that he can't even get out of the market.

In other words, you are saying that those who are expounding the idea of limits are really going to make matters worse for the small investor.

It is absolute lunacy. It is a law that is being proposed for the benefit of sophisticated institutional investors.

Your earlier comment implied that, prior to the soybean trade, you always traded the long side of the markets. Is that right?

Yes. I never went short. I felt it was un-American. After the soybean trade, I realized that the business I was in was the height of capitalism, and it really made no difference what side of the market you were on. All I could think about was that the people who were short made money and I lost money.

How long did the emotional impact of this experience last?

Months. I didn't want to trade commodities anymore. I ripped every chart off my walls. I tore up everything in my house that had anything to do with commodities.

When did you begin trading again?

After a few months, I started trading AMEX stocks, but I found it amazingly slow. I missed the leverage of the commodity markets. I didn't think I could successfully support myself trading stocks.

Around that time, I ran into a friend who is a great options trader. I told him about my experiences and he suggested that I join him. In my first week at his office he told me to buy Teledyne calls right before expiration because he was sure they were going up. I followed his advice, and the calls completely collapsed.

How much did you lose?

About $40,000. I felt extremely hostile, but I didn't want to show it because he never promised me any results. I was so upset that I walked out of the office and didn't come back for two days. He tried reaching me during that time, but I didn't return his calls. Finally, he got a message to me through a mutual friend.

Was he upset that he had given you bad advice?

When I came back to the office, he told me that he had done the exact opposite trade in another account, and that the trade was mine. So I didn't really lose any money.

That sounds like an awfully odd type of practical joke.

It wasn't a practical joke. He was trying to teach me not to place blind trust in anyone—even him. It was his way of teaching me the importance of self-reliance in being a good trader.

How did you do after that point?

I did pretty well. My friend was a phenomenal options trader. He knew everything about the market and I learned a tremendous amount from him.

Did you trade options based on the methodologies he taught you?

Yes, combined with my own technical analysis.

Your friend didn't use technical analysis?

No, he didn't believe in it. He was a tape reader.

Has the fact that you have been extraordinarily successful as a 100 percent technical trader changed his mind about technical analysis?

Not at all. He thinks technical analysis is just a crutch for me, and the real reason I make money is experience. There was a point at which we separated for a few years. He came to my office one day and watched me trade. He embraced me like a father and said, "You finally made it." I told him that not only had I gained a lot of experience, but I had learned just about everything there was about technical analysis, including certain things I had created myself. He said, "You never give up, do you? It has nothing to do with technical analysis. You are trading that way because of experience."

Why did you and your option trading friend eventually separate?

There was a conflict in our trading styles. He was a great trader who was willing to take an occasional large loss, because he knew he would more than make up for it with large gains and come out way ahead in the long run. However, I was uncomfortable trading that way. I preferred trading for small profits and trying to eradicate losing trades. I wasn't willing to take the same type of risk. Also, my approach was purely technical, whereas he was basically a tape reader. Anyway, in 1980, I decided to go off on my own. We got together again years later.

I know you once entered an options trading contest. Can you tell me about it?

It was originally organized by two traders on the CBOE floor. They got 47 traders together, each of whom put up $5,000 in a winner-take-all contest. Each trader opened a $100,000 account with the same clearing firm.

How long was the contest for?

Three months.

What were your results?

I turned the $100,000 into over $900,000 without any *pyramiding* [using profits to increase leverage].

That's a rather phenomenal performance.

Yes, but the markets were very good at that time.

What did you trade when you went out on your own in 1980?

I traded everything. I continued to trade stock options. When stock index futures trading began in the early 1980s, that became a primary market for me. I also traded the commodity markets. In fact, during the last two years, my trading has shifted to nearly 90 percent commodities.

Do you remember your first soybean trade after the debacle in the 1970s?

For a long time, I avoided soybeans. But, as I began to find myself trading the commodity markets effortlessly, I knew deep down that I would eventually get back the money I lost in soybeans. I never forgot about it.

It sounds like you were looking for revenge.

Yes, exactly. Every time I looked at a commodity chart book, my eyes would edge over to the soybean chart, then I would quickly flip the page. I watched the market peripherally for years before doing anything. When soybeans went down to $4.75, I knew they were near a low, but I didn't want to buy them until I was sure I couldn't lose on the trade. I was like a Sicilian whose wife had been murdered ten years earlier, waiting for the perfect moment for revenge. When my technical analysis convinced me that the market had bottomed for real, I jumped in on the long side.

Where did you buy the beans?

Around $6.18. [This was shortly before the 1988 drought caused prices to skyrocket.]

Where did you get out?

I got out of some at $7.25, and the rest at $9.92. [The high of the move was $10.46.]

How much did you make on that trade?

Let's just say I made my money back in spades.

The way you talk about it, it sounds like that trade was a great relief for you.

Yes, it was a total catharsis. I realized that there was a reason why I had lost the money in the first place.

What was the reason?

Because I was inexperienced. I don't believe anyone ever gets wiped out in the market because of bad luck; there is always some other reason for it. Either you were off when you did the trade, or you didn't have the experience. There is always a mistake involved.

You mentioned earlier that one of the reasons you split with your former trading partner was that your own trading style was geared to extremely low risk. Since 1980, what was the worst percentage drawdown you have experienced?

I lose so infrequently that I don't really keep track of that type of number.

Well, let's put it this way: What was your worst single trading month?

I haven't had any losing months.

You have made money in every single month since 1980!

Yes. Of course, I could have made a lot more money if I wasn't so cautious, but that is the way I trade.

Do you remember your worst losing week?

I haven't had any losing weeks during that time, but I have had some losing days.

That is an incredible statement. How can you be sure that you are not simply forgetting about a few weeks when you lost money trading?

The reason I am sure is that I remember all my losses. For example, I have had three losing days in the last two years. Out of the thousands of trades I made during that time, I had 17 losers, but nine of them were because my quote machine was down, and when that happens I just get out of my position.

Most traders would be happy winning on 50 percent of their trades, and a win ratio of 75 percent would be spectacular, yet you are implying that your win ratio is somewhere in the vicinity of 99 percent—that is really hard to believe.

You can check with Leigh. I told him about hundreds of my trades during the past few years. [Leigh Stevens is a mutual friend who introduced me to Weinstein.]

OK reader, I know what you are saying: "'No losing weeks, but I've had some losing days.' Give me a break." Frankly, I admit Weinstein's statements sound preposterous. I could not verify his claims by examining account statements because his partners are vigorous in maintaining the confidentiality of the partnership's trading activity as it is a private trading firm, not open to the public. In fact, a number of his partners were adamantly opposed to this interview and were nearly successful in dissuading Weinstein from participating. The only account statement Weinstein was willing, or able, to show me was his independent entry in the option trading contest, which did indeed confirm that he multiplied a $100,000 account ninefold in three months with 100 percent winning trades.

Still unsatisfied, I spoke to Leigh, who has known Weinstein for years and has spent many days watching him trade. I have known Leigh for three years and can confidently describe him as honest, low-keyed, and levelheaded. Leigh confirmed that of about 100 of Weinstein's trades he had personally witnessed and several hundred more Weinstein told him about on the phone (right after he put them on), he could remember only one that was a loser. Even if because of faulty memory (I mean this literally, not as a euphemism for dishonesty), Weinstein's actual percentage winning rate is somewhat lower than he implies, I still believe his win/loss ratio is incredibly high.

How can he do it? Weinstein's own response to this query follows, but to put it in perspective, I thought some further elaboration would be helpful. Weinstein employs his own custom-designed state-of-the-art computer systems to monitor constantly technical indicators designed to measure changes in market momentum. Rather than use the standard values for these indicators, Weinstein uses his own values, which he frequently adjusts for changing market conditions. He combines this intensive real-time analysis with comprehensive chart analysis incorporating a variety of methodologies, including cycles, Fibonacci retracements, and Elliott Wave analysis. Finally, add to this one last essential ingredient: an uncanny sense of market timing. Only when nearly everything lines up right and he feels the timing is virtually perfect does he put on a trade. He passes up many trades that he believes have a high probability of working, but for which he lacks the same degree of near absolute confidence. Because of the combination of a lifetime devotion to studying the markets, intensive real-time analysis, innate market sense and incredibly rigorous trade selection, virtually all of Weinstein's trades are at least marginally profitable at some point within twenty minutes of entry. That is all Weinstein needs to assure a breakeven or better result.

It helps to understand that Weinstein usually plays for quick profits and covers his trades within hours or even minutes. Even on position trades, Weinstein will usually take some profits quickly to assure a net profitable outcome. He also trades markets in rotation, quickly shifting his profits from market to market, always seeking the profit potential with the lowest perceived risk. Finally, Weinstein enjoys the support of a floor network that often puts him on the right side of the bid-asked spread.

Weinstein's comments may sound like boasting on the written page, but that belies their tone—naiveté would be a much closer description. When Weinstein talks about trades, his comments are peppered with phrases such as, "It's obvious the market is going lower," "This market is so easy." It is clear he has no conception of how difficult trading is for the rest of us.

How do you explain your ability to win such a high percentage of the time?

Because I have a real fear of the markets. I have found that the greatest traders are the ones who are most afraid of the markets. My fear of the markets has forced me to hone my timing with great precision. When I am trading properly, it is like a pool player running racks. If my gut feel of market conditions is not right, I don't trade. My timing is a combination of experience and my nervous system. If my nervous system tells me to get out of the position, it is because the market action triggers something in my knowledge and experience that I have seen before.

I also don't lose much on my trades, because I wait for the exact right moment. Most people will not wait for the environment to tip itself off. They will walk into the forest when it is still dark, while I wait until it gets light. Although the cheetah is the fastest animal in the world and can catch any animal on the plains, it will wait until it is absolutely sure it can catch its prey. It may hide in the bush for a week, waiting for just the right moment. It will wait for a baby antelope, and not just any baby antelope, but preferably one that is also sick or lame. Only then, when there is no chance it can lose its prey, does it attack. That, to me, is the epitome of professional trading.

When I trade at home, I often watch the sparrows in my garden. When I feed them bread, they take just a little piece at a time and fly away. They keep on flying back and forth, taking small bits of bread. They may have to make a hundred stabs at a piece of bread to get what a pigeon gets at one time, but that is why a pigeon is a pigeon. You will never be able to shoot a sparrow, it is just too fast. That is the way I day trade. For example, there are times during the day when I am sure that the S&P is going up, but I don't try to pick the bottom, and I am out before it tops. I just take the mid-range where the momentum is greatest. That, to me, is trading like a sparrow eats.

Am I paraphrasing you correctly? The cheetah is your analogy for position trading and the sparrow is your analogy for day trading. The common denominator is that both animals wait for can't-lose circumstances.

Exactly.

How do you pick your trades?

I use many different types of technical input: charts, Elliott Wave and Gann analysis, Fibonacci numbers, cycles, sentiment, moving averages, and various oscillators. People think that technical analysis is unreliable because they tend to pick the one thing they are comfortable with. The problem is that no single technical approach works all the time. You have to know when to use each method.

How do you do that?

It is experience and gut feel. I use all forms of technical analysis, but interpret them through gut feel. I do not believe in mathematical systems that always approach markets in the same way. Using myself as the "system," I constantly change the input to achieve the same output—profit!

Is there anything you can single out as the most important element in deciding to put on a trade?

I am always looking for a market that is losing momentum, and then go the other way.

Having traded both the stock and commodity markets, would you say they behave differently?

Absolutely. In contrast to the commodity markets, the stock market very rarely gives you the opportunity to enjoy a meaningful trend.

Why is that?

Because when institutions and specialists sell out, they don't sell out at one price level, they scale out as the market goes up. Similarly, when they buy, they scale in as the market goes down. This leads to choppier price action and is the reason why many good commodity traders that I know lose every time they go into the stock market.

But you win consistently in the stock market, as well. What are you doing differently?

I don't try to figure out where the market is going before the action; I let the market tell me where it is going. Also, there is such a variety of technical input in the stock market (divergence, advance/decline, sentiment,

put/call ratios, and so on), that you will almost always get a signal before
the market is about to do something.

Is your method of technical analysis therefore different in the stock market than in the commodity markets?

I look at the individual stocks; they all have their own personalities. For
example, IBM and General Motors will usually rally before a major
market bottom and fail to rally before a major market top. As another
example, I have never seen a real good rally without the utilities leading
the market. The utilities go up when interest rates are expected to come
down, and when interest rates come down, portfolio managers jump into
stocks. I have done extremely well trading the indexes, because before
I ever traded index futures, I had become a very experienced trader of
stocks and options.

What do you think is the public's biggest misconception about the markets?

That people who trade the markets gamble. I know floor traders that have
made money for twenty straight years. You can't call that gambling.

Another major misconception is that people always expect the
market to react to news. For example, when John F. Kennedy was assas-
sinated, the market initially broke very sharply, but then quickly
rebounded to new highs. This price action baffled many people. Investors who sold on the news only to watch the market reverse blamed the
institutions for pushing the market higher. What they failed to realize is
that a market that is fundamentally and technically poised to move higher
is not going to reverse direction because of a news item—even a dramatic
one.

Another item I would place under the category of misconceptions
is the way the media reports the reasons for the market being down. They
are always saying that the market is down because of profit taking. I think
it would be wonderful if everybody was always taking profits. But, the
truth is, most people lose money, and the reason markets go down is because they take their losses. I know educated people who watch the news
and wonder why the hell they lost money when everyone else is taking

profits. The media owes it to the public to report that the market goes down not only on profit taking, but on a lot of loss taking as well.

What are the trading rules you live by?

1. Always do your homework.
2. Don't be arrogant. When you get arrogant, you forsake risk control. The best traders are the most humble.
3. Understand your limitations. Everyone has limitations—even the best traders.
4. Be your own person. Think against the herd, as they must lose in time.
5. Don't trade until an opportunity presents itself. Knowing when to stay out of the markets is as important as knowing when to be in them.
6. Your strategy has to be flexible enough to change when the environment changes. The mistake most people make is they keep the same strategy all the time. They say, "Damn, the market didn't behave the way I thought it would." Why should it? Life and the markets just don't work that way.
7. Don't get too complacent once you have made profits. The toughest thing in the world is holding on to profits. That is because once you have attained a goal, you then set a second goal that is usually the same as the first one: to make more money. Consequently, for many people, attainment of that second goal is not as rewarding. They may begin to question what they really want from trading and trigger a self-destruct process in which they wind up losing.

Any final advice you have for the beginning trader?

You have to learn how to lose; it is more important than learning how to win. If you think you are always going to be a winner, when you lose, you will develop feelings of hostility and end up blaming the market instead of trying to learn why you lost.

Limit losses quickly. To paraphrase from *Reminiscences of a Stock Operator*, most traders hold on to their losses too long because they hope the loss will not get larger. They take profits too soon, because they fear the profit will diminish. Instead, traders should fear a larger loss and hope for a larger profit.

342 *Mark Weinstein*

Weinstein's most traumatic trading experience occurred when he let a material goal interfere with his trading. This is a common theme that has surfaced in other interviews. It invariably seems to be a mistake to translate the potential profit or loss of a trade into material terms.

The cornerstone of Weinstein's trading approach is to wait for those trades in which everything appears to be lined up exactly right, and the odds of winning seem overwhelming. Even though most of us can never expect to remotely approach Weinstein's confidence in the trades he selects, the concept of waiting for only those trades one feels most confident about is sound advice that is echoed by a number of traders in this book.

Although viewing markets as nonrandom over the long run, I have long believed that very short-term market fluctuations (i.e., intraday price movements) were largely random. Weinstein has shaken this belief.

Part IV

The View from the Floor

Brian Gelber

Broker Turned Trader

Brian Gelber began his career as a broker, managing a major brokerage firm's financial futures operations on the floor of the Chicago Board of Trade. After successfully advising institutional clients, he began trading for his own account. In the early days of T-bond futures trading, Gelber enjoyed the dual distinction of being one of the most (if not *the* most) prominent brokers on the floor and one of the largest local traders.

In January 1986, Gelber expanded his trading to include the direct management of customer accounts. In addition to his own trading, Gelber supervises a group of traders in both cash and futures in government securities and other markets. He is the president of a group of companies: Gelber Group, Gelber Management, and Gelber Securities. These companies are involved in clearing, brokerage, and money management.

Gelber's relaxed personality seemed almost out of place with his profession. Instead of the high level of intensity expected of someone who trades and supervises trading in multimillion dollar bond positions daily, I found a man who talks about his work as if he were describing a pleasant vacation.

Although our meeting took place during trading hours, Gelber did not seem to be overly concerned with the bond market. In fact, he seemed quite relaxed, despite leaving the trading desk for his private office to conduct our interview. "I'll probably do better by staying here," he remarked, obviously reflecting what he perceived to be a low-opportunity market at the time.

In response to a query regarding other traders I was interviewing, I mentioned that one, Tony Saliba, had made the cover of the current issue of *Success* magazine. Gelber asked me if I had a copy. I pulled out the magazine from my attaché case and handed it to him. He smiled as he read the bold headline describing Saliba's experience during the week of the October 19, 1987, stock market crash: "Victory! He Made $4 Million in Seventy-Two Hours." Jokingly, Gelber asked, "I made $4 million in twenty minutes on that day; how come I'm not on a magazine cover?" It was not meant to be boastful. It did, however, very specifically summarize a basic truth about great traders: Many, if not most, maintain relatively low profiles and are therefore virtually unknown to the public.

How did you get started in this industry?

After graduating from college in 1976, I backpacked around the country. In Salt Lake City, I answered an ad for a commodity broker position. I didn't have any idea what it was, but I figured it was something like a stockbroker. I got my license while working for a guy who was basically running a boiler room operation.

You really started out on the wrong side of the business.

When I walked in, there was a guy seated at the back end of a penny stock office. He spent his days on the phone trying to convince people to give him $5,000 or $10,000 to speculate on his charting system. It was a real fly-by-night operation.

I was keeping his charts for him, while getting registered. I kept saying to myself, "This guy is pretty much of a crook." I got my license and quit. Then I bummed around for another few months, just working temporary jobs to pay the rent.

What kind of jobs?

Unloading railroad cars. Then one day I walked into a Thomson McKinnon office and said, "Hey, I have a broker's license." The fellow there said he would pay me $800 a month. That was a large amount of money for me at the time. All I had to do was go in and cold call; any accounts I opened would be mine.

But you knew virtually nothing at all about markets at that time.

I had read a couple of books, and I knew something about charts—having kept them for the first fellow I worked for.

What books did you read? There weren't too many around at that time.

The book I learned the most from was *Technical Analysis of Stock Trends* by Robert D. Edwards and John Magee (John Magee, Inc., 109 State Street, Boston, MA).

What other books would you recommend to people?

The first book we have our traders read is Edwin Lefevre's account of Jesse Livermore, *Reminiscences of a Stock Operator* [Reprinted in 1985 from the original 1923 edition by Trader Press, Inc., Greenville, SC.] I've read it at least a dozen times.

Anyway, around the time that I started at Thomson McKinnon, the Ginnie Mae market was just coming into its own. Thomson McKinnon had just hired a trading group to run a Ginnie Mae desk. I told them I was interested in learning more about the Ginnie Mae market.

Why were you attracted to that market?

It was a new market and seemed more manageable than the conventional commodities. I figured my business would grow more steadily if I focused on that market. Also, I had made a number of trades in Ginnie Maes. The first trade was a winner, but the following ones were all losers.

It was magnetic; I felt I could make money there, but I kept losing, and that made me want to learn more about it.

It sounds like you had a minor compulsion to pursue it.

Yes, because I had failed. Anyway, the traders at the Ginnie Mae desk taught me a few things, and I went out and opened almost every mortgage banker account in Salt Lake.

Did you understand the Ginnie Mae market at that time?

When I first started opening accounts, I didn't understand anything about it.

How then did you sell people on yourself?

I snowballed them at first, but I listened and I learned from the questions they asked me. Initially, I was confused by what they were doing, and they were equally confused by what I was trying to sell them.

At least you understood futures as an instrument.

Right. And with that limited knowledge, I bumbled through my first few meetings. Then I really got pretty good at it.

Were these hedging accounts?

Yes, all pure hedging accounts. By May 1977, I was making $2,000 a month in commissions. That was a tremendous amount of money for me.

Was this all in the Ginnie Mae market?

At that point, yes. Previously, I had done some brokerage in other commodity markets such as wheat, hogs, and pork bellies.

Who were those trades for?

Just accounts I had opened by cold calling—people who really didn't understand that they could lose, and when they lost, they were always upset.

Were you giving them trading suggestions?

Pretty much.

Using chart analysis?

Believe it or not, more off the research of Thomson McKinnon analysts, and secondarily off my charts. Newer brokers definitely tend to rely on their firm's research.

Did your customers lose because the research was wrong?

No. They lost because their time horizon was mostly day to day, while the research was longer term.

So there was a mismatch?

Exactly. I think that is a basic problem between most brokers and their customers. It is almost impossible to get market information to your customer quickly enough for the customer to act on it.

What you are saying is that even if a broker can actually beat the market trading short term, he can't translate that to the customer.

Insurmountable odds, because you have two people who have to pull the trigger, and the information changes so quickly.

So, one of the points of advice you would give to speculators is to trade with a longer-term perspective?

Yes, you have to.

Let's talk about floor trading. I know, at one point, you were both a floor broker and trader in the T-bond futures market. The question I think a lot of people would ask is: If you receive a large customer sell order at the same time you're thinking of closing out your own long position, how do you handle it?

I never scalped, so the idea of being long and having a large customer order move the market against me 2 or 3 ticks never made any difference. Besides, I had so many customers that they were often going opposite ways.

OK, that's an easy one. But what if some important news was breaking, and all your customer orders were going one way against your own position? Did you ever end up trapped in a position because you had to execute all the customer orders first?

Yes, that happened to me about half a dozen times, and it probably cost me a grand total of a half million dollars over a number of years. But measured against the amount of money I was making, it didn't kill me.

That was the cost of doing business?

Right.

It must be a gut-wrenching situation though, knowing you want to get out, but not being able to act because of a conflict with customer orders.

Usually, you are too busy acting as a broker and thinking, "OK, I have to sell 1,000 lots; how can I do it best?" Then, when you are done with the order, you might say to yourself, "Oh damn, I'm still long; I have to get out of this thing."

Is there a built-in disadvantage for a floor trader who also handles customer orders?

Absolutely. As I tell the people I hire, "If you are a broker, you are not a trader; if you are a trader, you are not a broker."

But you were.

It was a wild time. I was the biggest trader and the biggest broker in the same market. I worked very long hours and was totally exhausted when I went home. Then I would just get up the next day and do it again. This went on for three years, and while it was a great experience, I really shouldn't have done it. You can't be a great broker *and* a great trader. I did a good job, but it probably took years off my life.

Are most of the significant size traders on the floor just traders, or do some also handle customers?

They all are either brokers or traders now. That is the only way to go; there is no doubt about it.

Is that true of most floors, or just the T-bond floor?

Primarily, the T-bond floor. In the S&P and in the New York markets, some of the big brokers are also big traders.

Given today's increased scrutiny, are people who violate the confidence of *dual trading* [handling customer orders and trading one's own account] likely to get caught?

It is still very difficult to create a flawless audit trail in an open outcry market.

Say bonds are trading at 95.00 and the market gets hit with some bearish news. The broker executes a large amount of orders for customers and his own account, and the market goes straight from 95.00 to 94.00. His fills are 94.31, 94.30, 94.29 and all his customers get fills at 94.27 or lower. [Bond prices trade in 32nds.] How does he explain his way out of that one?

He could give his order or his customers' orders to another broker. Or he could fill both orders and put another broker's number on his own order. There are always ways to get around extra scrutiny. The smart crooks will always be difficult to catch.

Is the temptation in dual trading too great?

No. After having been through it, I would say that dual trading is good
for efficiency in the marketplace, but it is too heavy a burden for the individual.

Should the rules be changed to disallow dual trading?

That is a difficult question. What is more important, the efficiency of the
market or the integrity of the individual? There is no doubt in my mind
that dual trading adds tremendous liquidity to the system, and that is
probably more important than the fact that a small percentage of dual
traders may cheat. Besides, even if dual trading were banned, the stealers
would still find a way to steal. That is their perception of how to make
money in this business.

When did you first get involved in the T-bond market?

In September 1977, I moved to Chicago and became a broker on the T-
bond floor. I was just twenty-five and I got lucky. I went to New York
in November 1977 and met with eight big-name companies, seven of
whom opened accounts. I was at the right place at the right time.

When did you start trading for your own account on the floor?

In 1979.

**Were you tempted to give up your floor brokerage so that you could
concentrate on trading?**

Actually, it was just the opposite. I had started out as a customer's man,
and from 1979 through 1981, I built a massive customer base. We were
a powerful force in the market at that time. Probably the saddest thing I
ever did was to became a trader too. I was a great broker in my twenties,
and if I had parlayed that for ten years, I probably would have ended up
where I am now without enduring all the pains of trading. I consider trading to be an unrewarding, unglamorous game.

It's odd you say that, because you have been far more successful than most traders.

I guess my point is that as a broker I was at an even higher echelon. I was really good at it, and it suited my personality.

So, why did you get into trading?

I started trading because some of my customers said, "You know the market so well, why don't you just trade?" I resisted at first, but after six months of holding out, I started trading. From there it just evolved.

Do you remember your first trades?

My first trade was a long position, and I made some money. Then I put on a long bond/short Ginnie Mae spread, which was almost like being long. The market went down, and I lost all the money I had made, plus $50,000 more. Since I was making about $50,000 per month as a broker, my attitude was that I basically broke even that month. But I didn't like the feeling at all. So, I cut my position size down and started trading a little more actively. This happened during the bear market of 1979. The problem was that I was bullish all the way down.

Why were you bullish?

My customers kept telling me that rates couldn't go much higher.* For example, I was handling the orders for CitiBank and Citicorp and they were buying all the way down. These were renowned people saying that they had an opinion and backing it up with deeds.

*Bond prices fall when interest rates rise. This is a basic concept that is sometimes confusing to the novice. The reason that bond prices decline if rates increase can be explained as follows: If rates rise, it means that all existing lower-yielding instruments are less attractive to investors. To induce an investor to purchase these lower-coupon bonds, their prices must fall sufficiently so that the return is equivalent to the return on the higher-coupon bond purchased at face value.

What would you do today in the same situation?

Now, I know the characteristics of various institutions. Let's take Citi-Bank. Back then, I was buying because they were buying. Now, if Citi-Bank was buying, I might conclude that they were just reallocating their assets or changing the duration of their portfolio. Today, I have little regard for the views of portfolio managers, because their outlook tends to cover a much longer time perspective than mine. I didn't understand that back then.

So, you don't pay much attention to those types of opinions anymore?

I listen to them in passing. I don't read the *Barron's* interviews of portfolio managers anymore. It never did much for me, and I don't think it does much for any trader.

In other words, the problem wasn't the fact that you were listening to other people, but that you were listening to the wrong people.

I didn't know how to decide which were the right or wrong people. I was a naive kid saying, "Here is a major account that is buying a lot of stuff; the market should go up."

You really had no strategy, no plan, no system. You were just shooting from the hip.

That's right. Then over time, I started to get a grip on how to make money. As opposed to saying, "I have an opinion and I want to express it in the market," I started asking, "How do I make money out of all this?"

What had you learned by that point?

I had learned that an opinion isn't worth that much. It is more important to listen to the market. I became a reactive trader as opposed to an opinionated trader.

In 1980, one of my customers was Solomon Brothers. At the time, they were bearish on bonds from 65 to 80. If I had listened to my big customers as I had done in 1979, I would have thrown away money all over again.

What told you not to listen to your customers then?

The 1979 experience of losing money based on someone else's opinion—a sound opinion by intelligent people that was just absolutely wrong.

Where were your successes coming from?

I learned how to read the tape and developed good instincts. We were such big players in bonds back then—we, meaning my customers and myself—that the spots we picked to trade could virtually stop the market. We were actually creating some of the support and resistance points. It didn't take that much to do it back then. I think there was a streak of months when I hardly had any losing days.

Could you have done it without the commercial accounts?

I would hope that I could have done it without them; that it wasn't a self-fulfilling prophecy. But if it was, fine. I don't know.

When did that streak end?

From a trading standpoint, I never had a losing year until 1986, although I did struggle in 1985 during the mid-stages of the bull market in bonds.

Was your trading success a matter of being able to read the tape?

Yes. I was attentive and had good instincts.

It sounds like you are saying that either you are born to be a good trader or you are not.

Well, to a certain extent, that may be true. My feeling is that you don't have to be, but it helps.

Is it a matter of having a sixth sense about the market?

Yes. Your gut often tells you what to do.

Are people who don't have the natural instincts for trading wasting their time? Or can almost anybody be successful if he or she works at it hard enough?

Working hard has nothing to do with it. About two weeks ago, a very bright fellow who works for me said, "This is a very frustrating business. It doesn't matter how hard I work; it has no bearing on whether I make money or not." You have to know yourself and put that knowledge to work in the market.

That sounds like a cliché. What do you mean by "know yourself"?

I'll give you an example. I think I'm a good trader, but there is a guy working for me who is better. I could go out there and beat my head against the desk and try to outdo him, or I can just be myself. Let him make whatever he can, and I'll make whatever I can.

This is my view of a year in the life of a trader: Four out of twelve months you are hot. You are so excited that you can't sleep at night. You can't wait to get to work the next day; you're just rolling. Two months out of the year, you are cold. You are so cold, you are miserable. You can't sleep at night. You can't figure out where the next trade is going to come from. The other six months out of the year, you make and lose, make and lose. You can't sleep, because you are trying to figure out how you are going to make money.

The net result is that you never sleep, because you are constantly thinking too much about trading. It is an all-consuming thing. That is why you need to know yourself—to moderate your emotions. If you don't, then after a big success, you are high as a kite. You are not prepared when just around the corner, the market suddenly brings you back to earth. Or, in the opposite situation, when you are consistently losing, you might end up jumping out of a window. Why did I leave the floor? Again, because I know myself. I need to interact with people and that doesn't happen there.

Being on the floor sounds like a very intense thing to be doing day in, day out. Does it physically grind you down?

Absolutely. You can see that in the older fellows. When you are in your twenties and thirties, you can rebound pretty well from the physical and mental stress. As you get older, you don't rebound as well, and you have to push harder to maintain your performance.

It sounds like professional sports. You get to a certain age and no matter how good you were—

That's right. It's exactly like that.

Out of every 100 people who go to the floor to become traders, how many will make at least a million dollars within five years?

Maybe five or less.

How many will end up losing everything they came in with?

At least half.

You have been more successful than most traders. What do you attribute your success to?

The reason I have been so consistent is that I'm a great listener. I probably talk to about twenty-five traders each day. Most traders don't listen to your opinion; they only want to tell you their opinion. I am different because I honestly and truly listen to what they say and how they say it. For example, if one of the major locals calls me up three days in a row when the market has rallied, and he is asking me what I think, I know that he has been selling and is not sure of his position.

What does that tell you?

If it is in line with what the other traders I talk to are doing, it tells me the market will probably go higher.

So if you talk to twenty-five people, and twenty of them are nervous about the market going higher because implicitly they are short, does that tell you that you should be trading on the long side?

Yes. I know a large number of people in the industry and that is a big plus. I listen to them. I go with the people who are hot. Sure, I can form my own opinion, but that is not what makes me do the things I do in the market. Sometimes, I know my opinion is right, and I'll go with it. Sometimes, I know somebody else is hot, and I'll go with their opinion. I'm not picky about how I make my money. It doesn't matter if my opinion is right or wrong. All that matters is whether I make money.

Doesn't it get confusing when you talk to twenty-five people and fifteen are bullish and ten are bearish?

Sometimes, but I've been doing this since 1976. I've always been able to read people very well, even though no one thinks I listen. For example, I have one trader here who is cold as ice right now. All I have to do is listen to him. Last night, he told me he wanted to be short. I knew that I was going to be long.

As long as he is cold?

Right, and the one time he gets hot, fine. When the guy is cold, he is cold. You can't say to a trader, "You're cold, you can't trade." You have to let them run their course.

Is reading other traders a key component of your personal trading right now?

Yes, I'm pliable. I know these people, so I understand how to read them. I don't want to hear what Jack Schwager says, because I don't know him. I only want to talk to people I know very well.

What other things are important to your trading success?

The realization that when you don't care, you do well, and when you try too hard, you don't do well.

By "trying too hard," do you mean pressing when there is no trade?

Pressing is one of the reasons I'm sitting in here with you for so long during trading hours. The markets haven't traded well in weeks, and we are proud of ourselves for not having thrown a lot of money away.

So when the opportunities aren't there, you just lay fairly low?

Don't misunderstand me. I'm not that good at that, but I have gotten better as I've gotten older. I've learned that lesson over the last couple of years. After Richard Dennis left the floor, he said: "The first year I left the floor was the most painful experience for me, and I have paid the largest tuition I ever have." It was the same with me.

What was the motivation for coming off the floor, since you were so successful there?

I felt that the industry had developed to the point where my brokerage skills were no longer needed. All anyone wanted to know was: "Where's the next tick?" "How can I move size?" The price to be paid for my particular skills was too low.

You are talking in terms of customer business?

Customer business and trading. The market had gotten so voluminous that my style of swing trading was worthless. It got to the point where I was just trying to read the next tick instead of the next 8 ticks.

Why couldn't you play the same game?

The volume was too big; capitalization was too big. I couldn't read the market from the floor.

Because there were too many players?

Exactly. In the early days of T-bond futures trading, the depth was low and you could read when people were overextended long or short. You couldn't do that anymore.

Did your performance start decreasing; did you see the handwriting on the wall?

In 1985, I made under a million dollars trading for the first time and I knew something was wrong. I had always been a very consistent trader, making more money each year. I looked at my results and found that my profits were smaller, meaning 3 and 4 ticks, and my losses were greater. My first reaction was to become a much more active pit trader. I found that I was taking on tremendous positions and the risk/reward was insane. That was when I became convinced that I had to make a change.

Were you just lucky that you didn't get hit really hard during that period on any particular trade?

Actually, I did get hit pretty hard a couple of times, but I had some good winners too. The point is that as I worked harder and harder, I found that all I was doing was running in place. I don't like to work hard at trading, and here I was just mentally and physically exhausting myself.

If you had been doing as well as in previous years, would you have stayed in the pit?

Yes. The pit is a very stimulating environment. Off the floor, you have to force yourself to be motivated each day. That was a very difficult transition.

Is it harder to trade off the floor?

Not in the long run. My profitability in 1987 and 1988 has been pretty good.

You mentioned that your first year off the floor was very difficult. Was the main problem that you were still trying to trade the market as you did on the floor?

Yes, that was the number one reason. The second reason was that the transition occurred during the 1986 runaway bull market. I was bound to lose because my style was not based on following trends.

Is that still true?

No, it has changed. I've gotten better. I can still countertrend trade real well, but I found you can also make a lot of money trend following.

Do you use trading systems?

No, we are "discretionary traders." We only use technical indicators and systems as trading tools. One particularly interesting system we have developed is based on quirks related to volatility. Our belief is that volatility offers clues to trend direction. Although we've found through backtesting that this system gives you good signals, we do not blindly follow the trades.

For an automated, computerized system, what would you consider good results in terms of average annual return?

About 40 to 50 percent, with maximum equity drawdowns under 10 percent.

But systems will always have larger maximum drawdowns than that.

That is why we haven't directly traded money on them.

Do you think any system can compete with a good trader?

I haven't seen one yet, although there may be one somewhere.

There are some traders who have the skills, but who don't succeed. What is it that keeps them from becoming successful?

Most traders who fail have large egos and can't admit that they are wrong. Even those who are willing to admit that they are wrong early in their career can't admit it later on. Also, some traders fail because they are too worried about losing.

In other words, successful trading is a matter of trying to avoid losses, but not being afraid of them.

That is a good way to put it. I'm not afraid to lose. When you start being afraid to lose, you're finished.

Is the ability to accept losses a characteristic of a winning trader?

Yes. Tom Baldwin is a good example. He only trades the market; he doesn't trade size or equity. By that I mean, he doesn't say to himself, "I am long 2,000 contracts. Oh my God, that is too many, I have to sell some." He never looks at it that way. He will sell either when he thinks the market has gone up too far, or when he thinks that his position is wrong.

In your trading experience, is there one particular trade that stands out as the most dramatic?

In 1986, when the long bond was being cornered by the Japanese, there was a big, emotional rally on a Monday morning. I had thought the market was too high at 90.00, and here it was trading over 91.00. So I sold 1,100 contracts scale-up above that level. The market backed down and was offered 1,000 lots at 91.00. Just as I was thinking that I had this trade nailed, in less than five minutes the market reversed and soared to 92.00.

I was down $1 million, and the market was only a few ticks away from limit bid. I had never lost so much money, so fast, and it was because I did things differently than I normally do.

What specifically?

I usually don't trade that big early in the year. I like to make money gradually at first and then play with the money I have made.

It sounds like part of your money-management philosophy is based on treating each year independently.

Right. Anyway, I sold a little bit more up at the highs, and from that point on, I was only concerned with covering. I waited patiently, and the market started coming back down. I ended up losing only $400,000 for the day, not all that bad considering where I was earlier. But that trade had a big emotional impact on me. I was flabbergasted by the market action. I had forgotten that markets could run away like that. I couldn't believe how wrong I had been.

What did you mean earlier when you said the Japanese cornered the market?

When the Japanese want to buy something, their big thing is market share. This was the first time the U.S. got a good feel of how the Japanese buy securities—they buy them all.

Was this the move that drove us to the highs in the bond market?

That's right.

So, apparently, the Japanese weren't as fazed by the yield being so low for all the risk implied in a long bond position.

I don't think they look at it in terms of yield. Rather, they view things as whether prices are going up, and if they are, they buy. Every time they would buy, prices would go up, and they would buy some more.

The bond market has collapsed again since then; did they get out of their position in time?

Sure. Do you know who bought the most at the highs? The U.S. dealers who desperately needed to cover because they had sold on the way up.

Are the Japanese smart traders then?

No, they just have a style. They are cannonball traders. They go one way, and they all go together. A friend of mine at one of the Japanese shops told me about a Japanese trader who bought just about every long bond on the screen. About fifteen minutes later he called back and asked, "Why is the *basis* [the price spread between cash T-bonds and T-bond futures] going out?" Naively, the Japanese trader had noticed that cash prices had gone way up, while futures didn't go up very much. My friend told him, "Well, you just bought every bond available. Of course, the basis is going to go out." They didn't really understand the impact of their trading.

The Japanese did much the same thing in the U.S. equity market in 1987 as they did in bonds in 1986. They practically took control of it, buying because prices kept going higher.

I'll never forgive myself for not buying stocks and selling bonds in 1987. That was going to be my number one trade in 1987.

Was the reasoning that the bond market had already run way up, while stocks hadn't? Did you just believe the two markets were out of line valuewise?

That's right. Also, we knew the Japanese were buying the high-capitalization U.S. stocks. Having already learned their buying style in the bond market, the trade was even more obvious.

Then why didn't you do it?

The spread between the S&P and the T-bond contract was trading between $19,000 and $25,000 on a one-to-one contract value basis. I went on a four-day vacation, and in just a few days, Japanese buying in the stock market had pushed the spread to $30,000.

Why didn't you buy the spread before the vacation, since you had the idea?

I was waiting for the spread to break out above its trading range. I wanted to buy it above $26,000. At a $30,000 spread, I just couldn't pull the trigger.

What is the key trading rule you live by?

Never add to a loser.

What does the average trader do wrong?

He overtrades and begs for tips.

How do you handle a losing streak?

I instinctively trade smaller and sometimes I just take a break. It is a good habit to wipe the slate clean and start fresh.

When you are going bad, but still have some good positions on, do you liquidate them as well?

Absolutely. They are bound to turn against you too.

I found the subjects of dual trading and the Japanese impact on the U.S. T-bond market among the most interesting portions of my conversation with Brian Gelber. These subjects, however, did not provide any insights into the art of trading. On a more practical note, one of the primary caveats provided by Gelber concerned the misuse of brokerage research. He noted a tendency for the broker and client to use longer-term research for short-term trading. This misapplication of information often leads to trading losses, even when the research is right.

Clearly, flexibility and suppression of ego are key elements of Gelber's success. Referring to hot traders, he notes, "I'll go with their opinion. . . . It doesn't matter if I'm right. All that matters is whether I make money."

Finally, Gelber's reaction to losing streaks is one cited by a number of traders. He advises wiping the slate clean and starting fresh. Getting out of everything allows the trader to achieve greater clarity. Liquidated positions, if they still appear attractive, can always be reentered once the trader has regained his confidence.

Tom Baldwin

The Fearless Pit Trader

The trading pit of an active futures market is an imposing place. Scores of traders push over each other, while shouting buy and sell orders at the top of their lungs. To the uninitiated, it seems miraculous that this institutionalized bedlam actually functions efficiently as a process for executing orders. In the frenzied world of futures pits, the T-bond ring, with over 500 traders, stands out as the unchallenged giant. The pit is so large that one side of the ring often does not know what is happening on the other side.

By most accounts, Tom Baldwin is the single largest individual trader in the T-bond pit. His trading size puts him in the same league as the primary institutional players. Single trades as large as 2,000 contracts ($200 million face value T-bonds) are not unusual for him. On a typical day, he may trade over 20,000 contracts (the equivalent of $2 billion in face value T-bonds). Baldwin is in his early thirties, having begun trading T-bonds a scant six years ago.

Baldwin's entry into the world of floor trading sounds more like a recipe for failure than success. In 1982, with no prior trading experience, Baldwin left his job as a product manager for a meat-packing firm to lease a seat on the Chicago Board of Trade. His stake was only $25,000. Out of this skimpy capital base, he had to pay over $2,000 per month to lease the seat, and at least another $1,000 per month for living expenses. As if this were not enough, his wife was pregnant at the time.

Obviously, Baldwin is not one to play it safe. His aggressive risk-taking posture is one of the key elements of his success. He turned a profit from the beginning. He was a millionaire before his first year was up and has never looked back. Although he declines to discuss the extent of his winnings, $30 million appears to be a conservative estimate. The true figure could be significantly higher.

I considered an interview with Baldwin essential to this project, because of his prominence as the most successful floor trader in the world's largest futures market. Baldwin, however, was not eager to be interviewed. Although he had done some interviews in the past, he had obviously grown reluctant to do any more. Without Brian Gelber's generous intervention—the two are friends and admire each other's trading abilities—this interview would never have taken place.

Gelber had warned me that Baldwin could be either abrasive or gracious, but to be prepared for the former. As an example, Gelber said that Baldwin would probably answer the question of how he first got involved in trading with the curt response: "I went down to the floor and began trading." As it turned out, this was very close to the spirit of his answer.

I arrived at Baldwin's office several minutes after the end of the day's trading. Baldwin arrived a few minutes later. Since he had just moved to new offices and the furniture had not yet been delivered, the interview was conducted sitting on a window sill.

Baldwin's attitude was neither abrasive nor gracious; aloof might be the best way to describe it. I had the distinct impression that the minute I hesitated in asking the next question, Baldwin would be gone. It was St. Patrick's Day, and this impression was intensified each time someone left the office saying that he or she would meet Baldwin at a local bar. I could sense that Tom was anxious to join them. I decided to conduct the interview completely impromptu, shooting off a new question the second he finished answering the prior one. Often his responses were quite short. I felt like a photographer stalking a rare bird; one false step and the bird would fly off.

I knew that, at some point, I would not be able to think of an immediate follow-up question. This happened about forty minutes into the interview. I quickly glanced down at my index cards, searching for a lead. Unfortunately, my eyes focused on a question I had already touched upon, and though I tried to ask it from a different perspective, it was too late. The game was over. Baldwin said he had to get going and excused himself.

How did you first get interested in trading?

I had taken some classes in commodities in graduate school. I wanted to trade, but I didn't have the money to buy a seat. In 1982, I found out I could lease a seat, and that's when I began.

Did you always want to trade as a local as opposed to any other type of trading?

Yes.

How did you learn to trade?

One lot at a time. I always had an opinion. All day long I stood there and developed an opinion. As I came to see that my opinion was right, I was reinforced, even if I didn't make the trade. Then when I traded, I knew from standing there six hours a day, every day, that most of the time I was right. I would see the same scenarios develop over and over again.

Are you talking about market patterns or traders doing certain things?

Both. Market patterns would occur over and over again, or market players would do the same thing over and over again, and you just trade it.

What were your first few months like? Were you profitable initially?

I think the most I was ever down was 19 ticks, so I pretty much started out profitably.

Coming to the pits with no background, what was it that gave you enough of an edge to be right on the market?

I worked hard. I stood there six hours a day, all day, every day.

But you didn't have any experience to fall back on.

You don't need it. You don't need any education at all to do it. The smarter you are, the dumber you are. The more you know, the worse it is for you.

For your type of trading—that is, scalping—when you put on a trade, what are you looking for?

To get as much as I can get out of it. I've taken full points or just 1 tick out of a trade. You just never know. You have to watch the market, get a feel for it, and if you are in the right position, just go with it.

On average, though, your trades will net out at a few ticks?

Yes. I probably average 4-tick profits on big positions.

I assume your holding time is probably very, very short.

I try to make it short.

Are we talking about minutes?

Yes, or seconds. Just because that is less risk. The object is always: Minimize your risk.

Have you always been a scalp-type trader?

Well, I evolved from a pure scalper to a combination of scalper and speculator.

Right now, what percentage of your trades are position versus scalp?

A small percentage, well below 10 percent.

Basically then, you are still using the same basic trading style you started out with.

Right.

Do you use any technical input?

Yes. I use charts.

Do you use intraday charts, since you are trading short term?

No. Bar charts covering the past six months.

If you look at the charts and say, "I'm basically bullish," do you primarily scalp from the long side?

Not necessarily. I would start with an opinion, but if I saw something to change my mind, I would adjust.

Is the fact that you started off with a chart-influenced trading bias a key element behind your winning?

Yes.

Were there periods when you were unsuccessful, or did you remain consistent?

Consistent.

Didn't you have any losing months?

Yes, I had one or two.

But not two together?

No, never.

What percentage of those who come to trade on the floor are still around after five years, versus losing their stake and dropping out?

Less than 20 percent. That is really the rule of thumb, and it's probably less than that.

What percentage are successful to the point of making and keeping at least a couple of million?

One percent.

In other words, a very small fraction of traders.

Right. It is like any other industry. How many people get to be president of General Motors?

Do you have an opinion about what separates the 1 percent from the other 99 percent?

Yes. It is a lot of hard work, for one. It's perseverance. You have to love to do it. Also, in our business, you have to have a total disregard for money. You can't trade for money.

Do you mean as long as you like the position, you stay with it? That you can't think, "I'm losing $1 million on this trade, and with $1 million I could have bought a great house." You can't translate it into real terms.

Exactly. Most people do.

I guess another way of saying it is you have to have almost no fear.

Right.

Is that a characteristic of winning traders: They have less fear than the losers?

Yes.

Can you size up a new trader on the floor and tell if he is going to make it or not?

Yes.

What kind of things would tip you off that he is a loser?

Most important, losers don't work hard enough. Most people walk in and think there is a 50/50 chance on any trade. They don't think there is anything more to it than that. They don't concentrate. They don't watch the factors that affect the market. You can see it in their eyes; it is almost as if there is a wall in front of their face.

By factors, do you mean fundamentals?

No. Paying attention to what other markets are doing, such as the Dow Jones or gold. Watching the traders in the pit.

Patterns?

Yes.

In other words, they are not paying enough attention. They are standing there trying to pick a trade here and there, but they are not absorbing everything that is going on.

Right. Also, their expenses are usually way too high. They can't stand there and hack it long enough to pick it up. Because it is like any job, if you stand there long enough, you have to pick it up. It is just a matter of how long you can afford to stand there before you do.

Do you really believe that?

Well, the average guy might not be a million-dollar trader, but if he stands there for five years, he would have to pick it up. It is just like a job. You don't start any job and feel comfortable in the first six months.

You did.

Yes, but I did start as a one-lot trader. And I wasn't really comfortable, because I *had* to make money. I only had $25,000 to my name.

At what point were you confident that you were going to be successful at it?

That is an interesting question. You are never really confident in this business, because you can always be wiped out pretty quickly. The way I trade is: Live by the sword, die by the sword. There is always the potential that I could get caught with a big position in a fluke move with the market going the limit against me. On the other hand, there is no doubt in my mind that I could walk into any market in the world and make money.

What percentage of your days are losers?

One day out of ten.

Has that percentage changed over time?

That is over a long period of time.

From your perspective, what does the average trader—that is, public trader—do wrong?

They trade too much. They don't pick their spots selectively enough. When they see the market moving, they want to be in on the action. So, they end up forcing the trade rather than waiting patiently. Patience is an important trait many people don't have.

Waiting for the right spot?

Right, I bet most people are probably ahead after their first five trades. They think, "This is great, like free money." But then they forget that the reason they made money on their early trades was because they waited a long time. They said, "I bet this is a good spot to buy it because I've seen the market act this way a lot of times." And they made money. But all of a sudden, they are doing a trade every day.

The next thing that happens is they lose on a few trades, and invariably don't know how to take a loss. They made money to start, and before they know it, they are even. Now they hesitate. "Where do I get out?" The minute they hesitate, the market just keeps going. Now they are losing money and they say, "If I sell it here, I'm going to lose $1,000." They don't like to lose $1,000, when they're getting paid $500 a week. Now, all of a sudden, they are thinking about the money.

Once you think about the money, you are dead?

Yes. That is what usually happens to the public.

What is your own way of handling losses?

Get out.

Quickly?

If I can. My point is that I have a lot of patience and I wait. If I know it is a losing trade, I wait for what I think is the optimum time to bail out. Then I try and reverse.

So, if you realize you don't like the trade anymore, you'll get out, but you'll pick your time?

Right, but I will get out.

Let's say you are doing that on a day when the market is a one-way street. At what point do you just have to cough it up?

It depends how far it has gone against you. If it's against you a long way, at some point you just throw it in. Those days happen maybe three or four times a year. You just start bailing out.

But you usually have a feel for when that is the thing to do?

Yes, because it has happened before.

But normally, if you are just a bit behind in a trade, you are better off if you let the market move a little in your direction and try to sell on strength, or buy on weakness, instead of just trying to dump it in a hurry?

Right.

Is that a key element to your trading style?

Yes. Never give up on a trade. Many traders who are in a losing trade will just get out because they were taught that you have to have discipline. Great. Those traders will always be around. But if they just had some patience and said, "Yes, it is going to be a losing trade, but instead of getting out here at 7, maybe if I wait and just sweat it out for another minute, I can sell at 10."

Is it a matter of just wanting to get out to stop the pain? And if they were willing to stand the pain a little longer, they would be better off. Is that a fair way of putting it?

Yes. They give up too quickly. In most cases, if you don't give up, you might be able to turn a five-yard loss into a two-yard loss.

Your trading size has obviously grown quite dramatically since you first got into the business. Has that made it harder to trade?

Yes, you have to adapt. You need to change your method of buying and selling, because the market is continually changing in subtle ways.

What changes have you seen in the bond market since you got in?

Well, you can trade bigger size. Now you can usually trade a couple of hundred at each tick. It doesn't move the market as much.

How about a thousand lots?

It depends on the liquidity at the time. Lots of times you can get out. It is amazing how much liquidity there is when you want to get out.

On average, if you had to dump a thousand, how much would that move the market?

Depending on the time of day and the liquidity, maybe 1 or 2 ticks.

Not much at all?

No, not much.

Has size been an impediment at all if the liquidity is that good?

Yes, it is harder. Generally, when you get into a big position, the rest of the floor knows about it because they stood there and watched you. At least they think they know. They all put their hands down and wait when they think you are wrong. It is natural for a trader to be skeptical.

I would almost think that because you have a long-term record of success, they would more often coattail you.

Lots of times that is true, and that also makes it harder to get in and out. When you go to offer them, they are all offering too.

How do you handle those situations?

You have to pick your spot. You have to wait for the big paper order to come in and then go for it.

Does it become like a chess game, where you sometimes want the pit thinking that you are selling when you are really buying?

Yes, sometimes. But generally, you can't trade big size when you are doing that.

So, frequently, if you are long and want to liquidate, you just wait for the bid to come in?

Right.

What kinds of things do you look for in a chart?

Key points such as the high and low for the week, the halfway back point, and consolidation areas.

Do you use charts for short-term or long-term perspective?

Short term.

Short term in your case meaning?

I guess as short as possible. You get in a trade, make money as fast as possible, and minimize your risk.

I've noticed that a lot of times, bonds will take out one- and two-week highs or lows by a few ticks and then pull back. The price action almost seems like a trap for the breakout players. Is that a pattern in the bond market?

Yes. It always has been.

Do you use fundamentals?

Whenever any important fundamental numbers come out, I use them.

Do you use the fundamentals indirectly, that is, by seeing how the market responds to the new information?

Yes, but also by being the first one to trade off the new fundamental information. I know what I am going to do if a number comes out one way or the other, and I usually have the opportunity to be first.

You want to get there before the crowd does. Are you normally right on that type of trade?

Yes.

You've done tens of thousands of trades. Does any single trade stand out as particularly emotional?

The first 100-lot I did. It was a milestone.

What kind of jump was that for you?

You tend to go from one lot to five lots to ten lots to twenty lots to fifty lots.

So, you probably went from 50 to 100? Do you remember that trade?

Yes, it was a much bigger risk. The market was trading at 64.25 and a broker bid 25 for 100 lots. But he didn't put a size on it, he just bid 25. So I said, "Sold." He thought I was being funny and said, "I'll buy the 100," knowing I had never traded that big before. So I said, "Well, I'll sell you 100." The market went to 24 offered instantly.

It almost sounds like you did your first 100-lot as a dare?

Well, almost. But I wasn't a very good trader then. I immediately bought ten, then ten more. I was trying to bid at 23, and the market went to 22 offered. By the time I got out, I had ten different people in the trade, because I didn't know how to cover 100 lots.

But the trade worked out for you?

Oh yes. Well, actually, the word got out that this small trader had done a 100-lot. So I had to go up to the office to talk to the clearing firm after the close.

How long had you been trading at that time?

Six months.

That was pretty early on. I assume your capitalization was really inadequate to handle 100 lots?

Right. I had probably made $100,000 by then. Maybe not even that.

Even at $100,000, that wouldn't cover you for much of a move.

Yes, only 1 *point*. [In bonds, 1 point equals 32 ticks (the smallest price movement).] I told them, "Look, I just thought it was a great trade at the time, and I'll probably never do it again."

How long was it before you traded 100 lots again?

Two days.

You just never thought about the risk side of it?

No, if a guy bids 25 for 100, and I think that it is a great trade, I just say "Sold."

Is there any element in your mindset as a trader that says: I had better be careful that I'm always in the game?

That came later.

Are you always in control, or are there days when you have lost control?

There were days when I've lost control.

Any that stand out?

A couple. You have to say that about any day you lose a couple of million dollars.

Were those days one-way street markets?

Yes, one-way streets. Because I'm a market maker, I take the other side of the trend. So, if the market goes one way for 50 ticks, I can guarantee you I'm going the wrong way, and at some point, it is going to be a loss.

What was your position at the October 1987 low in bonds?

I was long.

When did you start getting long?

Five points higher.

Five full points! You mean 81?

Yes. The day it broke below 77, I was long thousands of contracts. Other traders were also heavily long.

That was the day we gapped sharply lower. Who was selling?

The commercials just kept selling.

Did you have second thoughts?

Yes.

**Did you think if the market went down to 76, maybe it could go to
70?**

No. At that point, you had to say it was all over and done.

Why?

Technical analysis and experience.

**Was that an example of your being patient in picking your spot to
get out, even when the initial trade was wrong?**

Right.

Do you ever use any trading systems for anything?

No. They wouldn't be there if they weren't wrong.

Do you think trading systems are a losing game?

Sure. Why do they exist?

You tell me.

Because people aren't confident in their own ability. If you had a really
good trading system, you could make millions. Why would you sell it
for $29.95?

Does luck have anything to do with trading?

Trading is like any other job. You work hard, put in the time and effort,
and make your own luck. I was lucky that the first 100-lot I sold was a
winner. But why was I lucky? Because I stood there all day for over six
months, developing and honing market feeling. When the opportunity
occurred, I didn't hesitate.

You have to pay your dues to get the luck.

Right.

Are there people on the floor who are not good traders, but are way ahead because they just happened to do a couple of big trades on the right side of the market? Can anybody really get by just on luck?

No, not for long. The rule of thumb is if you have lasted a year, you will make it, but it is hard.

Are there traders that you are influenced by because you respect what they are doing?

Oh, yes. They are indicators.

So, that is actually part of your trading approach. For example, if trader X is a good trader, and he is on a roll, and you are thinking of selling—

And he does, then you know you're right.

But if he is buying?

Then you hesitate. Maybe you don't get into the trade.

Are there traders who can't succeed because their ego is too big to ever be influenced?

Yes.

Is part of the success a willingness to not always do your own thing?

Right. You have to adapt to your success. If you make a lot of money, all of a sudden you start to think you are infallible. You forget the reason you were right was because of all those little factors that you followed. As soon as you think, "I'm the guy who is going to lead the way," you get slammed.

So, it really doesn't make a difference whether it is your idea or somebody else's. Winning or losing is all that counts. Where the idea came from isn't important?

Right.

Do you have to be somewhat of an egomaniac to be a good trader?

Actually, the best traders have no ego. To be a great trader, you have to have a big enough ego only in the sense that you have confidence in yourself. You cannot let ego get in the way of a trade that is a loser; you have to swallow your pride and get out.

After you get way ahead, is there a temptation to say, the extra money doesn't mean anything anymore, maybe I should cash in the chips?

I never thought that way. Obviously, when I started, I needed to make money to support my family, but I never had a goal to make a million dollars. I said, "Hey, this is great, maybe I can make $100,000."

You passed that a very long time ago. Do you have any other goals?

No.

You just do what you do because you enjoy it?

Yes. And I hope it lasts.

Baldwin's incredible trading achievements made him an ideal interview candidate for this book. However, I did not really expect his comments to be pertinent to myself or other off-the-floor traders. After all, what could a floor trader, whose time horizon is measured in minutes and seconds, say that was relevant to traders who hold positions for weeks or months?

To my surprise, the interview yielded some relevant insights. Perhaps the most important point made by Baldwin was his emphasis on not viewing trading in terms of money. To him, money is only a means of keeping score. By contrast, most traders tend to think of gains and losses in terms of their monetary implications—a frame of mind that only gets in the way of making trading decisions.

For example, assume you originally planned to risk up to $5,000 on a trade, and quickly find yourself down by $2,000. If, at this point, you start to think of the trade in terms of money (for example, "the extra $3,000 can pay for my vacation"), you might well liquidate the position, even though you still believed in the trade. It is one thing to get out because you no longer like the position, but it is quite another matter to liquidate on impulse simply because you have translated the risk into tangible terms.

Another interesting point made by Baldwin is an unconventional one: Don't get out of a losing trade too hastily; instead, wait and choose your time. This advice seems to fly in the face of most trading advice. After all, isn't one of the basic tenets of trading success to cut your losses quickly? However, I don't think Baldwin's statement contradicts the rule. I believe he is saying that often the worst time to bail out of a position is during a violent price move against you. Baldwin's point is that by bearing the pain just a little longer, you may be able to find a more favorable circumstance for liquidating. Of course, this philosophy should be applied only by disciplined traders: those with the ability to maintain a risk control strategy.

Tony Saliba

"One-Lot" Triumphs*

Tony Saliba came to the floor of the Chicago Board Options Exchange in 1978. After a half-year of clerking, Saliba was ready to try it on his own. He found another trader to back him for $50,000, and after a favorable start, nearly self-destructed. He pulled back from the brink of disaster by altering his trading techniques, and has been successful ever since.

Saliba's trading style can be described as trying to do a little better than treading water day in, day out, while being positioned to take advantage of the rare spectacular trading opportunity. His fortune has been built largely by exploiting only a handful of such events. Two of these situations—the Teledyne price explosion and the October 1987 stock market collapse—are discussed in the interview.

The impressive aspect of Saliba's trading achievements is not the few spectacular gains he has registered in his career. Rather, it is that these gains have been achieved by using a trading approach exemplified by incredible risk control. In fact, at one point, Saliba managed to string together seventy consecutive months of profits exceeding $100,000. Quite a few traders have become multimillionaires by scoring several big hits. A much smaller number have managed to hold on to their gains. Only the rare trader can boast both occasional dramatic gains and consistent trading profits.

*Readers unfamiliar with options may wish to first read Appendix 2 in order to understand the trading-related references in this chapter.

Although the homework required for Saliba's successful trading is extensive, he has nonetheless managed to diversify into a wide range of other ventures, including real estate investments, a software company, and a restaurant chain. Overall, his extracurricular business endeavors have proven only modestly profitable, but they have indulged his appetite for variety.

During the time these interviews were being conducted, Saliba was involved in the most important business venture of his life: negotiating with a French bank to back him with several hundred million dollars to form a major trading company. His goal is to discover and train a generation of successful traders.

Saliba is a likable person who makes you feel like you're one of his best friends within five minutes of meeting. He is a person who genuinely likes people—and it shows.

On the evening before our scheduled meeting, Saliba had a minor accident, slipping on the marble floor at the health club in the Chicago Board Options Exchange building. As I showed up at the scheduled time, his aide told me that Tony would not be in that morning due to the accident. I left a message. Saliba called later that day, and to spare me the inconvenience of missing my flight that evening, or making another trip to Chicago, he arranged to meet me several hours later.

We talked at the LaSalle Club bar, which was sufficiently empty to not cause a major distraction. Initially, I was too intensely focused on directing the interview to pay any attention at all to the large movie screen at the front of the bar. Later on, however, as I relaxed, I glanced at the screen as Saliba was answering one of my questions. I instantly recognized the train scene from the movie *Risky Business* in which the sensuous Rebecca DeMornay seduces Tom Cruise.

I have a bad habit of severely overscheduling my appointments, and as Saliba was my third interview of the day, I was beginning to feel the strain. My first thought was, "Keep your eyes off the screen, you are having a hard enough time keeping your mind focused as it is." My second thought was, "It would be incredibly rude not to pay full attention to Tony, especially after he literally hobbled over to spare me the inconvenience of having to reschedule our interview." My third thought was, "Thank God I'm the one facing the screen."

What led you to become a trader?

I was a caddy for some grain traders when I was in high school. In college, a friend of mine asked me if I would like to be a broker. I thought that he meant doing the same thing as the guys I had caddied for. So, I said, "Yes. Great! Where?" "Indianapolis," he answered. I said, "What exchange is in Indianapolis?" "None," he said, "you do it on the phone." I had this impression of: "Hello New York, buy; Chicago, sell." When I got there, I found out I was a salesman.

After a few months, I asked the guys in the office, "Who makes all the money in this business?" They said you have to be on the floor. Right there I decided to go to the Chicago Board Options Exchange. On the floor, I met one of the traders I had caddied for years ago, and he grubstaked me with $50,000.

Isn't that unusual, giving $50,000 to a kid who used to caddy for you?

It was, except that he was very wealthy and needed to get off the floor because of his high blood pressure. He owned a seat that he had bought for only $10,000, and just needed the ability to trade in a customer account. I was going to help him do that.

What made him think you could make it as a trader?

He had heard some rumors around the floor that I was a hotshot clerk, and he basically took a chance on me.

What happened?

I went from $50,000 to about $75,000 in the first two weeks. I had put on all these *volatility spreads* [an option position that will gain if the market becomes more volatile] and they were getting pumped up.

Did you think, "Boy, this is easy"?

I thought, "This is it!" I mean, I was a genius. But what I was really doing was taking the opposite side of positions the other brokers were liquidating, letting them out of the market with their profits, while I was left holding the bag. This was spring 1979 and implied volatilities were very high because 1978 was a very volatile year. Well, the market went nowhere, and the volatility and option premiums collapsed. Within six weeks I had lost almost everything. The original $50,000 was down to only about $15,000. I was feeling suicidal. Do you remember the big DC10 crash at O'Hare in May 1979, when all those people died? That was when I hit bottom.

Was that a metaphor for your mood?

Yes. I would have exchanged places with one of those people in that plane on that day. I felt that bad. I thought, "This is it; I've ruined my life."

Did you feel guilty because you had lost someone else's money?

Yes, and I felt like a failure.

Had you started out confident?

Initially, I was very confident because before I started trading on my own, I had clerked for a broker for four months and picked his brain clean.

And now you thought the game was over?

Yes. In June 1979, I decided that I better find another job. I went to the Levy brothers, who owned a chain of restaurants that my dad built for them. They said, "Any time you want a job, you can run one of our restaurants." So, I said, "Hold that line. I am going to give it one more month."

Did you feel better because you had a cushion?

Yes. I said, "This is great, I've still got fifteen grand in my account."

You had a stop on your life so to speak?

Exactly, exactly. I had a stop on my career. So, I decided to go back and give it one more shot.

Did the fellow who staked you know how much you had lost? Did he ever say anything?

Oh, good question, Jack. He called me every night. I've grubstaked many guys since then, and three or four of them have lost more than fifty grand each. This man was a multimillionaire, and he acted as if this was the end of the world.

Did he ever ask you for the rest of the money back?

No, he just moaned and groaned. He had become wealthy through inheritance and money he made in another business. He really didn't know much about option trading. He had bought the seat to have something to do with his life. He told me, "If you lose $5,000 more, we'll pull the plug." So, I spent the next few weeks winding down my positions.

During that time, I sought advice from the more experienced brokers on the floor. They said, "You have to be disciplined and you have to do your homework. If you do those two things, you can make money down here. You might not get rich, but you can make $300 a day, and at the end of the year that's $75,000. You have to look at it that way." It was like a light bulb went on. I realized that this chipping away approach was what I should be doing, not putting myself at a big risk, trying to collect a ton of dough.

At the time I was in Teledyne options, which was a very volatile market. So, I switched to Boeing, which was a very tight, narrow range type of market. I became a spread scalper trying to make a quarter or an eighth of a point on a trade.

I stuck strictly to my goal of trying to average $300 a day and it was working. This period taught me to be regimented and disciplined.

To this day, I live by the credo of hard work, homework, and discipline. I teach my guys that.

Anyway, at this same time, I still had the remnants of a big spread position in Teledyne that I was in the process of liquidating. It was a position that would lose in a rising market. One day after I had been trading Boeing for about five weeks, Teledyne started moving up sharply. I was not going to let it get me again. I rushed into the Teledyne pit to take my position off. I was hearing floor brokers come in with orders, and all of a sudden I found myself responding to them. I was adapting the same technique I had learned in Boeing to Teledyne, except instead of scalping for an eighth or a quarter, I was scalping for halves and dollars.

What size were you trading at the time?

I was doing one lot at a time. The guys didn't like me because I was getting in their way. They wanted to do ten- or twenty-lot orders.

In other words, you were just a nuisance.

Exactly.

How did you get someone to take one lot?

On the options floor, it's first come, first served. If you have 100 to sell and someone bids first for just one, you have to do his one before you do 99 with the number two guy. The broker could ignore you if he wants, but if he does, he's breaking the rules.

Were you ignored?

The brokers never did, but the market makers on the floor did.

By brokers, you mean order fillers?

Yes. The floor brokers are the order fillers, and the market makers are the locals who trade for themselves. On the options exchange, the two are separate.

Were you the only one-lot trader in Teledyne?

For the most part, yes.

Did you take a lot of ribbing?

Oh, did I! They called me "one-lot" for the longest time. The individual who gave me the hardest time was the best trader in the crowd. He had made millions and was virtually a legend in his own time. He started leaning on me and ribbing me right from the beginning. He made my life miserable.

Did your ego get dented by these really successful traders railing you?

Oh, yes. And, it went on for almost a year, day in, day out.

Were you tempted to pick up your trading a little bit?

I did, but not for that reason. My backer, who had given me such a hard time when I was down, was the prod. Although he didn't know that much about trading, he did give me one piece of very useful advice. Once I started turning it around, he told me to increase my size. He said, "Tony, a banker makes his first loan and he is very careful, but as he gets more comfortable, he makes his loans bigger. You need to increase your size."

How did the harassment you were taking on the floor finally end?

When they introduced puts in June 1980, the lead trader, who had given me the hardest time, hated them. He said they were bad for the business and he didn't want to trade them. I seized that opportunity to really study what puts would mean to us, and I was one of the first market makers to start trading puts.

Actually, it opens up a whole range of new strategies.

Oh, unbelievable. These other guys were set in their ways, even though they had only been there a couple of years. Sooner than you might think, this number one trader befriended me and suggested that we work together. We started working on advanced strategies, getting real creative and abstract.

Were you working these out on a computer?

No, we did everything by hand. Writing out all these "what-ifs."

Didn't you still have to be guessing right on price and volatility direction?

You would have to guess right on volatility. However, we didn't have to peg market direction, because we were setting up spreads that had a big edge. For example, one option might be highly overvalued because it was popular among the member firms.

Eventually, I felt I was doing more of the work, while this top trader in the pit was counting on his ability to muscle the market. He would also stray from the strategies we had worked out and even started doing things to try to hurt me. I would say, "What are you doing?" He would just answer, "I changed my mind."

Finally, I just said, "Forget it, I'm working on my own." I started taking on more size. When interest rates went through the roof in 1981 and early 1982, my strategies worked really well and I started making a lot of money. Then in the bull market in 1982, I had days when I was making $200,000 a day. The guys in my clearinghouse couldn't believe the sheets; there was just tons of paper.

What kind of trades were you doing?

I was doing everything. I consider myself a matrix trader. I trade everything on the screen as it interrelates to everything else. My basic strategy, however, was buying *butterflies* [a long or short position at one strike price balanced by an opposite position in higher and lower strike options—for example, long one IBM 135 call, short two IBM 140 calls, and long one IBM 145 call] and offsetting that with an explosion position.

By buying butterflies, do you mean you were long the middle or long the wings [that is, the higher and lower strike price options]?

Long the wings. Your risk is limited, and if the market does not move widely, time decay works in your favor. [Barring a favorable price move or an increase in volatility, the value of an option erodes steadily over time. In a relatively flat market, the premium erosion in options with a strike price near the market price—"middle" in butterfly spread—will be greater than that of options further removed from the strike price— "wings" in spread.] Of course, I tried to buy the butterflies as cheap as I could. If I chained enough of them together, my profit zone would be fairly wide. Then I would do an explosion position in a more distant month.

What do you mean by the term "explosion position"?

That's basically my own term. An explosion position is an option position that has limited risk and open-ended potential, which will profit from a large price move or an increase in volatility. For example, a position consisting of long out-of-the-money calls and long out-of-the-money puts would be an explosion position.

It sounds like the basic unifying feature of the explosion position is that as the market moves, the *delta* [the expected price change in the option position given a one-unit change in the price of the underlying market] increases in your favor. So, you are really betting on volatility.

Exactly.

In effect, this is the opposite of what you do with the butterfly.

Yes. I put on the butterfly in the front month, where time is working for me, and the explosion position in the mid- or back-month. Then I complement that with scalping to help pay for the time decay in the explosion position.

In other words, the explosion position is your money bet in case of a big move, while your scalping is paying the bills, that is, the time decay cost of the explosion position.

Exactly.

Were you always offsetting one position with another? In other words, were you always *delta neutral*? [An option position in which total equity will remain roughly unchanged for small price changes in either direction.]

Usually, but once in a while I would take a significant net position.

What was your first really big trade?

Teledyne in 1984. The stock had dropped sharply and I was building up a position in the out-of-the-money October calls. Well, the stock started inching back up, but these guys from the Pacific Coast Exchange, where they also list Teledyne, were leaning on my longs. They just kept battering them on the close every night. Instead of shying away, I stepped up and would buy them. "You want to sell them at 1¼, I'm 1¼ bid for fifty." This went on for over ten trading days.

Why were these Pacific Coast traders leaning on the calls?

The stock had gone down from 160 to 138, and then inched its way back up to 150. I guess they didn't think it was going to go up anymore. On May 9 at 9:20 they stopped trading in Teledyne because of news pending. The news comes across the tape: "Teledyne Announces a Stock Repurchase Program at $200 per Share."

Buying back their own stock?

Yes. The stock was at $155, and I owned the $180 calls. Overnight, I made millions. The stock eventually went up to $300. The next four to five months were great.

What happened after that?

One of my goals in life was to become a millionaire before I was thirty and retire. Well, I was a millionaire before I was twenty-five. I had decided to retire when I was thirty. On May 5, 1985, my thirtieth birthday, I walked off the floor and said good-bye to everybody and that was it. I was never going to come back to the floor.

How far were you up then?

About $8–9 million.

Did you know what you were going to do?

I didn't really know. I thought I'd stay in the business somehow, but work off the floor.

How long did your retirement last?

About four months.

Were you bored?

Yes. I missed the markets. I missed the excitement.

So, in the beginning, money was the goal, but once you got there it became—

Yes, it became secondary. Maybe if I had a wife and kids, or someone special in my life, I might not have gone back. But trading was my life. It made me feel like something; it gave me a reason for being.

I understand one of your best trading periods was the week of the October 1987 stock crash. Tell me about it.

I was expecting a big move, but I didn't know if it would be up or down. So, I started building the same type position that I had in Teledyne.

The butterfly spread combined with the explosion position.

Yes.

What was the explosion position in this case?

In this case, it was formed by buying out-of-the-money puts and out-of-the-money calls in the back months. To counterbalance this position, I had butterfly spreads in the front month, which would profit from time decay.

What told you the market was going to have a big move?

You could feel it in the wild gyrations that were occurring by late September.

Did you expect the move to be on the downside by that time?

Actually, I thought it was going to be on the upside. At first, I thought we were going to attack the old highs again.

When did you change your mind?

On Wednesday of the week before the crash, the market fell apart. Thursday, it didn't bounce back, but kind of churned. Now, if it had rallied on Friday, then I would have been confused. But instead, the market cracked on Friday. At that point, I was sure we were going down.

Because it was the end of the week?

Yes, and there is a high correlation between the action on a Friday and the follow-through on the next Monday—at least on the opening.

Did you have any inkling of the size of the impending move on the following Monday?

Do you know what I really thought was going to happen Monday? I thought the market would open lower, go down sharply, and then bounce back to about unchanged. I actually bought out-of-the-money calls that Friday for protection.

But you said you thought the market was going down?

Yes, but I just wanted to have some insurance. A trader once told me, "Saliba, in stealing second, you never take your hand off first until your other hand is on second." That's the way I am; I always have insurance.

Still, you must have been awfully confident that the market was going sharply lower on Monday morning. According to the cover story in *Success* magazine [April 1988], it sounds like you knew the market would collapse. It says you even deliberately chose to go to the office instead of the floor to avoid being influenced out of your position by all the confusion on the floor. Isn't that highly unusual for you to go to the office instead of the floor on a trading day?

Yes, if I'm trading, I'm on the floor. But that article is completely misleading. They wrote it that way to sell magazines. They make it sound like I planned and plotted to avoid the floor that day. That's not the story. I was concerned about the positions held by my clearing firm. One guy in particular had a huge position, which he wasn't closing, and I had to spend a great deal of time on the phone. Now, that's not as dramatic as the way the magazine wrote it up, but that's what really happened.

Didn't you also sell your seat that day? You must have been really confident the market was going down to sell a seat.

I hit that seat before the market opened. I figured if I didn't hit the bid for the seat, someone else would. Anyway I had seven seats; I just sold one.

Was this the first time you traded a seat? I mean seats aren't exactly a liquid market.

Yes, it was the first time I did it like that: trading the seat round turn in one day. But I have traded seats before. I trade them depending on my mood in the market. On balance though, I want to be long seats. I believe in our industry.

But in that circumstance, it did seem like a good trade?

I figured, "Hey, I have a lot of exposure in seats—a few million dollars worth—I better take some protection." I sold that seat for $452,000 in the morning and bought it back the next afternoon for $275,000.

How much did you make that Monday?

That has caused me a lot of headaches. I would rather not say.

Obviously, your big money was made in the out-of-the-money puts. What percentage of that position did you keep as of Monday's close?

About 95 percent.

You kept most of it! But the profits were so huge. Wasn't it tempting to just take it?

The reason I didn't cover was because I felt my long puts hadn't gone up enough. They all went to parity. The puts that were thirty points in-the-money were trading at $30. In other words, the option premiums consisted almost entirely of intrinsic value; the market wasn't giving them any time value premium. Given the enormous market volatility, I thought that was crazy.

So, you figured you would wait till the next day.

Yes, and do you know what I did to hedge myself? I bought more insurance at the close on Monday. I covered hundreds of my short calls.

You were basically buying more volatility.

It was the best thing I could have done. The next day they didn't know what they wanted more of: Half the world wanted puts, and half the world wanted calls.

But everybody wanted volatility.

That's when the register really started ringing. It was the day that the sun was so close to the earth that everybody needed zinc ointment, and I was the only guy that had some left.

Let's take the other side of the fence: What did the traders who got buried in October do wrong?

They took for granted that Monday would be a normal day. They started out long, thinking the market was just correcting and was due for a bounce. Then they bought on the way down; they bought every dip.

Did some traders just freeze?

Sure, some did. I have one friend, who is a million-dollar annual earner. On Tuesday morning, I walk in and say, "Hey, Jack, what do you think? Are you going to get them today?" But he just stood there. He didn't say a word to me. He looked shell shocked. He just kept going over his sheets, looking for something to do, but not knowing what to do. So he missed all the opportunity.

Why was the way you responded to the market so different from the way your friend responded?

He wasn't sure what his position risk was. I always define my risk, and I don't have to worry about it. I walk into the pit every day with a clean slate, so that I can take advantage of what is going on.

A clean slate sounds like you come in with a flat position every day, but you obviously hold positions overnight.

I mean that I'm always hedged, and I'm always prepared.

Do you always know the maximum risk in a position that you hold? Do you always know what your worst case is?

Yes. Now, what could happen? The market sits, it explodes, or something in between. But no matter what happens, I know my worst case. My loss is always limited.

Why do so many traders who come to the floor end up losing everything?

I think the biggest problem with some traders that come on the floor is that they think they are bigger than the market. They don't fear the marketplace, and they lose sight of their discipline and the hard work ethic. Those are the traders who get blown out. But most guys on the floor really work hard.

What is the biggest misconception the public has about the marketplace?

The idea that the market has to go up for them to make money. You can make money in any kind of market if you use the right strategies. With futures, options, and the underlying markets, there are enough tools available to set up a game plan for any situation.

In other words, the public has too much of a bullish bias?

Yes, it is the American way: The market has to go up. The government never said anything about program trading when we were in a three-year bull market. Once the market started going down, all of a sudden, program trading became a major concern, and they set up commissions galore.

For the average person, like my mom or dad and their relatives, the biggest misconception is that they think when the market goes up, you make money, and when it goes down, you lose. People need to approach it from a more neutral standpoint and say, "I'm going to be a little long in this category and short in this category, but limit my short-side risk because it is infinite."

How do you handle a losing period?

How do you lose money? It is either bad day trading or a losing position. If it's a bad position that is the problem, then you should just get out of it.

Is that what you do?

Yes. I either liquidate it or neutralize it, because then you are back afloat. When you are in a boat that springs a leak, you don't drill another hole to let the water out.

What if your trading losses are due to your making bad decisions? What do you do then?

Take a day off. If I get myself all wound up, I like to lay out in the sun and bake for a while and let all the strenuous stuff go out of my head.

What are the elements of good trading?

Clear thinking, ability to stay focused, and extreme discipline. Discipline is number one: Take a theory and stick with it. But you also have to be open-minded enough to switch tracks if you feel that your theory has been proven wrong. You have to be able to say, "My method worked for this type of market, but we are not in that type of market anymore."

Trading rules you live by.

I scale in and scale out of my positions, so that I can spread out my risk. I don't like to do all of a large order right up front.

What else?

Always respect the marketplace. Never take anything for granted. Do your homework. Recap the day. Figure out what you did right and what you did wrong. That is one part of the homework; the other part is projective. What do I want to happen tomorrow? What happens if the opposite occurs? What happens if nothing happens? Think through all the "what-ifs." Anticipate and plan, rather than react.

When you made your first few million, did you sock some of it away to limit your worst case possibility?

No. My trading strategies were growing and I needed new capital. Then after I made some more, I started putting money into other investments: real estate, stores, exchange seats, and things like that. Then when the market crashed—I hate to use that term—on Monday, October 19, I realized that I didn't have a big chunk of cash anywhere, so I took a couple of million dollars out of the flow and bought T-bills. Then, a few weeks later, I used the money to buy an annuity.

I guess because your trading style is so focused on limiting losses, the first time you felt the need for a safety net was when the market seemed to be saying that a catastrophe could occur and have nothing to do with you.

Yes. What happens if you have $10 million in your trading account, but they shut down the game?

How do you set goals?

Until recently, I set goals on a monetary level. First, I wanted to become a millionaire before I was thirty. I did it before I was twenty-five. Then I decided I wanted to make so much a year, and I did that. Originally, the goals were all numbers, but the numbers aren't so important anymore. Now, I want to do some things that are not only profitable, but will also be fun. For example, I'm currently working on setting up a trading company and a software company. I also want to do the family-type thing.

How do you judge success?

I used to judge success as being the best in your field, like Bruce Springsteen in rock music. In my industry, it would have to be dollar-wise. Now, I think it is more quality of life. A lot of people think I'm a success, but I don't feel like I'm a success. I really don't. I feel like I've made a lot of money, and I've been successful at this one area in my life. I help the needy, but I don't have that family fulfillment. How do you judge success? I don't know. All I know is that all the money in the world isn't the answer.

You thought it was at one time.

Yes I did. And to be honest, money is important because it is influential. See that guy standing over there? I don't know him from Adam. But say he came over to talk to us. If he made a really bad first impression on me, I might not have much respect for him. But if you then told me that guy is worth $50 million, and he made it on his own, that would completely change my opinion of him. That may not be fair, but that's the way it is.

How does trading affect your personal life?

I'm able to handle it well from a business standpoint, but from a social standpoint it clobbers me. It doesn't allow me to give the time to women and friends that they require. People like to just sit and talk sometimes. Unless it is about business, like this with you, I'm out of here.

Are you always that conscious of time?

Yes. Most people aren't. They say, "Well, don't you ever just sit home and watch TV?"

Do you?

Well, I might have the TV on, but my head is always on trading. Last night I came back from a dinner date at midnight. I was tired and wanted to go to bed, but I was up until 2:00 A.M. figuring out trades. It's an addiction. I used to be much worse. I got lots of grief from former girlfriends because I would take my work with me on dates. I don't do that any more, but I'm always still thinking about trading.

What makes you different?

I think I can do anything, and I'm not afraid of hard work. Right now, for example, I'm working on a deal with a French bank to put together a trading company. I can't wait until this venture starts up, so that I can start working with these kids, training them to be traders. I don't know exactly how much the bank is going to give me, but I could have hundreds of millions to work with. I love that type of challenge.

It is important to realize that many of the great traders interviewed in this book were not immediately successful. Saliba's initial trading experience was so disastrous that it brought him to a near suicidal state of mind. However, what these traders share is a sense of self-confidence and persistence. In the case of early failure, these traits are enough to lead to eventual success. Besides allowing him to make a comeback from his early poor start, Saliba's persistence also came into play at other points in his trading career. For example, many others faced with the type of constant ridicule that Saliba was subjected to in the Teledyne pit might have abandoned their strategy.

This same Teledyne example also illustrates another important characteristic of the superior trader: the maintenance of rigid risk control, even in difficult circumstances. It must have been very tempting for Saliba to trade a larger position size in the Teledyne pit when he was being derided as "one-lot." Instead, he maintained his discipline and continued to trade small until his capital had grown sufficiently to allow him to increase his position size.

Working hard and examining many different scenarios so that he is prepared for all contingencies is a critical element of Saliba's success. By anticipating all the "what-ifs," he can take advantage of situations such as the October 19 stock slide, instead of being immobilized by such events. For many people, the concept of a great trader conjures up an image of someone using a shoot-from-the-hip approach, moving in and out of markets with great agility and a near sixth sense. The reality is far less glamorous. In the majority of cases, exceptional traders owe their success to hard work and preparation. In fact, similar to Tony Saliba, many of the very successful traders will do their "homework" every night, not allowing leisure or other business from interfering with their daily regimen of market analysis. When they stray from that discipline, it usually ends up costing them money. In Saliba's own words, referring to a recently missed trade due to his failure to have his orders in while on a business trip, "It cost me ten grand, and all those little ten grands can add up."

Part V

The Psychology of Trading

Dr. Van K. Tharp

The Psychology of Trading

Dr. Van K. Tharp is a research psychologist who received his Ph.D. from the University of Oklahoma, Health Sciences Center, in 1975. He has spent his career studying how stress affects human performance. His strongest interest is in the psychology of winning—especially as winning applies to the markets. In 1982, Dr. Tharp developed his Investment Psychology Inventory, a test that measures winning and losing traits. Thousands of investors and speculators—myself included—have taken this test, which includes a written evaluation and a ten-minute phone consultation. Dr. Tharp has written five books on successful investing which provide the core of his investment course. He is a contributing editor for *Technical Analysis of Stocks and Commodities* and has also written numerous articles for other financial publications. Dr. Tharp is a frequent guest on financial television and radio programs, and has spoken at many investment conferences.

Dr. Tharp currently devotes himself full time to counseling traders from his office in Glendale, California, and continuing his research on trading success. A recent focus of this research has been interviewing and studying top traders so that he could create a model for success. His basic theory is that by teaching the winning traits of the top traders (not specific trading methodologies), he can dramatically improve the performance of less successful traders and investors. In his most recent project, he is attempting to turn his most successful clients into "super-traders" by extending his normal program of two two-day sessions into an ongoing semiannual process.

After I interviewed Dr. Tharp, he asked whether he could do a video tape interview of me as part of his ongoing research. Since I thought such an interview might be helpful in improving my own trading performance, I eagerly agreed. The interview lasted for over four hours. Dr. Tharp has a particularly probing questioning style. After an initial response to a question, he would ask, "What else?" and repeat this process several times. When I could no longer think of any additional responses, he would have me shift the direction of my gaze (he later explained this instruction was intended to facilitate accessing different parts of my brain), and sure enough I would think of another point I had somehow overlooked. I felt that this interview yielded some important personal insights. (One of these self-realizations is briefly discussed in the next chapter.)

I would have liked to provide my personal impression of Dr. Tharp's basic course, which includes five books and four tapes. However, although I reviewed the material briefly as background for this chapter, the combination of simultaneously working at a full-time job and writing this book did not leave me with enough time (or energy) to give the course the serious attention it calls for—a personal project I plan for later. I can, however, attest to the fact that one of the traders interviewed in this book served as a subject in Dr. Tharp's project on modeling success and was duly impressed with his intellect and insight into successful trading.

How did you first get interested in the connection between psychology and trading?

My primary research interest after graduate school was how various drugs affect human performance. After receiving my Ph.D. in psychology, I spent about eight years doing fairly standard psychological research. For example, I helped standardize the current Field Sobriety Test Battery that police throughout the country are still using. While I was doing that, I also learned how to lose money trading options. In fact, I lost money so fast and so consistently that when I finally got out of the market, I had to conclude that the losses had something to do with me.

During that same time period, I enrolled in a class in prosperity at the local Church of Religious Science. One of the principles taught in that class is that what happens to you reflects your mindset. I had read a lot on the psychology of trading, and while I considered most of that information to be "folklore," I wanted to test it out. I decided to do so by developing my Investment Psychology Inventory, a test to measure investment strengths and weaknesses, as a creative project for that class. No one in the class would take it, so I sent it to R. E. McMaster, the editor of a newsletter to which I was subscribing. McMaster took it and then offered it to his subscribers. Overall, I received close to a thousand responses and that really roused my interest in this area as a career.

What did you learn in analyzing the responses to your test? Were there any major surprises?

I had several measures of success built into the test, so I could rank the responses according to "success level." The investment literature suggested ten different areas that might be important. As a result, I designed questions to measure each of those areas. I did a number of statistical analyses of the data and found a significant correlation between each area and investment success. In addition, I found that those ten areas could be grouped into three major clusters, which I label the psychological factor, the management and discipline factor, and the decision-making factor. Although I've since refined the test, I still use the same three major clusters. In addition, I still keep the ten original areas, and I've added an extra one—intuition.

What are the eleven areas you measure?

Well, the psychological factor has five areas. These include a well-rounded personal life, a positive attitude, the motivation to make money, lack of conflict, and responsibility for results. Motivation to make money is not significantly correlated with success, but I keep it in the test because lack of such motivation plus high conflict is very significant.

There are three factors in the decision-making area. These include a solid knowledge of technical factors in the market, an aptitude for making sound decisions without common biases, and the ability to think independently. Incidentally, knowledge of technical factors has little relationship to success based on the test scores.

Also, there are three management-discipline factors. One needs risk control and the ability to be patient. In addition, I also include intuition in this category. Although I have not found any relationship between intuition and trading success, I keep the factor in the test because it is interesting to me.

Given those areas, what are the characteristics of the losing trader?

The composite profile of a losing trader would be someone who is highly stressed and has little protection from stress, has a negative outlook on life and expects the worst, has a lot of conflict in his/her personality, and blames others when things go wrong. Such a person would not have a set of rules to guide their behavior and would be more likely to be a crowd follower. In addition, losing traders tend to be disorganized and impatient. They want action now. Most losing traders are not as bad as the composite profile would suggest. They just have part of the losing profile.

You now consult with many traders. How did you get started in that?

After I started using the test regularly, people began to ask me what to do about their particular problems. Since investment psychology is a rather unique area of study, I found I didn't know how to respond to many of their questions. As a result, I decided to write a pamphlet on each of the ten areas—both to learn about the areas myself and to provide investors with a source of help. The first pamphlet turned into a book. I decided at that point to cover the subject matter in five workbooks which would constitute a course in the psychology of investing/trading. After I finished the second workbook, I started training in Neuro-Linguistic Programming (NLP). NLP is really a science of how to duplicate success, and I was able to incorporate a number of those techniques into my course. The development of the course naturally led to a private consulting service.

Have your ideas and concepts changed from what they were early in your research?

I designed the test to predict who could win and who couldn't. Now, I believe that anyone can win if they are committed to do so. Primarily, it's just a matter of learning how.

Too many people get stuck by the beliefs they hold, yet they continue to cling to those old beliefs. My beliefs, in contrast, are constantly evolving, and I think it's because I value them according to their utility. Thus, I'm willing to admit most of my beliefs are probably wrong. For example, there may be people who could not be successful in trading even if they were committed to doing so. But right now, it's most useful for me to believe that anyone can win. When I hold that belief, I am much more effective at helping people become winners.

Could you provide some specific case examples of people who succeeded or failed in consultation?

One trader who came to me hadn't been able to trade for over a year. He wanted me to get him trading before he did the full consultation. As a result, I had him drop by one morning for about forty-five minutes. I gathered some information and made an educated guess that he had a conflict problem. He then went through an exercise that took about ten minutes. It took him two weeks to mentally integrate the results of that exercise, but after that he was trading again. He'd spent a lot of money and done a lot of things to correct the problem and none of it had worked. Yet, it only took a ten-minute exercise and two weeks of integrating the results to solve his problem.

I tried that with another person who was unable to afford my consulting fee, for whom a simple exercise of that nature didn't work. His problem had nothing to do with his investing. Although he was in his late forties, he was still a little boy in that he couldn't accept adult responsibilities. He still lived with his mother, and his whole lifestyle supported being a child. The only reason he wanted to trade was to be able to continue that lifestyle. I doubt that I could have helped him without a major commitment on his part to change his lifestyle, which he was unwilling to give.

Another client made minor adjustments after two days of consulting. He was reluctant to do the follow-up because he thought it would probably be superfluous. But he eventually decided to do it. I spent another two days listening to him talk and then we did a simple exercise together. At the end of that exercise, he was a totally changed person (although it probably took him a week to integrate the effects of that exercise). He called me two months later and said he had made over $650,000 trading in the markets.

In the case of a trader who uses a nonquantifiable approach (for example, "I buy or sell whenever I get a feeling about the market's impending direction from the chart patterns"), how do you distinguish whether trading problems are related to lack of skill or to psychological impediments to success?

Before I take someone on as a client, I need to know that they have some sort of methodology that they think works. I determine what evidence they have of that. Can they, for example, convince me? Have they tested that methodology? Does their testing amount to a hindsight evaluation, or is it based on actual trading signals that one can follow. I also am convinced that it is difficult to make money day trading or trading in a short time frame, so I am skeptical about anyone who wants me to help them day trade successfully.

At the same time, I think that lack of skill is, in itself, a psychological impediment to trading. People don't develop a systematic approach or don't test their approach because of poor judgment, lack of goals, internal conflict, etc. So, perhaps the area they need help in is overcoming internal resistance to developing a systematic approach to the market. If somebody came to me and said that was the problem they wanted help with, I would have no problem at all accepting that person as a client.

What are the primary psychological impediments that keep most people from being winning traders? How can they deal with each of those problems?

What typically happens is that when people approach the markets, they bring their personal problems with them. The markets are a natural place to act out those problems, but not to solve them. Most people end up leaving the markets, but a few decide that they need a system to trade more effectively. Those people who do adopt a systems approach usually just end up transferring their problems from dealing with the market to dealing with their system of trading.

One of the basic problems that most traders face is dealing with risk. For example, two primary rules to successful speculative trading are: Cut your losses short and let your profits run. Most people cannot deal with those two rules. For example, if making money is important to you—as it is to most people who play investment games—then you will probably have trouble taking small losses. As a result, small losses turn into moderate losses, which are even harder to take. Finally, the moderate losses turn into big losses, which you are forced to take—all because it was so hard to take a small loss. Similarly, when people have a profit, they want to take it right away. They think, "I'd better take this now before it gets away." The bigger the profit becomes, the harder it is to resist the temptation to take it now. The simple truth is that most people are *risk-aversive* in the realm of profits—they prefer a sure, smaller gain to a wise gamble for a larger gain—and *risk-seeking* in the realm of losses—they prefer an unwise gamble to a sure loss. As a result, most people tend to do the opposite of what is required for success. They cut their profits short and let their losses run.

If you think of trading as a game and that a mistake is not following the rules of the game, then it becomes much easier to follow these two rules. You should review your rules at the beginning of the day and review your trading at the end of the day. If you followed your rules, even if you lost money, pat yourself on the back. If you didn't follow your rules, then mentally rehearse what you did and give yourself more appropriate choices in the future.

The second major problem people have is dealing with stress. Stress really takes two forms: worry and the biological fight/flight response. Our brains have a limited capacity for processing information. If your mind is preoccupied with worry, that worry takes up most of the decision space, and you don't have enough capacity left to perform effectively.

One aspect of the fight/flight response is that it causes people to narrow their focus. They revert to earlier well-practiced response patterns. For example, a common decision that people make under stress is not to decide. They do what they did when they were a beginner. They do what their broker advises. In short, they do anything simple. Simple solutions are rarely correct. When people are stressed, they also tend to be crowd followers. The behavior of others provides a simple example to follow. Crowd followers don't have to make decisions, but crowd following is a sure way to lose money in the markets.

A second important effect of the fight/flight response is that it causes people to expend more energy. When faced with stressful events, people give more effort to the few alternatives they do consider. They keep on doing what they were doing—only they do it harder. Putting more energy into trading decisions does not help you make more money. Instead you will tend to make quick, irrational choices, which use up some of that excess energy. You probably put more energy into a losing position by actively resisting closing it out. The result is a bigger loss. In summary, the fight/flight response will decrease your performance by causing you to narrow your choices and concentrate more energy on the remaining alternatives.

The solution for dealing with stress is to work on the causes and to develop stress protectors. I would recommend that people with this problem go into a stress management program. Also, it is important to understand that many stressful events are such because of the way you perceive them. Change those perceptions and you will change the event itself. For example, winners typically differ from losers in their attitude about losses. Most people become anxious about losses, yet successful speculators have learned that an essential ingredient to winning is to make it OK to lose. Since most people in our culture are taught that only winning is acceptable, most investors must change their beliefs about losses to become successful.

The third major problem that people have is dealing with conflict. People have different parts of themselves, each of which has a positive intention. For example, someone might have a part to make money, a part to protect him from failure, a part to make him feel good about himself, a part which looks after the welfare of the family, etc. Now, once you establish these parts, you usually allow them to operate subconsciously. What happens is the parts continually adopt new behaviors to carry out their intentions. Sometimes, those new behaviors can produce major conflicts. This model of conflict is one of my most useful beliefs. I'm not saying that people actually have parts, but it is very useful in helping people solve their trading problems for me to believe that. You just have to make them aware of their parts and then conduct a formal negotiation between the parts so that each part is satisfied. If possible, you also want to integrate the parts so that they join together.

I find the concept of people having different parts in conflict with each other a little difficult to conceptualize. Could you provide an example?

I worked with a floor trader whose father was fairly successful. His father was not a good model for him, however, in that he was an alcoholic. As a result, he developed a part to protect himself from being like his father. He could make about $75,000 per year trading, but if he made any more than that, this part kicked in to make sure that he would not become too successful. He was the one who made $650,000 in about two months after we had completed the parts negotiation.

Are you implying that some people actually want to lose on a sub-conscious level because it fulfills some other positive intention? How common is that?

Half the traders I work with have problems of this nature. I think it's very common.

So far, you've cited poor risk attitudes, stress, and conflict as im-pediments to trading success. Are there any other major problems people have with the markets?

A fourth major problem is that many people allow their emotions to con-trol their trading. In fact, most trading problems appear to involve emo-tional control in some manner. I know of at least ten methods of helping people control their mental states. An easy method that people can adopt right away is simply to control posture, breathing, and muscle tension. If you change those factors, you will probably find that you change your emotional state.

Finally, the last major problem is making decisions. Although there are many facets to decision-making problems, what most people do is bring their normal method of making decisions to trading the markets. For example, think about what you go through in order to buy a new car. You have to think about the model, make, deal, service, cost, accessories, etc. And it probably takes you a week or more to evaluate those factors and make a decision. Most people bring that same method of making decisions to trading and it just doesn't work. It takes too much time. So, the solution is to adopt a trading system that gives you signals to act. But most people with a trading system continue to apply their normal method of making decisions to the signals given to them by their trading system. And, of course, that doesn't work. The best method that I've found of dealing with long, ineffective decision-making problems is to short circuit them through a process called anchoring. That process is a little too involved to explain here.

Do you believe that most people can be successful traders if they learn to eliminate negative emotions?

Well, that assumes that negative emotions are the cause of trading problems. I think they are just a symptom of the basic problem. In most cases, I don't believe it's even necessary to solve specific problems to produce success—you simply have to teach people to do things in an effective manner. The teaching process, however, involves working with how people think, and most trainers do not emphasize that.

Right now, I consider myself to be an expert modeler. By that, I mean that if someone can do something well, then I can figure out how they do it and teach those skills to anyone else. I'm concentrating on modeling trading and investment excellence. So naturally, I believe that I can teach anyone who is committed to being a successful trader to be one of the best.

Are superior traders better because of keener analytical skills, or because they have better emotional control?

Better emotional control, but I think that both of those factors are over-emphasized.

So what does it take to duplicate successful trading?

There are three primary factors involved in duplicating success—beliefs, mental states, and mental strategies. If you duplicate the way the best traders use those three factors for every aspect of the trading task, then you can duplicate their results. As a nontrading example, most martial arts experts believe that it takes years of practice to break a board with your bare hand. I was able to observe someone for about fifteen minutes and then break two ½-inch pine boards with my hand. I even showed my son (who was ten at the time) how to do it. That's the power behind modeling.

What happens with most experts is that they are unconsciously competent. They do things well, which means they do them automatically. For example, most people are unconsciously competent at driving a car. You don't even think about it when you do it. When someone who is unconsciously competent tries to explain what he or she is doing to someone else, much of what is important is left out. Thus, my focus is to discover the missing pieces and help people install those pieces.

Let's talk about the first factor: beliefs. How are beliefs important to trading success?

Let me give you an example from another modeling project. The Army modeled the rifle skills of the two best sharpshooters in the U.S. They were then able to develop a training class for Army recruits in which they reduced the training time from four to two days, while increasing the qualification rate from 80 to 100 percent. In addition, they were able to use the same knowledge to help the top shooters improve their skills. The information they gathered about shooting beliefs was particularly revealing.

The two top shooters, for example, believed:

- Shooting well is important for my survival.
- Hunting is fun.
- Mental rehearsal is important to successful performance.
- If I miss a shot, it has something to do with my performance.

One of the two top shooters, when they were in competition together, always won. And you could tell the difference between the two in accordance with their beliefs. For example, the best shooter believed that it was important to rehearse an entire 1,000-round match the prior evening, whereas the second best shooter only believed that mental rehearsal was important. In addition, the best shooter believed that it was important to hit the center of the bull's eye on each shot (even though you didn't get extra points for that), whereas the second best shooter believed that it was only important to hit the bull's eye. Can you understand why one was better than the other just from their beliefs?

Now, contrast the beliefs of top shooters with the beliefs of new recruits coming into the Army. The latter might believe:

- Guns are evil; they kill people.
- If they shoot this weapon too many times, they might go deaf.
- If they miss the target, it means the gun is misaligned.

I think, just on beliefs alone, you can begin to understand why the top shooters were so much better than the raw recruits.

Now, let me explain some of my findings in working with top traders. You might find some of these beliefs confirmed in other interviews in your book. Generally, I find that top traders believe:

- Money is NOT important.
- It is OK to lose in the markets.
- Trading is a game.
- Mental rehearsal is important for success.
- They've won the game before they start.

Although there are a lot more than five critical beliefs, I think these five are among the most important. Most people approach trading to make a lot of money, and that is one of the primary reasons they lose. Because money is so important, they have trouble taking losses and letting profits run. In contrast, when you think of trading as a game and play by certain rules, then it becomes much easier to follow those two golden rules.

In addition, because of mental rehearsal and extensive planning, top traders have already gone through all the trial and error in their mind before they begin. As a result, they know they are going to win in the long run, and that makes the little setbacks much easier to deal with.

You mentioned that winners know they've won the game before they start. Although I can easily see how such confidence would be beneficial for the established winning trader, might the impact of this trait actually be reversed for the novice trader? For example, in your first week on skis, confidence about your ability to go down the expert slope might not be such a great quality. How does the less expert trader distinguish between justified and misplaced confidence?

The top traders that I've worked with began their careers with an extensive study of the markets. They developed and refined models of how to trade. They mentally rehearsed what they wanted to do extensively until they had the belief that they would win. At this point, they had both the confidence and the commitment necessary to produce success. In addition, they also had the entire constellation of beliefs I just described. As a result, I believe that there are three major differences between justified confidence and misplaced confidence. First of all, justified confidence comes from a constellation of beliefs, such as the one I just described. If a trader has confidence and nothing else, he is probably in a lot of trouble. Second, justified confidence comes from extensive testing of some sort of model of trading. If you don't have a model that you have properly tested, then your confidence is probably misplaced. Third, justified confidence comes with an extensive commitment to being successful as a trader. Most people who want to be traders are not committed—they just think they are. There is a poem by W. N. Murray, of the Scottish Himalayan expedition, that says: "That the moment that one definitely commits oneself, then Providence moves too."

If you are really committed, then not only are you certain that you are doing the right thing, but somehow events just seem to occur to help you. If you are really committed to being a trader, then you probably have an understanding at some level of what I'm talking about. You probably even understand that those events that help you might be big losses. If you are not committed, on the other hand, then you are probably saying, "I don't understand what Tharp is saying. I'm committed, but events certainly have not been helping me."

Earlier, you mentioned "mental states" as the second critical factor in modeling success. Could you explain what you mean by that?

If you ask people to list their trading or investment problems, they are of two types—problems they don't own and mental state control problems. Problems they don't own consist of blaming the markets, blaming floor traders or locals, blaming insider trading, blaming their broker, or blaming their system for what goes wrong. We have a natural tendency to blame something other than ourselves for what happens. Society promotes it. For example, the recent media coverage of program trading virtually implies that investors who lost money in the stock market did so because of this activity, rather than because of any fault of their own. Yet, when you blame something other than yourself, you can continue to repeat the mistake because it was the result of something beyond your control.

The best thing an investor can do, when things go wrong, is to determine how he or she produced those results. Now, I don't mean that you should blame yourself for your mistakes either. I mean that at some point in time, for any situation, you made a choice that produced those results. Determine what that choice point was and give yourself other options to take when you encounter a similar choice point in the future. Change the decision at similar choice points in the future and you will change the results you get. And by imagining doing so now, you can make it easy to select those alternatives in the future.

When people own their own problems, they discover that their results usually stem from some sort of mental state. Common examples are:

- I'm too *impatient* with the markets.
- I get *angry* at the markets.
- I'm *afraid* at the wrong time.
- I'm too *optimistic* about what will happen.

These are just a few examples of mental state problems. Once you identify a mental state problem, you can do something about it because this sort of problem is within your control. I've already mentioned how one can use body posture, breathing, and muscle control to manipulate one's mental state. To try this out for yourself, go into a shopping mall and notice how other people walk. Duplicate a dozen or so walks for yourself and notice how your mental state changes with each one.

I'm not saying that controlling your mental state is the magic solution to trading success. It's just part of the answer. But when you admit that the answer is within yourself, you've come a long way. The realization that you are responsible for the results you get is the key to successful investing. Winners know they are responsible for their results; losers think they are not.

Can you give a practical example of how someone can control their mental state?

Well, mental state manipulation is what most people call discipline. I teach people a very simple procedure that they can use right away. For example, suppose you are at your desk and you become aware that you are in a mental state that you would like to change. Get up out of the chair. Walk away about four feet and then look at how you looked in that chair. Notice your posture, your breathing, your facial expressions. Then imagine how you would look if you had the sort of mental state you would like. When you can see that clearly, sit down in the chair again and assume the position that you just imagined. That exercise works for almost any situation as it involves several important principles—changing your body posture, seeing yourself from a more objective viewpoint, and imagining a more resourceful state.

Please elaborate on mental strategies—the third element you cited earlier as critical to duplicating success. Could you provide some examples?

To understand strategies, you have to understand how people think. People think in the same modalities as their five senses, that is, in terms of visual images, sounds, feelings, and for some people, tastes and smells. Those five modalities are to mental strategies as the alphabet is to a great novel, or as musical notes are to a great symphony. It's not the elements, but the way in which the elements are put together. A mental strategy is really the sequence in which you think.

Rather than explain a complex topic in detail, which I think is beyond the scope of this interview, let me give you two examples. First, imagine that you have a trading system that gives you specific signals. Since most signals are visual, such as a particular chart pattern or certain signals on your computer, imagine that your system gives you visual signals. Now, try on the following strategy:

- See the signal.
- Recognize that it is familiar.
- Tell yourself what might go wrong if you take it.
- Feel bad about it.

Could you trade effectively using that strategy? Would you even take the signal? Probably not! What if you used the following strategy?

- See the signal.
- Recognize that it is familiar.
- Feel good about it.

Could you trade from that signal? Probably. So even though the two strategies are quite similar, they lead to very different results in terms of trading. If you are trading a system, you need a simple strategy like the last one in order to use it effectively.

Two of the top traders that you used in your research in modeling success have completely different trading styles. One is very mechanical, while the other uses a much more intuitive approach. Could you contrast their differences and compare their similarities?

First, let me talk about their similarities, because they are extensive. In fact, when you find extensive similarities between two excellent traders who seem so different, then you can begin to assume that those similarities are essential to successful trading. Both traders, for example, developed models for how the markets work and did extensive research to test those models. Although their ideas are very different, I think the process of developing and testing some sort of model is probably very important. In addition, both traders share all the same beliefs that I mentioned earlier as common to successful traders. Third, both traders are very aware of their purpose in life and as a trader. They believe they are part of a "bigger picture" and they just go with the flow.

The mechanical trader is very logical. He constructs his models visually in his imagination. He is very precise in his language and thinking. His models tend to focus on his concept of how to trade successfully and of how the economy works. He does not believe that his models are adequate until they can be converted into algorithms for the computer that match his own mental processes. As a result of this belief, he has computerized his models, modifying both his constructed image and his computer output, until both models match—in his words, "until they both look right." This is a very slow and laborious process. I think it hinders his decision making on everyday events, and he tends to agree with me, but it helps him in the long run. When his mental image and the computer model match, he virtually takes himself out of the trading picture. The computer does everything, so at that point, decision making is easy for him.

The intuitive trader, in contrast, has developed a model of how he thinks markets operate, rather than a model of how to trade successfully. He also believes that the markets are constantly evolving and that it is more important to keep up with changes in the market than to test his models by developing an algorithm to computerize them. He trades from his expectations of what the markets will do, which are visualizations. But I think that he tends to convert his visualizations into feelings. Feelings actually are a mode of thinking, but they are difficult to communicate to others or to computerize. As a result, he believes that exercises such as computerizing a trading system are a waste of time. Remember that his main emphasis is to explain how markets work (rather than how to trade), and he believes that the markets are constantly evolving. As a result, he has difficulty explaining how he trades to anyone else. He just calls it intuitive. At the same time, he makes day-to-day decisions easily—a distinct contrast to the mechanical trader who is uncomfortable until he has proven his work by computerizing it.

What are the most difficult problems to solve?

I think there are only two difficult problems. One is lack of commitment to trading. People are not going to do what I tell them to do unless they are committed to becoming a good trader, so I don't see many noncommitted traders. It's only occasionally, when I do a free or reduced-rate consultation, that I see traders with this sort of problem. The man who wanted to remain a little boy, and was trying to use trading as a means of accomplishing that, was a classic example. I don't make the mistake of seeing noncommitted traders too often.

The second most difficult situation is the trader who does not own his problems. This person can continue to repeat his problems because he never gets at the source. Once again, I usually don't see these people. When people come to me, they realize that they produce their own problems, although, to some extent, everyone has problems that they don't own—even my clients.

Among the people who come to see me, I think the most difficult type is the compulsive gambler. Since these people typically crave the action of the markets, they are not likely to want my help until they are heavily into debt. At that point, I refer them to Gamblers Anonymous or to some local source for help. However, I have had one compulsive trader among my clients. He's now in my super-trader program. I've simply channeled his compulsiveness from the markets into working on himself.

I'm not sure that correcting trading problems is always the answer though. For example, one approach to teaching a class on trading would be to give everyone the fundamentals in the first session and a simple trading system in the second. You could then spend the remaining sessions dealing with their problems trading that system. That would probably be a very effective class. On the other hand, you could conduct the same class by giving them the fundamentals. Then you might give them the beliefs, mental states, and mental strategies necessary to trade the system. Finally, you might give them the system. I'm willing to bet that the second method would be more effective than the first. At least that is the direction I'm heading.

Talk about the origins, concepts, and direction of your super-trader program.

It all began on Christmas Eve one year, when that one trader called and told me that he had made $650,000 in the two months since I had finished working with him. In a sense, I felt that we had only started working together. The more I thought about it, the more the question kept popping into my mind: "What if we pushed this to the limits? What is he capable of accomplishing?" So the idea of the super-trader program was born from those thoughts. I called him up and suggested the idea to him. Naturally, he was all for it.

About four of my clients have now graduated to the super-trader program. It simply means that I continue to work with these people on a regular basis (usually semiannually). The idea is to stretch their performance to the limits. Many people aren't ready for that, but I have enough among my clients who are. Who knows, in three or four years, I might just have about fifty top traders that I work with on a continual basis! Incidentally, I find that my best clients now make excellent models to use to study top traders.

I sometimes have dreams which involve impending market direction. Although these are rather infrequent, they prove right a high percentage of the time. Is this unusual?

I imagine that it's quite common because people tell me that all the time, especially top traders. For example, both the mechanical and intuitive super-traders that we talked about earlier expressed that they had dreams about the market that were amazingly accurate. But most traders say that such dreams are infrequent enough so that they could not trade on them regularly. This phenomenon may even occur more frequently than one might imagine—in symbolic form. But most people do not bother to interpret their dreams, so they miss the symbolic predictions. However, I must admit that although it interests me, I have not investigated this area very extensively.

I know of lots of people of genius level who claim that some of their creativity comes from their dreams. Michael Jackson claims he doesn't write his songs—they just come to him. Paul McCartney said that he heard the song "Yesterday" in a dream. Einstein essentially dreamed the theory of relativity. I think there are probably a lot of famous examples of this sort. It all boils down to what intuition really is, but don't ask me to explain it. I don't understand it—YET!

I assume that the reason you have not tried trading again is that you perceive that it would interfere with your objectivity in dealing with your clients. Yet, given all that you have learned about successful trading during the past five years, I imagine there must be some temptation to try it again. How do you handle this conflict? What do you envision as the long-term resolution?

There are two reasons I don't trade. The first is the reason you mentioned about objectivity with clients. If I'm helping someone trade and I have conflicting positions, then I may not be very objective about what they are doing. An equally important reason, however, is that I am fully committed to doing what I am doing. I love helping other people, writing, giving talks, and so on. I'm very happy doing that. It is also a sixty-hour per week job right now. If I wanted to start trading, then I would have to devote almost as much time to doing that, at least at the beginning. Why should I do that and give up what I already know I love doing? Player coaches, in the history of most sports, usually are not that effective at either coaching or playing.

Your question also assumes that I am committed to trade, and as a result there is a conflict. Actually, I find that as I get more and more into helping others become successful, I have less and less interest in trading myself. I'm investing in myself and in my business right now. I constantly work at improving my skills and knowledge, and that is paying off for me. Why should I dilute that effort? Perhaps some time in the future, I will decide that I have done everything I can do, or perhaps I'll want to change what I'm doing, or perhaps I'll just want a break. For example, three to four years from now I might just be working with fifty or more top quality traders. If that happens, then maybe I'll also trade. But for the near future, it doesn't seem very likely.

The Trade

A Personal Experience

In the course of conducting the interviews for this book, I came to realize that one of my primary motives for the entire project was a quest for self-discovery. Although I have been a net profitable trader over the years (substantially multiplying a small initial stake on two separate occasions), I had a definite sense of failure about my trading. Given the extent of my knowledge and experience about markets and trading, as well as the fact that on numerous occasions I had correctly anticipated major price moves, I felt that my winnings were small potatoes compared to what I should have made.

In one of my trips for this book, on one evening, I was interviewed at length about my trading by Dr. Van Tharp, and the very next evening, I had a probing conversation about my trading with the very perceptive Ed Seykota. This back-to-back experience caused me to focus intensely on the flaws that had prevented me from reaching what I perceived to be my true potential as a trader.

As a result of this self-examination, I came to realize that one of my great errors had been failing to exploit major price moves that I had correctly anticipated. Invariably, my initial position would be far too small, given the potential I perceived in such trades. This mistake was then compounded by a highly premature liquidation of the position. Typically, I would take profits on the first leg of the price move, with the intention of reentering the position on a correction. The problem was that subsequent corrections usually fell short of my reentry points and, refusing to chase the market, I ended up watching the rest of the price move unfold while I was on the sidelines. I vowed to myself that the next time such a situation would arise, I would make a concentrated effort to come closer to realizing the true potential of the trade.

I did not have to wait very long. Two weeks later, while on a plane to Chicago to conduct some further interviews, I was thinking about my review of the price charts the previous evening. I recalled that I had come away with the distinct impression that precious metal prices were ready to move higher, even though the foreign currency markets appeared vulnerable to further price erosion. Suddenly, the trade I should have made became crystal clear. Given my combination of expectations, a trade of long precious metals and short foreign currencies would be particularly attractive. (Since these markets normally move in the same direction, the combined position implied less risk than an outright long position in precious metals.) I made a mental note to generate some charts on this trade at my first opportunity.

The next morning, I found a quote machine capable of generating price charts and sat down to evaluate various price relationships. First, I looked at the interrelationships between silver, gold, and platinum and decided that silver was my preferred buy among the metals. Then I reviewed the interrelationships between the various foreign currencies and decided that the Swiss franc appeared to be the weakest currency. Having made these two determinations, I then reviewed charts of the silver/Swiss franc ratio for various time spectrums, ranging from ten years to one month.

This analysis led me to the conclusion that we were at the brink of a possible multiyear advance of silver relative to the Swiss franc. Although I had intended not to trade because my traveling prevented me from paying attention to the markets, the potential of the trade seemed so dynamic that I had to put on at least a base position. To be done properly, a ratio trade requires approximately equal dollar positions in each market. I quickly calculated that at the prevailing price levels, it would require approximately three long silver contracts to balance one short Swiss franc contract.

I looked at a short-term chart of the silver/Swiss franc price ratio. To my dismay, the price ratio had already moved sharply in the direction of my intended trade since my realization about it the previous morning. Even on that morning's opening, the trade could have been implemented at much more favorable price levels. As I was trying to decide what to do, the silver/Swiss franc ratio continued to move higher and higher. I decided that I had to act to prevent the possibility of missing this trade altogether. I immediately called in an order establishing the minimum position of long three silver contracts and short one Swiss franc contract. No sooner had I placed the order than the price ratio seemed to reach its peak and began retreating. The ratio pulled back further during the next two days. As it turned out, I had managed to implement the trade at the exact worst possible moment in time since the inception of my idea. However, the silver/Swiss franc price ratio quickly recovered, and a few days later I was well ahead.

At this point, I thought about my recent realization regarding my continued failure to adequately profit from major price moves. I decided to maintain my position and, moreover, selected a reaction point for doubling up the position. The correction came about a week later and I followed my game plan. My timing proved good, as the trade once again rebounded in my favor—this time with double the initial position. Given my account size (approximately $70,000 at the time), the long six silver/short two Swiss franc position was about twice as large as the one I normally would have held. My efforts to correct my aforementioned trading flaw seemed to be paying off, as the trade raced in my favor during the following two weeks. Within a month of putting on the trade, my account was up over 30 percent,

I now faced a dilemma: On the one hand, my new-found realization suggested that I hang on to the trade for the long run. On the other hand, one of my other rules is that if you are ever lucky enough to realize a very large profit on a trade very quickly, take it, because you will usually get an opportunity to reenter the trade at considerably more favorable levels. The second rule came to mind when the silver/Swiss franc price ratio began falling.

A cursory examination of the price charts suggested it might be prudent to take at least partial profits. I should have done more analysis to reach a decision. However, the combination of having undertaken a new job, while at the same time writing this book, left me with very little time and energy to focus on other areas—trading included. Instead of doing the necessary work, I made a snap judgment to stay with the trade.

The trade now moved swiftly against me, and within a week, I had given back a significant portion of my earlier gains.

Although a week earlier, I had rationalized that my substantial profits would give me enough of a comfort cushion in the event of a reaction, now that such a reaction had occurred, I found that I had seriously misjudged my comfort level. Suddenly, I was concerned that I might give back all my profits, and possibly even ride the trade into a loss. I could not decide whether to blow out of the trade or stay with it as initially planned.

That night I had a dream. I was talking to a friend of mine, who is a developer of software for the analysis of futures and options markets, but not a trader. In my dream, he had begun trading. We were talking about trading and my current dilemma regarding the silver/Swiss franc position.

My friend commented on my predicament, "Everybody gets what they want out of the markets." I replied, "You sound just like Ed Seykota." This sounded a bit odd to me, since as far as I knew, he did not even know Seykota. To my surprise, he answered, "I have been talking to Ed Seykota for a while and I have been winning in my trading ever since."

He had a sheet in front of him, with one of the columns indicating his month-to-month ending equity. I glanced at the sheet and was astounded to see that the last figure exceeded $18 million. I exclaimed, "Bert, you have made $18 million in the market! I hope you plan to take a few million out for safekeeping." "No, I need all the money for trading," he replied. "But that is crazy," I said. "Take $3 or $4 million out, and that way you will be sure then that no matter what happens, you will come out way ahead." "I know what I am doing, and as long as I do my homework on the markets every day, I am not concerned," he replied.

His answer had implied, quite correctly, that I did not diligently do my homework on the markets every day. His point, although unstated, was quite clear: If I did my work on the markets every day, I wouldn't have any trouble understanding why he did not need to pull out several million dollars in profits from his account to feel confident that he would not lose back all his profits in trading.

"You say you don't have enough time each day to do your work on the markets. You are too busy with your new job and writing your book. Here, let me show you something." He started citing assumptions regarding the sales of my book, royalties per copy sold, and the total hours I had spent writing the book. He then scribbled various calculations on a yellow pad. He arrived at a final figure of $18.50 per hour. "Here," he said, "this is what you are making on your book." The tone of his voice implied that I was crazy to jeopardize tens of thousands of dollars in my trading for such a paltry sum. (Actually, the $18.50 estimate is probably wildly overinflated, but remember this was a dream.)

It was no coincidence that this dream occurred the night after editing the section of the Marty Schwartz interview dealing with his diligence in doing his daily homework on the markets. I realized that there are no shortcuts. If you want to be a good trader, you have to do your work on the markets every day. If there is not enough time, you have to make time. The costs for straying from this daily discipline, in terms of lost profit opportunities as well as losses, can be very substantial. The message my subconscious seemed to be crying out was: If you are going to be serious about trading, you have to reestablish your time priorities.

Postscript

Dreams and Trading

The relationship between dreams and trading is a fascinating subject. Readers may look up Seykota's and Tharp's comments on this matter. There was another interview in which this topic was prominently discussed. In that instance, the trader decided to rescind his approval for use of our conversation in the book. I was somewhat puzzled by his decision, since the chapter was basically complimentary. "What could you possibly have found so offensive as to back out completely?" I asked. "Absolutely nothing," he replied. "In fact, you made me sound almost human." It turned out that he was upset about his inclusion in a recently published book and that he was adamantly opposed to his appearance in any book. Even the offer of anonymity failed to change his decision. I did, however, manage to get his permission to use the dream-related portion of the interview. (The name references in the following conversation have been changed.)

In 1980, the year when corn set its record high, I was long the position limit. One night I had the following dream. I'm talking to myself and I say, "Hey Jerry, where is corn going to?" "To $4.15." "Where is corn now?" "$4.07." "You mean you are taking all that risk for an extra eight cents? Are you crazy?" I woke up in a flash. I knew I had to get out of my entire corn position as soon as the market opened the next day.

The next morning, the market opened up a little higher, and I started selling. The market moved a little higher, and I sold more heavily. The market moved up some more. For a minute, I thought the floor broker had executed my order backwards. He hadn't.

Anyway, a few minutes later, I'm completely out of my position and the phone rings. It's my friend Carl, another good trader, who had also been long corn. He says, "Jerry, is that you doing all the selling?" I tell him, "Yes, I just got out of my entire position." "What are you doing?" he shouts. I say, "Carl, where is corn going to?" "About $4.15–4.20," he replies. "Where is corn now?" I ask him. I hear an immediate click over the phone. He didn't even waste any time saying good-bye.

And was that the top of the corn market?

It might have gone up another day, but that was just about the high. Once it started falling, I could never have unloaded a position of my size.

I found this trader's narration of his dream particularly fascinating, since I have occasionally had similar experiences. Usually, I have found that when you feel strongly enough about a trade (either getting in or getting out) to dream about it, the message should be heeded. Of course, like anything else, this does not work all the time, but I believe it places the odds more in your favor.

As I interpret it, the dream is the means by which our subconscious penetrates the barriers we sometimes erect in accepting the true analysis of a market. For example, if I am bullish and not in a market, I might rationalize that it is prudent to wait for a reaction before entering the trade—even if a realistic assessment would suggest that such a development is unlikely. This is because entering the market at a higher price is a confirmation that, to some extent, I have already failed (that is, by not buying sooner)—a distasteful acknowledgment. In such a case, a dream that the market was going to run away on the upside might be the subconscious' way of breaking through mental impediments.

Final Word

There is no holy grail to trading success. The methodologies employed by the "market wizards" cover the entire spectrum from purely technical to purely fundamental—and everything in between. The length of time they typically hold a trade ranges from minutes to years. Although the styles of the traders are very different, many common denominators were evident:

1. All those interviewed had a driving desire to become successful traders—in many cases, overcoming significant obstacles to reach their goal.
2. All reflected confidence that they could continue to win over the long run. Almost invariably, they considered their own trading as the best and safest investment for their money.
3. Each trader had found a methodology that worked for him and remained true to that approach. It is significant that discipline was the word most frequently mentioned.
4. The top traders take their trading very seriously; most devote a substantial amount of their waking hours to market analysis and trading strategy.
5. Rigid risk control is one of the key elements in the trading strategy of virtually all those interviewed.

6. In a variety of ways, many of the traders stressed the importance of having the patience to wait for the right trading opportunity to present itself.

7. The importance of acting independent of the crowd was a frequently emphasized point.

8. All the top traders understand that losing is part of the game.

9. They all love what they are doing.

Appendix 1

Program Trading and Portfolio Insurance

One subject that has received widespread publicity in recent years is program trading. Perhaps never in the history of financial markets has there been more criticism about a trading approach that was less understood. I would venture a guess that less than one out of ten people opposed to program trading even know the definition of the term. One source of confusion is that *program trading* is used interchangeably to describe both the original activity and as a more general term encompassing various computer-supported trading strategies (for example, portfolio insurance).

Program trading represents a classic arbitrage activity in which one market is bought against an equal short sale in a closely related market in order to realize small, near *risk-free* profits, resulting from short-lived distortions in the price relationship between such markets. Program traders buy or sell an actual basket of stocks against an equal dollar value position in stock index futures when they perceive the actual stocks to be underpriced or overpriced relative to futures. In effect, program trading tends to keep actual stock and stock index futures prices in line. Insofar as every program-related sale of actual stocks is offset by a purchase at another time and most program trades are first initiated as long stock/short futures positions (because of the uptick requirement in shorting actual stocks), arguments that program trading is responsible for stock market declines are highly tenuous. Moreover, since the bulk of economic evidence indicates that arbitrage between related markets tends to reduce volatility, the relationship between increased volatility and program trading is questionable at best.

Portfolio insurance refers to the systematic sale of stock index futures as the value of a stock portfolio declines in order to reduce risk exposure. Once reduced, the net long exposure is increased back toward a full position as the representative stock index price increases. The theory underlying portfolio insurance presumes that market prices move smoothly. When prices witness an abrupt, huge move, the results of the strategy may differ substantially from the theory. This occurred on October 19, 1987, when prices gapped beyond threshold portfolio insurance sell levels, triggering an avalanche of sell orders which were executed far below the theoretical levels. Although portfolio insurance may have accelerated the decline on October 19, it could reasonably be argued that the underlying forces would have resulted in a similar price decline over a greater span of days in the absence of portfolio insurance. This is a question that can never be answered. (It is doubtful that program trading, as defined above, played much of a role in the crash of the week of October 19, since the severely delayed openings of individual stocks, tremendous confusion related to prevailing price levels, and exchange restrictions regarding the use of the automated order entry systems severely impeded this activity.)

Appendix 2

*Options—Understanding the Basics**

There are two basic types of options: calls and puts. The purchase of a *call option* provides the buyer with the right—but not the obligation—to purchase the underlying item at a specified price, called the *strike* or *exercise* price, at any time up to and including the *expiration date*. A *put option* provides the buyer with the right—but not the obligation—to sell the underlying item at the strike price at any time prior to expiration. (Note, therefore, that buying a put is a *bearish* trade, while selling a put is a *bullish* trade.) The price of an option is called a *premium*. As an example of an option, an IBM April 130 call gives the purchaser the right to buy 100 shares of IBM at $130 per share at any time during the life of the option.

The buyer of a call seeks to profit from an anticipated price rise by locking in a specified purchase price. The call buyer's maximum possible loss will be equal to the dollar amount of the premium paid for the option. This maximum loss would occur on an option held until expiration if the strike price was above the prevailing market price. For example, if IBM was trading at $125 when the 130 option expired, the option would expire worthless. If at expiration, the price of the underly-

*Adapted from Jack D. Schwager, *A Complete Guide to the Futures Market* (John Wiley & Sons, New York, NY, 1984).

ing market was above the strike price, the option would have some value and would hence be exercised. However, if the difference between the market price and the strike price was less than the premium paid for the option, the net result of the trade would still be a loss. In order for a call buyer to realize a net profit, the difference between the market price and the strike price would have to exceed the premium paid when the call was purchased (after adjusting for commission cost). The higher the market price, the greater the resulting profit.

The buyer of a put seeks to profit from an anticipated price decline by locking in a sales price. Like the call buyer, his maximum possible loss is limited to the dollar amount of the premium paid for the option. In the case of a put held until expiration, the trade would show a net profit if the strike price exceeded the market price by an amount greater than the premium of the put at purchase (after adjusting for commission cost).

Whereas the buyer of a call or put has limited risk and unlimited potential gain, the reverse is true for the seller. The option seller (often called the *writer*) receives the dollar value of the premium in return for undertaking the obligation to assume an opposite position *at the strike price* if an option is exercised. For example, if a call is exercised, the seller must assume a short position in the underlying market at the strike price (since by exercising the call, the buyer assumes a long position at that price).

The seller of a call seeks to profit from an anticipated sideways to modestly declining market. In such a situation, the premium earned by selling a call provides the most attractive trading opportunity. However, if the trader expected a large price decline, he would usually be better off going short the underlying market or buying a put—trades with open-ended profit potential. In a similar fashion, the seller of a put seeks to profit from an anticipated sideways to modestly rising market.

Some novices have trouble understanding why a trader would not always prefer the buy side of the option (call or put, depending on market opinion), since such a trade has unlimited potential and limited risk. Such confusion reflects the failure to take probability into account. Although the option seller's theoretical risk is unlimited, the price levels that have the greatest probability of occurrence (i.e., prices in the vicinity of the market price when the option trade occurs) would result in a net gain to the option seller. Roughly speaking, the option buyer accepts a large probability of a small loss in return for a small probability of a large gain, whereas the option seller accepts a small probability of a large loss in exchange for a large probability of a small gain. In an efficient market, neither the consistent option buyer nor the consistent option seller should have any significant advantage over the long run.

The option premium consists of two components: intrinsic value plus time value. The *intrinsic value* of a call option is the amount by which the current market price is above the strike price. (The intrinsic value of a put option is the amount by which the current market price is below the strike price.) In effect, the intrinsic value is that part of the premium that could be realized if the option were exercised at the current market price. The intrinsic value serves as a floor price for an option. Why? Because if the premium were less than the intrinsic value, a trader could buy and exercise the option and immediately offset the resulting market position, thereby realizing a net gain (assuming that the trader covers at least transaction costs).

Options that have intrinsic value (i.e., calls with strike prices below the market price and puts with strike prices above the market price) are said to be *in-the-money*. Options that have no intrinsic value are called *out-of-the-money* options. Options with a strike price closest to the market price are called *at-the-money* options.

An out-of-the-money option, which by definition has an intrinsic value equal to zero, will still have some value because of the possibility that the market price will move beyond the strike price prior to the expiration date. An in-the-money option will have a value greater than the intrinsic value because a position in the option will be preferred to a position in the underlying market. Why? Because both the option and the market position will gain equally in the event of a favorable price movement, but the option's maximum loss is limited. The portion of the premium that exceeds the intrinsic value is called the *time value*.

The three most important factors that influence an option's time value are:

(1) *Relationship between the strike and market price*—Deeply out-of-the-money options will have little time value since it is unlikely that the market price will move to the strike price—or beyond—prior to expiration. Deeply in-the-money options have little time value, because these options offer positions very similar to the underlying market—both will gain and lose equivalent amounts for all but an extremely adverse price move. In other words, for a deeply in-the-money option, the fact

that risk is limited is not worth very much, because the strike price is so far from the prevailing market price.

(2) *Time remaining until expiration*—The more time remaining until expiration, the greater the value of the option. This is true because a longer life span increases the probability of the intrinsic value increasing by any specified amount prior to expiration.

(3) *Volatility*—Time value will vary directly with the estimated *volatility* [a measure of the degree of price variability] of the underlying market for the remaining life span of the option. This relationship is a result of the fact that greater volatility raises the probability of the intrinsic value increasing by any specified amount prior to expiration. In other words, the greater the volatility, the greater the probable price range of the market.

Although volatility is an extremely important factor in the determination of option premium values, it should be stressed that the future volatility of a market is never precisely known until after the fact. (In contrast, the time remaining until expiration and the relationship between the current market price and the strike price can be exactly specified at any juncture.) Thus, volatility must always be estimated on the basis of *historical volatility* data. The future volatility estimate implied by market prices (i.e., option premiums), which may be higher or lower than the historical volatility, is called the *implied volatility*.

Glossary

Advance/decline line. The cumulative total of the daily difference between the number of New York Stock Exchange stocks advancing and the number declining. Divergences between the advance/decline line and the market averages, such as the Dow Jones Industrial Average (DJIA), can sometimes be viewed as a market signal. For example, if after a decline, the DJIA rebounds to a new high, but the advance/decline line fails to follow suit, such price action may be reflective of internal market weakness.

Arbitrage. The implementation of purchases in one market against equivalent sales in a closely related market, because the price relationship between the two is viewed to be out of line.

Arbitrageurs. Traders who specialize in arbitrage. Arbitrageurs seek to make small profits from temporary distortions in the price relationships between related markets, as opposed to attempting to profit from correct projections of market direction.

Averaging losers (averaging down). Adding to a losing position after an adverse price move.

Bear. Someone who believes prices will decline.

Bear market. A market characterized by declining prices.

Boiler room operation. An illegal or quasilegal phone sales operation in which high-pressure tactics are used to sell financial instruments or commodities at excessive prices or inflated commissions to unsophisticated investors. For example, contracts for precious metals (or options on precious metals) might be sold at prices far above levels prevailing at organized exchanges. In some cases, such operations are complete frauds, as the contracts sold are purely fictitious.

Breakout. A price movement beyond a previous high (or low) or outside the boundaries of a preceding price consolidation.

Bull. Someone who believes that prices will rise.

Bull market. A market characterized by rising prices.

Call option. A contract that gives the buyer the right—but not the obligation—to purchase the underlying financial instrument or commodity at a specified price for a given period of time.

Chart. A graph that depicts the price movement of a given market. The most common type of chart is the *daily bar chart*, which denotes each day's high, low, and close for a given market with a single bar.

Chart analysis. The study of price charts in an effort to find patterns that in the past preceded price advances or declines. The basic concept is that the development of similar patterns in a current market can signal a probable market move in the same direction. Practitioners of chart analysis are often referred to as *chartists* or *technicians.*

Congestion. A price pattern characterized by extended sideways movement.

Consolidation. See *congestion.*

Contract. In futures markets, a standardized traded instrument that specifies the quantity and quality of a commodity (or financial asset) for delivery (or cash settlement) at a specified future date. For a more detailed explanation, see the "Taking the Mystery Out of Futures" section (page 3).

Contrarian. One who trades on contrary opinion (see next item).

Contrary opinion. The general theory that one can profit by doing the opposite of the majority of traders. The basic concept is that if a large majority of traders are bullish, it implies that most market participants who believe prices are going higher are already long, and hence the path of least resistance is down. An analogous line of reasoning would apply when most traders are bearish. Contrary opinion numbers are provided by various services that survey traders, market letters, or trading advisors.

Cover. To liquidate an existing position (i.e., sell if one is long; buy if one is short).

Day trade. A trade that is liquidated on the same day it is initiated.

Discretionary trader. In a general sense, a trader who has the power of attorney to execute trades for customer accounts without prior approval. However, the term is often used in a more specific sense to indicate a trader who makes decisions based on his own interpretation of the market, rather than in response to signals generated by a computerized system.

Divergence. The failure of a market or indicator to follow suit when a related market or indicator sets a new high or low. Some analysts look for divergences as signals of impending market tops and bottoms.

Diversification. Trading many different markets in an effort to reduce risk.

Downtrend. A general tendency for declining prices in a given market.

Drawdown. The equity reduction in an account. The *maximum drawdown* is the largest difference between a relative equity peak and any subsequent equity low. Low drawdowns are a desirable performance feature for a trader or a trading system.

Earnings per share (EPS). A company's total after-tax profits divided by the number of common shares outstanding.

Elliott Wave analysis. A method of market analysis based on the theories of Ralph Nelson Elliott. Although relatively complex, the basic theory is based on the concept that markets move in waves, forming a general pattern of five waves (or market legs) in the direction of the main trend, followed by three corrective waves in the opposite direction. One aspect of the theory is that each of these waves can be broken down into five or three smaller waves and is itself a segment of a still larger wave.

Equity. The total dollar value of an account.

Fade. To trade in the opposite direction of a market signal (or analyst). For example, a trader who goes short after prices penetrate the upside of a prior consolidation—a price development that most technically oriented traders would interpret as a signal to buy or stay long—can be said to be fading the price breakout.

False breakout. A short-lived price move that penetrates a prior high or low before succumbing to a pronounced price move in the opposite direction. For example, if the price of a stock that has traded between $18 and $20 for six months rises to $21 and then quickly falls below $18, the move to $21 can be termed a false breakout.

Federal Reserve Board (Fed). The governing arm of the Federal Reserve System, which seeks to regulate the economy through the implementation of monetary policy.

Fibonacci retracements. The concept that retracements of prior trends will often approximate 38.2 percent and 61.8 percent—numbers derived from the Fibonacci sequence (see next item).

Fibonacci sequence. A sequence of numbers that begins with 1,1 and progresses to infinity, with each number in the sequence equal to the sum of the preceding two numbers. Thus, the initial numbers in the sequence would be 1, 1, 2, 3, 5, 8, 13, 21, 34, 55, 89, etc. The ratio of consecutive numbers in the sequence converges to 0.618 as the numbers get larger. The ratio of alternate numbers in the sequence (for example, 21 and 55) converges to 0.382 as the numbers get larger. These two ratios—0.618 and 0.382—are commonly used to project retracements of prior price swings.

Floor trader. A member of the exchange who trades on the floor for personal profit.

Frontrunning. The unethical—and in some cases illegal—practice of a broker placing his own order in front of a customer order that he anticipates will move the market.

Fundamental analysis. The use of economic data to forecast prices. For example, fundamental analysis of a currency might focus on such items as relative inflation rates, relative interest rates, relative economic growth rates, and political factors.

Futures. See the "Taking the Mystery Out of Futures" section (page 3).

Gann analysis. Market analysis based on a variety of technical concepts developed by William Gann, a famous stock and commodity trader during the first half of the twentieth century.

Gap. A price zone at which no trades occur. For example, if a market that has previously traded at a high of $20 opens at $22 on the following day and moves steadily higher, the price zone between $20 and $22 is referred to as a gap.

Hedge. A position (or the implementation of a position) used to offset inventory risk or risk related to an anticipated future purchase or sale. An example of a hedge trade is a corn farmer who, during the growing season, sells corn futures with a delivery date subsequent to his anticipated harvest. In this illustration, the sale of futures effectively locks in an approximate future sales price, thereby limiting risk exposure to subsequent price fluctuations.

Hedger. A market participant who implements a position to reduce price risk. The hedger's risk position is exactly opposite that of the speculator, who accepts risk in implementing positions to profit from anticipated price moves.

Implied volatility. The market's expectation of future price volatility as implied by prevailing option prices.

Interbank market. See "The Interbank Currency Market Defined" section (page 7).

Leverage. The ability to control a dollar amount of a commodity or financial instrument greater than the amount of capital employed. The greater the leverage of the position, the greater the potential profit or loss.

Limit position. For many futures contracts, government regulations specify a maximum position size (i.e., number of contracts) that a speculator may hold.

Limit price move. For many futures contracts, the exchanges specify a maximum amount by which the price can change on a single day. A market that increases in price by this specified maximum is said to be *limit-up*, while a market that declines by the maximum is said to be *limit-down*. In cases in which free market forces would normally seek an equilibrium price outside the range of boundaries implied by the limit, the market will simply move to the limit and virtually cease to trade. For an advancing market, such a situation is referred to as *locked limit-up* or *limit-bid*, while for a declining market, the analogous terms are *locked limit-down* or *limit-offered*.

Liquid market. A market in which there is a sufficiently large number of trades daily so that most reasonably sized buy and sell orders can be executed without significantly moving prices. In other words, a liquid market allows the trader relative ease of entry and exit.

Liquidity. The degree to which a given market is liquid.

Long. A position established with a buy order, which profits in a rising price market. The term is also used to refer to the person or entity holding such a position.

Lot. In futures markets, another name for contracts.

Mark to the market. The valuation of open positions at prevailing settlement prices. In other words, if a position is marked to the market, there is no distinction between realized and unrealized losses (or gains).

Mechanical system. A trading system (usually computerized) that generates buy and sell signals. A mechanical system trader follows the signals of such a system without regard to personal market assessments.

Money management. The use of various methods of risk control in trading.

Moving average. A method of smoothing prices to more easily discern market trends. A *simple moving average* is the average price during the most recent fixed number of days. Crossovers (one series moving from below to above another, or vice versa) of price and a moving average—or two different moving averages—are used as buy and sell signals in some simple trend-following systems.

Naked option. A short option position by a trader who does not own the underlying commodity or financial instrument.

Open interest. In futures markets, the total number of open long and short positions are always equal. This total (long or short) is called the open interest. By definition, when a contract month first begins trading, the open interest is zero. The open interest then builds to a peak and declines as positions are liquidated approaching its expiration date.

Options. See Appendix 2.

Overbought/oversold indicator. A technical indicator that attempts to define when prices have risen (declined) too far, too fast, and hence are vulnerable to a reaction in the opposite direction. The concept of overbought/oversold is also often used in association with contrary opinion to describe when a large majority of traders are bullish or bearish.

Outright position. A net long or short position (as opposed to spreads and arbitrage trades, in which positions are counterbalanced by opposite positions in related instruments).

Pattern recognition. A price-forecasting method that uses historical chart patterns to draw analogies to current situations.

Pit. The area where a futures contract is traded on the exchange floor. Also sometimes called the *ring*.

Portfolio insurance. See Appendix 1.

Position limit. See *limit position*.

Price/earnings (P/E) ratio. The price of a stock divided by the company's annual earnings.

Program trading. See Appendix 1.

Put option. A contract that provides the buyer with the right—but not the obligation—to sell the underlying financial instrument or commodity at a specific price for a fixed period of time.

Put/call ratio. The volume of put options divided by the volume of call options. A put/call ratio is one example of a contrary opinion or overbought/oversold measure. The basic premise is that a high ratio, which reflects more puts being purchased than calls, implies that too many traders are bearish and is hence considered bullish. Analogously, a low put/call ratio would be considered bearish.

Pyramiding. Using unrealized profits on an existing position as margin to increase the size of the position. By increasing the leverage in a trade, pyramiding increases the profit potential as well as the risk.

Reaction. A price movement in the opposite direction of the predominant trend.

Relative strength. In the stock market, a measure of a given stock's price strength relative to a broad index of stocks. The term can also be used in a more general sense to refer to an overbought/oversold type of indicator.

Resistance. In technical analysis, a price area at which a rising market is expected to encounter increased selling pressure sufficient to stall or reverse the advance.

Retracement. A price movement counter to a preceding trend. For example, in a rising market, a 60 percent retracement would indicate a price decline equal to 60 percent of the prior advance.

Reversal day. A day on which the market reaches a new high (low) and then reverses direction, closing below (above) one or more immediately preceding daily closes. Reversal days are considered more significant ("key") if accompanied by high volume and a particularly wide price range.

Ring. A synonym for *pit*.

Risk control. The use of trading rules to limit losses.

Risk/reward ratio. The ratio of the estimated potential loss of a trade to the estimated potential gain. Although, theoretically, the probability of a gain or loss should also be incorporated in any calculation, the ratio is frequently based naively on the magnitudes of the estimated gain or loss alone.

Scalper. A floor broker who trades for his own account and seeks to profit from very small price fluctuations. Typically, the scalper attempts to profit from the edge available in selling at the bid price and buying at the offered price—a trading approach that also provides liquidity to the market.

Seat. A membership on an exchange.

Sentiment indicator. A measure of the balance between bullish and bearish opinions. Sentiment indicators are used for contrary opinion trading. The put/call ratio is one example of a sentiment indicator.

Short. A position implemented with a sale, which profits from a declining price market. The term also refers to the trader or entity holding such a position.

Skid. The difference between a theoretical execution price on a trade (for example, the midpoint of the opening range) and the actual fill price.

Speculator. A person who willingly accepts risk by buying and selling financial instruments or commodities in the hopes of profiting from anticipated price movements.

Spike. A price high (low) that is sharply above (below) the highs (lows) of the preceding and succeeding days. Spikes represent at least a temporary climax in buying (selling) pressure and may sometimes prove to be major tops or bottoms.

Spread. The combined purchase of a futures contract (or option) and sale of another contract (or option) in the same or a closely related market. Some examples of spreads include long June T-bonds/short September T-bonds, long Deutsche marks/short Swiss francs, and long IBM 130 call/short IBM 140 call.

Stop order. A buy order placed above the market (or sell order placed below the market) that becomes a market order when the specified price is reached. Although stop orders are sometimes used to implement new positions, they are most frequently used to limit losses. In this latter application, they are frequently called *stop-loss orders.*

Support. In technical analysis, a price area at which a falling market is expected to encounter increased buying support sufficient to stall or reverse the decline.

System. A specific set of rules used to generate buy and sell signals for a given market or set of markets.

Systems trader. A trader who utilizes systems to determine the timing of purchases and sales, rather than rely on a personal assessment of market conditions.

Tape reader. A trader who attempts to predict impending market direction by monitoring closely a stream of price quotes and accompanying volume figures.

Trading range. A sideways price band that encompasses all price activity during a specified period. A trading range implies a directionless market.

Technical analysis. Price forecasting methods based on a study of price itself (and sometimes volume and open interest) as opposed to the underlying fundamental (i.e., economic) market factors. Technical analysis is often contrasted with fundamental analysis.

Tick. The minimum possible price movement, up or down, in a market.

Trend. The tendency of prices to move in a given general direction (up or down).

Trend-following system. A system that generates buy and sell signals in the direction of a newly defined trend, based on the assumption that a trend, once established, will tend to continue.

Uptick rule. A stock market regulation that short sales can only be implemented at a price above the preceding transaction.

Uptrend. A general tendency for rising prices in a given market.

Volatility. A measure of price variability in a market. A volatile market is a market that is subject to wide price fluctuations.

Volume. The total number of shares or contracts traded during a given period.

Whipsaw. A price pattern characterized by repeated, abrupt reversals in trend. The term is often used to describe losses resulting from the application of a trend-following system to a choppy or trendless market. In such markets, trend-following systems will tend to generate buy signals just before downside price reversals and sell signals just before upside price reversals.